D1736367

To
the Lesser Heights
of Morningside

Rexford G. Tugwell, 1932 (Photo by Leon H. Keyserling)

To
the Lesser
Heights
of
Morningside:
A Memoir

REXFORD G. TUGWELL

University of Pennsylvania Press
Philadelphia
1982

Copyright © 1982 by the University of Pennsylvania Press
All rights reserved

Library of Congress Cataloging in Publication Data

Tugwell, Rexford Guy, 1891–
  To the lesser heights of Morningside.

  Includes bibliographical references and index.
  1. Tugwell, Rexford Guy, 1891–   .
2. Economists—United States—Biography.
3. Political scientists—United States—Biography.   I. Title
HB119.T83A37   330'.092'4   [B]   81–43528
ISBN 0–8122–7827–5   AACR2

Printed in the United States of America

Contents

Introduction

by Leon H. Keyserling

Rexford Guy Tugwell was a very great and exceptional man—in mind and heart and spirit, in courage and intellectual integrity, in a range of abilities that transcended his chosen specialties, and in the discernment and soundness of the positions he took on economic and social matters affecting the lives and livelihoods of all the people of this country, which he loved so much. The results of his efforts and influence have, even after his death, benefited many who did not know him, as well as those who did, and these benefits would continue to grow if the public and its leaders in the United States drew more fully upon what he said and did.

An account of my relationship with Rex and of my opportunities to work with him may help to "qualify" me as an evaluator of his legacy. During 1925–26, his seminar course in economics inspired me more as a sophomore at Columbia and did more to help formulate my own thought and action in later years than any other course at that college. Two years later, in one of the Monday night general honors weekly seminars, in which he was one of three professors who led discussions of great books written over several millennia, I came to marvel at his knowledge of many disciplines and his capacity to bring ideas together. During 1931–32, after I graduated from Harvard Law School, I returned to Morningside for more study in economics and collaborated with him in the editing and writing of two books.[1] He brought me to Washington in early 1933 and was mainly

---

1. *Our Economic Society and Its Problems* (New York: Harcourt Brace, 1934) and *Redirecting Education* (New York: Columbia University Press, vol. 1, 1934; vol. 2, 1935).

responsible for my becoming in April 1933 the one legislative assistant to the great Senator Robert F. Wagner, which more than anything provided the foundation for all my later activities. I lived with Rex and his family for a short time at the beginning of the New Deal and maintained other working and personal contacts with him during his years in the federal government. My contacts with him continued, although not as intensely, during more than four decades after he left the federal government, and we maintained an active correspondence, especially in his later years. He had more than one dinner at our home in Washington, D.C., one as late as 1977 occasioned by a hotel gathering of more than one thousand New Dealers to celebrate the work of FDR.[2] One of my visits to his home in Santa Barbara was within a year of his death, and I spoke at the memorial service for him when he died at the age of eighty-eight in 1979. But the man was so great in his personal attributes, and such a significant figure in public life and other activities, that any "bias" due to my association with him cannot distort much my judgment of his worth.[3]

The current volume, published as a posthumous autobiography, recounting Rex's thoughts and experiences during his studies at the Wharton School from 1911 to 1917 and his teaching at Columbia between 1920 and 1932, would be of value and interest to a general readership even if he had never left the academic groves and never done anything much noticed by the public. The book exhibits his truly beautiful writing style, poetic at times. Viewing his literary gifts and sensible discernment of everything around him, it did not surprise me three years ago when Dorothy Rosenman (wife of the late Samuel I. Rosenman, Franklin D. Roosevelt's longest and most valuable and valued helper) told me that Tugwell's book *The Democratic Roosevelt*[4] was the best of the many books written about the president. The current autobiography is also a marvelous description of what

2. My years as chairman of the Council of Economic Advisers (although not accompanied by substantial contacts with Tugwell) enlarged my awareness of the problems he faced in government service and influenced my evaluation of his contributions toward finding solutions.

3. An excellent, and in some respects definitive, account of Tugwell's ideas and works is contained in Bernard Sternsher, *Rexford Tugwell and the New Deal* (New Brunswick, N.J.: Rutgers University Press, 1964). But Sternsher did not have the benefit of appreciable personal contacts with Tugwell.

4. New York: Doubleday and Co., 1957.

university life and thought were like so long ago and of the academic powers with whom Tugwell had to contend—in part successfully and in part unsuccessfully. The memoir sheds much light upon what Tugwell later accomplished and could not accomplish by revealing his primary attachment (frequently at high personal cost) not to the conventional bigwigs in academia with their commitment to the past and to outdated thinking, but to such advanced trailblazers as John Dewey, Simon Nelson Patten, Herbert Croly, William F. Ogburn, and Carlton Parker (my mother, when I was still in high school or college, had me read a book about Carlton Parker by his gifted wife, Cornelia Parker).

But the chief value of the current autobiography is the luminousness and force with which it reveals the attributes of Tugwell that had so large a bearing upon his later successes and disappointments as a distinguished public servant. This revelation is not based on any claim that his university experiences occurred during "formative" years that were atypical of what he thought and did later on; the truth is that he made manifest a remarkable consistency from beginning to end. Fundamentally, the "formation" had already taken place when he was a first-year man at Wharton, where even then his gifts were abundantly apparent. Rex grew, but he did not become really different.

If I were asked what one trait of Rex Tugwell still stands out most in my mind, I would turn to a statement about him that I submitted to a journal a few years ago when asked which people had influenced me most and why. I named my father, William Keyserling, for inculcating in me a sense of social responsibility; Senator Wagner for his demonstration of political courage; and Tugwell for his uninterrupted and unalloyed intellectual integrity—a rare quality indeed among high-level public employees in the nation's capital.

What Rex stood for in his earlier years is of double significance; what he taught and wrote about and fought for at that time is of permanent value to all of us; by the same token, we have all suffered a great loss in areas where what he stood for has been disregarded. This disregard helps to explain why national economic policies that affect the *lives of people* as much or more than all else have yielded such deficient results in the past decade or so. The whole nation would benefit immensely by a renewed dedication to the principles Tugwell stood for more than half a century ago.

A telling example of this is the passage in the current autobiography that reveals, in Tugwell's elegant style, his position on economic thought, writing, and teaching when he was at Columbia. I cite this passage because of its current relevance:

> Classical economic theory had become a hardened logical system in circumstances quite different from those of the twentieth century. It could not, therefore, be taken as a generalization from contemporary economic experience or a hypothesis for the solution of future problems. It was dangerously close to being merely a speciously attractive, highly elaborated abstraction, relevant to nothing in the real world. It could not be concluded that, because its central subject matter was the valuation of goods and services, there was any special relevance to what went on in the market place. It was more precisely an exercise with artificial conditions: a series of theories, all of whose elements were assumed, and if any attempt was made to substitute actual observed elements, the whole edifice crumbled. In other words, it did not explain.

Tugwell at Columbia did far more than think or write about this problem. He fought to bring about much-needed change. Some of his efforts were eminently successful. These included his leadership and participation in the freshman Contemporary Civilization course, which soon spread to many other colleges and which used a review of Western civilization from the beginning—economic, governmental, political, historical, and even philosophical—to put into focus what we had become and still needed to do. He was also largely successful in his insistence upon the need for the integration of various disciplines, such as economics, history, sociology, the governmental process, and some philosophy and psychology—all reflected in part by the "C.C." course. While at Columbia he also wrote, with the assistance of Thomas Monroe and Roy E. Stryker, *American Economic Life and the Means of Its Improvement.*[5] This book drew upon empirical observation of the facts of our economic life and scrutinized the three levels of living—poverty, comfort, and riches— to define our real economic and related social problems and to suggest what ought to be done about them. The book was used as the main reading in the seminar to which I have referred, but was *not* sanctioned in the introductory course in economics. It was also used in some other colleges but not nearly enough. During 1931–33, at Co-

---

5. New York: Harcourt, 1925.

lumbia and in Washington, I undertook for Tugwell a complete revision of this book, concentrating heavily upon the first years of the Great Depression and including description and evaluation of early New Deal programs.[6]

As previously stated, one of the two books I collaborated with Rex in writing and editing during his Columbia years was *Redirecting Education*, which urged that college and university teaching, especially in the social sciences, be related more closely to the economic and social problems of the times. We also did work together for the General Education Board of the Rockefeller Foundation, including essays and visits to colleges around the country, all geared to the same purpose. One of our travels took us on a visit of several days to my family home in Beaufort, South Carolina.

The successes I have mentioned were accompanied by a strong admixture of frustration and disappointment at Columbia. This autobiography reveals much about the latter, which is of current significance because the reasons for it remain relevant for the teaching of and writing about economics today. Tugwell felt that he was highly respected and supported by the nationally eminent economists in the graduate school as an efficient administrator of economics in the college, but that he was undervalued by them as one who would not make much of a contribution to "economics." According to Tugwell, they felt he "was not likely to develop into a real economist"; younger men were given preferred positions at the graduate level; and even Professor Wesley C. Mitchell, the then most-honored student of the business cycle, at one time dissented from the decision that Tugwell be retained at Columbia. A current examination of Mitchell's work on the business cycle will reveal how far he fell short of explaining its real causes or proposing effective solutions. Tugwell was far more penetrating than Mitchell on this.

One of the factors contributing to Tugwell's loss of standing among the senior economists at Columbia was that he objected to their using the college as a means of providing financial support for

---

6. Tugwell and Hill, *Our Economic Society and Its Problems* (New York: Harcourt Brace, 1934). Hill's name was on the book as a high school textbook expert, but he had nothing to do with the writing of a line of it. By around 1935, Harcourt Brace requested that an updated volume be undertaken in my name alone, but by then I was too engrossed in other matters. Rex was then deemed "too political" for a textbook, due to reactionary criticism of him.

young instructors working toward their Ph.D.'s. Tugwell insisted that the most important students of economics in the college were not those who were going to become professional economists, but rather those who were going into the outside world where their thinking about economics would greatly influence the functioning of business and the determination of national economic policies. He therefore wanted these students to have the best economists and teachers the university could offer. Much later on, when Tugwell attempted to return to Columbia after repeated leaves of absence, he was turned down and asked to resign, which he did.

Other ideas Tugwell advanced while at Columbia were that income redistribution was fundamental to economic performance, and that more progressive income distribution was desirable on human grounds as well; that the behavior of the private sector needed profound modification; that all economic policies, especially at the national level, needed to be guided by a view of the economy as a whole and a reconciliation of divergent policies; and that more international cooperation and organization—*not* "one world"—needed to replace rampant nationalism. None of this won much support at Columbia, and very indicative of current as well as earlier circumstances are Tugwell's reports of his intellectual and practical battles with College Dean Herbert E. Hawks and the powerful Professor John J. Coss. Rex explained these difficulties, with characteristic generosity and penetration, by saying that these two gentlemen were not too much to blame because they were caught up in the culture in which they lived.

Yet Tugwell was never a "radical" as that term is frequently used today, although he was certainly radical in his persistent demand for fundamental solutions involving fundamental change. He was a determined pragmatist and realist and a "moderate" in the best sense. That he was not radical in the commonly used sense is indicated by his statement as a New Dealer that we should aim not toward anti-business action but toward a situation in which "business became government and government became business." This statement was not "fascist" in nature. It merely indicated that the two groups should work cooperatively toward common purposes and mutually reinforcing policies, with an integrated attitude toward the whole economy, and with the federal government necessarily taking the lead.[7] Thus,

---

7. A complete agenda for this is the Humphrey-Hawkins Full Employment

from his first to his last years, including his participation in the New Deal, Rex never joined in the antitrust commitment (much larger in words than in deeds), or in the so-called "Second New Deal," which turned toward inflammatory criticism of big business and attempted punitive legislation against it. He did not want to see business battered or threatened, but rather educated, influenced, elevated, and helped toward participation with government in common goals and achievements through improved policies, both public and private. An example of this was the 1933 National Industrial Recovery Act's enactment, in which he was so much involved. This act had much to be said for its purposes and achievements. It might well have been of permanent usefulness in its original or revised form if it had not been declared unconstitutional in 1935, partly because of the National Recovery Administration's improper assumption of powers not delegated to it by Congress, and mainly because the Supreme Court had not yet reached a broad enough interpretation of the Constitution's commerce clause; soon thereafter, the Court did so rise in its 1937 decisions *in re* the National Labor Relations Act, the Social Security Act, and so forth. FDR lost the battle but won the war in his 1937 "Court-packing" plan.

Rex's views on the relationship between business and government are further indicated by the statement in this autobiography that after his trip to Russia in 1927, he found communism even more "distasteful" than current capitalism. He protested the frequent identification of dictatorship with limited national planning under a system of responsible free government and responsible free enterprise. Maintenance and enlargement of the personal freedoms remained always firm in the mind and heart of Rex Tugwell. But he never confused these freedoms with economic laissez-faire or private license to plunder the public.[8]

I would be happy to be able to report that the decades that have rolled by have brought a strong movement toward what Tugwell stood for. To be sure, as indicated in his book *The Brains Trust*[9]

---

and Balanced Growth Act of 1978, honored thus far only in the breach, about which Rex and I had considerable correspondence *after* it was in the works.

8. Tugwell's attitude toward our business system is well illustrated by his books *Industry's Coming of Age* (New York: Columbia University Press, 1927) and *The Industrial Discipline and the Governmental Arts* (New York: Harcourt Brace, 1933).

9. New York: Viking, 1968.

(recounting his advisory work with Roosevelt as governor of New York) and later on by the influence of his work during the early years of the New Deal, there was much good done: the accent upon public employment to take care of the unemployed; public works in general; the early farm and resettlement programs; the original social security program; some aspects of housing; and the dedication to bold experimentation. But for Rex, the New Deal would have been very different and much inferior; he was, in my view, the most influential figure during the early New Deal for much of what proved over time to be good and useful in what the New Deal accomplished, and his early departure was a significant factor in its diminishing effectiveness.

But especially during the last decade, attention to Tugwell's ideas and work has waned, and the cumulative loss has been tremendous. The teaching and writing of most of the "leading" economists and the preeminent role of economists in giving advice to the president through the Council of Economic Advisers under the Employment Act of 1946 have moved increasingly backward. American economics today falls far short even of the 1940s and 1950s, when economists like Alvin H. Hansen and Sumner Slichter were honored and followed. Econometrics has come to the fore in recent years, and a perfect description of it is contained in the long quotation from Tugwell that I have set forth above. Value judgments have been broadly denigrated, if not ignored, although the ultimate purpose of all economics should be to recognize that "the well-being of the people is the supreme law." Income redistribution has, in general, become a subject too "controversial to be dealt with."[10] Goals have been set (but not adhered to) for aggregate economic performance that neglect the balance among private consumption, public investment, and private investment, which Tugwell identified as being at the heart of the entire economic problem and which is essential to achieve the goals. Improvised and ad hoc policies, generally not cohesive and sometimes inconsistent, have replaced an overall view and a systematic, long-range approach.[11] And it is no secret that the

10. One published report of the Council of Economic Advisers contained the amazing statement that it was *neutral* on the subject of income distribution. Yet every important economic policy affects income distribution, and *how* it is distributed shapes the performance of the whole economy.

11. See my "What's Wrong with American Economics?" *Challenge*, May–June 1973.

practical consequences of these wayward approaches to public policy have been distressingly obvious for a long time. Those who need guidance in straightening out national policymaking would do well to examine Tugwell's books.

Although our failure to benefit from what Rex stood for may seem recent, there were some important examples of it during his relatively short experience in the federal government. In the Department of Agriculture, where he served as assistant and then undersecretary, he was unable in 1933 to prevent the purge from the department of liberals, such as Jerome Frank and several others. Moreover, Tugwell himself was first shifted from one responsibility to another, and then his New Deal service terminated of his own choice in 1937. And the New Deal never developed an integrated policy and program. Later, he was appointed governor of Puerto Rico, and there he had freer rein to bring about significant improvements in that country—whose trials he describes in his book *The Stricken Land.* [12]

Tugwell's successes were aided considerably by his fine and even winning appearance, his obvious forthrightness and genuineness, his capacity to be liked even by most of those who disagreed with him in substance, and above all by his superb abilities and clarity in conveying his positions. But he was impeded, although by no means stopped, by his lack of "political" gifts, as these are commonly defined, in part because he did not give enough attention to these matters, but also in part because his strengths were not in this direction. An outstanding example of the latter was his unsatisfactory performance at the Senate hearings for his confirmation as undersecretary of Agriculture, where he was somewhat romped over by that noble example of all that can be worst in a politician, Senator Bailey of North Carolina. Another reason for Rex's "difficulties," if they can be regarded as such, was the absolute intellectual integrity, to which I have referred, although he did have a good sense of allowable action in the environment in which he worked. While in government service, he spoke out at times and remained quiet at others; he refrained from saying all that he believed, but he believed all that he said and did not fear to say it. He was superbly loyal to President Roosevelt, but he was not servile and did not avoid telling

---

12. Garden City, N.Y.: Doubleday, 1947.

FDR when he thought he was wrong. For example, some later books about presidents, including President Kennedy, were unvarnished eulogies that would have been appropriate in a short funeral tribute but were not appropriate in several hundred pages of what were offered as scholarly appraisals. In vivid contrast, Rex's *The Democratic Roosevelt* blended warmth and praise of merit as he saw it with dispassionate and unreserved indictment of defects as he saw them.

During the last three decades or so of his life, Tugwell practically abandoned his work as an economist proper, although in his very latest years he did a few economic articles for the Center for the Study of Democratic Institutions in Santa Barbara, where he long served as a permanent associate. He turned instead toward political science and brought forth a number of excellent books dealing in the main with presidents from Washington forward. That Rex made this transition so completely meant that in his later years he identified himself in *Who's Who in America* as a political scientist rather than an economist. The reasons for the switch were many, some unknown to me, but he once told me that he had made it because of his distress, if not disgust, with the turn American economics was taking. This again was evidence of both his intellectual integrity and his pragmatic realism, plus his growing conviction that economic policies and conditions were determined less by ratiocination than by the nature of the men who were elected president. His last monumental work, *The Emerging Constitution*, [13] was only a limited departure from his inbred instrumentalism and pragmatism. He recognized that none or almost none of his recommendations for the rewriting of the Constitution would be accepted. But he properly felt that it was important to state comprehensively why he believed we needed a new approach to the basic structure of our government.

If Rex had exerted himself more often with regard to the little niceties in personal relationships, he *might* have accomplished even more than he did. But he was essentially warm in his relationships with others and did for others a great deal more than shake hands and smile when he found them meritorious. There was an essential reserve and modesty in his avowal of his attitude toward others, as

---

13. New York: Harpers Magazine Press, 1974. As soon as this book appeared, Rex inscribed a copy to me "With the author's gratitude for services to him and our country."

when he wrote to me that "I applaud what you are doing, if ever so faintly." And as late as April 1, 1977, he wrote to me, in commenting on one of my published productions, that "I don't know whether in this case it is a virtue but we have been consistent throughout—at least generally." And still later, at the age of eighty-seven in 1978, he wrote me a remarkable five-page letter, arguing in detail why he still believed that the reforms of the New Deal and some later on were inadequate patchwork, and that we needed to turn to the planned reconstruction of economic thought and action that he had stressed in 1932[14] and much earlier as well as later.

In conclusion, I feel profoundly convinced that it is a public service to publish the current autobiography and any other material that would enlarge our understanding of Rexford Guy Tugwell and his accomplishments. More important, it seems to me vital to appreciate how much better off our country and people will be if at long last we come to draw more fully upon Tugwell's precepts and example.

---

14. See *The Brains Trust.*

To
the Lesser Heights
of Morningside

I

PHILADELPHIA

1911–1917

The Past improves. Soldiers find that even the squalors and boredoms of war after a while seem to have been incidents in a romantic enterprise; adults forget the terrors and tensions of childhood and recall mostly interludes of security and gaiety. Mean seasons seem presently to have had a high interest, and even personal enmities soften and seem in time to have been more comic than tragic. No wonder the bright college years of song and story seem in retrospect so idyllic. The light of other days is kindly and mellowing.

Even under later examination, these particular passages of time, quite aside from the gloss of recollection, do retain authentic values. Then the struggle to become one of the small number who will survive from preparatory school is over; then the youth who is not quite a man is suddenly freed from parental supervision; then he is granted, out of pride, the most that can be spared from the family income; and, moreover, he has none of the burdens so soon to weigh him down: dependents, career, civic duties, the risks and infirmities of maturity. Clearly, these days are precious.

The mind begins to open. Orthodoxies, theretofore unquestioned, seem suddenly not too sacred for examination, and the apparatus for analysis first becomes available. The great teacher is discovered—he seems to exist nearly everywhere and nearly always —and under his guidance, character is firmed and shaped.

Almost at once genuine creativeness may set in. A surprising number of contributors to civilization have been at their most productive between twenty-five and thirty, although their contributions often go unrecognized for a long time. The rest of life for them is often merely an elaboration of the conceptions that swirled magically into being out of the jar of youth, possibly somewhat vague and disembodied at first, but gradually becoming firm and integrated.

While the youth is thus coming into his cultural inheritance and throwing his new perceptions like nets into the outer darkness to see what he may draw in, the unfolding man within is being initiated into other varieties of experience. Those who have preceded him by just a little, and who are therefore his best mentors, are at this time most influential. He becomes a really social animal; he has his first experience of sublimated sexual fondness; he learns what loyalty is and what friendship can be; there loom on his spiritual horizon the faiths likely to sustain him until his dissolution; and he assumes attitudes he will never quite abandon.

A comparison of the kind of young man I was and what the Wharton School was like would probably have found us thoroughly unsuited to each other. For what I wanted, it would have been better to have gone, say, to Columbia, Harvard, Chicago, or another institution with a wider offering; I might at least have opted for the liberal arts course at Pennsylvania, rather than the Wharton School. Yet I should never have many regrets; and I do not think now that any other environment would have proven for me more helpful in furnishing what I wanted, in drawing out what I had to give, and certainly in introducing me to agreeable experience.

The Wharton School was primarily a place for learning how to become a good executive, but it was also a place for learning how to be effective in one or another kind of public service. That would often require opposition to the intentions of business, and it was a great advantage to have learned something about them. My later criticisms of the system, or, anyway, of many of its parts, were, thanks to the Wharton School, informed ones. Also there were new discoveries opening out of the techniques of industry and commerce, and they went far beyond money-making, becoming disciplines in their own right. Geography was more than a set of principles determining factory placement or favorable sales territories; it revealed the world's places and resources so that almost at once I sensed its essential oneness. Insurance was more than the study of ways to sell individual immunities from risk; it became for me a conception of shared uncertainties giving a certain security to harassed people.

So it went with most of the preparatory studies for business: commercial law, transportation, real estate, finance, and so on. In addition, there were three departments with only the most general relation to commercial training: economics, sociology, and political science. There was only an historic reason why these were in the Wharton School rather than the College. It did make falling into intimacy with them somewhat easier, but probably I should have found them anyway. I had no trouble finding English literature or history in the College of Liberal Arts. My undergraduate experience gave me no more than introductions to psychology and philosophy, for instance, which I should have liked to cultivate further; but this was not so unfortunate for me as for some others. I should have other opportunities.

Anyway, that is how it was. Joseph Wharton, the wealthy iron-master, had, in 1881, presented the university with a substantial part of his holdings to found a school for training young men in the way he felt they ought to go. He had rather definite notions about education, or, at any rate, about the education of future executives. From his covering letter and from the terms of the gift, it is clear that he intended to establish instruction not for the needy but for the sons of the well-to-do. It was no longer practical to think of apprenticeship in ancestral counting houses and factories. "Since," he said, "systematic instruction cannot be expected from the overworked heads of any great establishment, the novice mostly depends on what he can gather from the salaried employees of the house. . . . Increasing numbers of young men, possessing, by inheritance, wealth, keenness of intellect, and latent power of command or organization," were neglected. By the very felicity of their circumstances, the channels of proper instruction were closed to them.

When they left college at the age of twenty to twenty-five years, they were, he said:

> already too old to be desirable beginners in a counting house or to descend readily to its drudgery. No country can afford to have this inherited wealth and capacity wasted for want of that fundamental knowledge which would enable the possessors to employ them with advantage to themselves and to the community. Yet how numerous are the instances of speedy ruin to great estates, and indolent waste of great powers for good, simply for want of such knowledge and of the tastes and self-reliance which it brings.

The Wharton School was to graduate, about equally, businessmen, teachers, and public servants of various kinds—something more improbable in theory than it was in fact. Administration for profit-making or for the governance of "great estates" involved accounting and legal and financial arrangements. It was technically not so different from public administration, especially that part concerned with business regulation. James and Patten[1] had a theory about that; Patten often elaborated it in private. "If," he said, "we train enough experts, businesses will simply not be able to hire all of them and some will become available for the public service. In that way business regulation will become effective enough so that many present abuses, caused by business hiring away from government every one who threatens to become troublesome, will be greatly reduced."

One passage in the Wharton Trust was justification for such departments as economics, public law, sociology, and other disciplines of this generalized sort. It read as follows:

> Nor can any country long afford to have its laws made and its government administered by men who lack such training as would suffice to rid their minds of fallacies and qualify them for the solution of the social problems incident to our civilization. Evidently a great boon would be bestowed upon the nation if its young men of inherited intellect, means and refinment could be more generally led so to manage their property as, while husbanding it to benefit the community, they could be drawn into careers of unselfish legislation and administration.

This was a sufficient mandate. Our benefactor, then at the height of his money-making career, first gave stocks and bonds (of the Delaware and Boundbrook Railroad Company and the Schuylkill

---

1. Edwin J. James, organizer of the first courses of instruction under the Wharton trust and chairman of the Department of Economics until his departure in 1896. He left to become a professor at the University of Chicago and was subsequently president of the University of Illinois.

Simon Nelson Patten, who was to be influential in my development. He was educated in the American Midwest and at Halle in Germany. He came to Pennsylvania in 1888. After James departed, Patten became chairman of the Committee on Economics of the College Faculty and so head of the educational work of the Wharton School. I shall not recount the struggles, before my day, of the school to make its way against the conservatism of Philadelphia and the hostility of the liberal arts professors. Not until 1904 did the faculty gain sufficient administrative autonomy to have its own director (James T. Young); and not until 1912 was it finally taken out of the jurisdiction of the dean of the college. By this time it was the largest school in the university (625) and obviously destined to be very much larger. In fact, by the time I should finally leave in 1917, the enrollment would be twice as large. If the arts faculty had not let it go, that faculty, as was well understood, might have become a mere appendage of the upstart scion.

Navigation Company) valued at $79,000. Additional contributions increased the amount to some $806,700 (in 1948). This was generous; it was also one of the earliest of the large bequests to a university that got, on the whole, far less support from its community of wealthy men than had Harvard in Boston, Columbia in New York, or, even, later on, the University of Chicago. But after the first few years, the yield from it was never enough to cover more than a small part of the Wharton budget. The school succeeded, not because of its endowment, but because, for many students, at least, it departed from purely classical education and brought them into a freer and livelier atmosphere of learning.[2]

Wharton had one *idée fixe*. He believed the protective tariff to be a principle the United States ought not in any circumstances to depart from; and he made it quite clear that he expected the school's instructors to indoctrinate their students in its beneficence. In his letter of 1881 to the trustees he said:

> Although care has been taken to embody, not only my own convictions, but also some valuable suggestions from your . . . members, the elaboration of details . . . may bring to light further improvements which I should welcome, but I should object to any important alteration of the general scheme, and would therefore ask your decision upon it in its present shape; especially should I object to such lowering of tone in regard to national self-protection by means of tariff as some of your members seem inclined to favor. . . . It suffices, however, to express, in whatever paper of conveyance may be executed, that forfeiture shall occur upon such failure . . . as would be adjudged by the U.S. District Court . . . to be sufficient cause.

From this it can be seen how firm he was in the intention that his well-born young men not only should have competence in commerce but also should adhere to the protectionism so dear to Pennsylvania's manufacturers—but, as he obviously suspected, so little honored by the university's economists. The stricture about protection was influential in the choice of the first professor of economics (Patten, of whom I have spoken) but in not much else. Patten, having

---

2. The passages quoted here from the Wharton Trust and the letters of transmittal are published in one pamphlet entitled *Agreement: Joseph Wharton and the Trustees of the University of Pennsylvania*, made available to me by the university librarian.

been trained in Germany, and having made a clean escape from the free-trade influence of the English school, had written a defense of protection. If they had understood it, few of the manufacturers would have approved his reasoning, but it met the terms of the bequest.[3]

The small original group of professors, of whom Patten was the most prominent, had grown by 1911 to a faculty able to offer instruction in "accounting, marketing, commerce, transportation, insurance, industry, corporation finance, banking, and real estate, with each of these subjects being taught by specialists in their respective fields."[4] By stretching the Wharton mandate to cover the public service, the wider fields now had competent and even distinguished coverage. Besides Patten himself, there were, for instance, Leo S. Rowe, James T. Young, and Clyde King in political science; George B. Roorbach and J. R. Smith in geography; Roswell McCrea, Scott Nearing, and Eliot Jones in economics; Carl Kelsey and J. P. Lichtenberger in sociology; E. S. Mead and Thomas Conway in finance; S. S. Huebner in insurance; Emory R. Johnson and G. Huebner in commerce; and Ward Pierson in commercial law. If this stretched the terms of the bequest beyond recognition, Wharton never objected, and he lived for thirty years after making his original gift.

The school had become by 1911 not only an active center of training for business executives and industrial technicians, but also a genuine seat of learning and free research in all the social disciplines. It was by now so large, and the yield of the bequest was so small a percentage of its revenues, that Wharton students finished their courses of study without more than a casual acquaintance with old Joseph's intention for them. The district court was never called on

---

3. Patten's book was called *The Economic Basis of Protection*. It developed an ingenious theory at variance with free-trade thought but with a long enough history in German economics. Friedrich List was the best known of this nationalist school. There had been American defenders of protection: Henry C. Carey, for instance, a prominent Philadelphian (1793–1879) of a former generation. Manufacturers like Joseph Wharton had not only their own interests to influence them, but also respectable academic support, even if by now it represented a minority view. Perhaps the best account of these conflicting doctrines is to be found in Joseph Dorfman's *The Economic Mind in American Civilization*. Carey's views are described in chapter 29 of that work (New York: Viking, 1946).

4. Emory R. Johnson, dean. *The Wharton School: Its First Fifty Years—1881–1931*. This pamphlet is available at the University Library. It was privately published.

to enforce their indoctrination in the principles of protectionism.

That many or most of us were of the lively, optimistic, and prosperous breed so influential in the next generation gave the school a very special character. Most came from middle income families. We were used to prosperity. We had a tradition of working hard and being generously rewarded for it, and we carried ourselves with the assurance of a favored group. The Wharton tradition had become one of assiduity in study, frankness in discussion, and fairness in examination. There was a completely successful honor system—one of the few I was ever to see in my educational experience—administered by the students themselves with almost no fuss or trouble. There was no such thing elsewhere in the university, and we thought ourselves superior even in ethics, and perhaps we were.

Such a school, with so many sons of merchant and manufacturer families, might have been expected to be somewhat more adequately housed than it actually was. Logan Hall had undoubtedly seen better days. It had, in fact, been built in the era of green serpentine, as had College Hall.[5] It was, perhaps, preferable to that nightmarish monstrosity of red brick and terracotta, the library,[6] sitting uneasily close by its pale green neighbors. By 1911 the Victorian days were well in the past, and there were none to praise its architectural relics. The Medical School had recently abandoned Logan Hall, in fact, for its new quarters across Spruce Street.[7] And there was still evidence of that occupancy in class and lecture rooms. The bull-pit lecture halls, especially, were obviously designed so that surgeons could operate with several hundred students gazing down at their victims. The heating system was overefficient, and ventilation, in spite of an obviously complex contraption whose enormous pipes ran everywhere and seemed to end nowhere, completely unsuccessful. It was a poor setting for so much budding success. But we made do with it; and, of course, in later years, we would say that the crowding it imposed had been especially valuable—like that of the British House of Commons!

---

5. In 1871. The style would be called, I believe, Victorian Gothic. The architect was T. W. Richards, professor of Architecture. Logan Hall was built in 1874.

6. The masterpiece of Furness, Evans, and Company (Philadelphia architects), built in 1890.

7. In 1904. Until then the Wharton School had been an uneasy tenant in College Hall.

Perhaps it was true that its closeness did have advantages. Only a few steps were required to get from one place to any other place. Since class sizes were reaching their limits, it was logical to limit matriculation. The students were, for that time, of really high quality, even though growth was taking place at a rapid rate. This expansion would eventually break down the homogeneity and common acquaintance we had in my time and force the reconstruction of Logan Hall and eventually the building of an entirely new home.[8] The intimacy of our day created that remarkable esprit de corps responsible for the honor system. We were a select group. The only trouble was that we were so proud of it that the other schools were annoyed —especially the College. The College drew a disproportionate number of day students from the city of Philadelphia who had none of those fine airs we carried in so lordly a way. The students there could hardly be blamed for being somewhat resentful.

The campus as a whole was fairly lost in the nondescript wilderness of West Philadelphia. It was just across the Schuylkill from the old city, and was, if not so imposing as it later became, at least romantically vine covered. And the dormitories, after all, as the undergraduates' homes, were wholly satisfactory. They were built in house units, good solid Tudor.[9] Many of us moved into fraternity houses sooner or later, but we nevertheless kept a special affection for the dorms. In my time the "little quad" and the "big triangle" had a satisfactory appearance of age, but only one side of the "big quad" had been completed. Behind the dorms lay the Biological Gardens, romantic adjunct of the natural science departments, whose otherwise rural alleys were disturbed by the continuous frantic outcries of the dogs being immolated in the adjoining vivisection laboratory.[10] Over beyond the gardens lay Woodlands Cemetery, once William Hamilton's estate, and farther along, at Fifty-fourth Street and Eastwick Avenue, Bartram's Gardens.[11] How historic a spot we inhab-

---

8. This, so long hoped for, would not be begun until 1950.

9. The dormitory construction had begun in the 1890s. The triangle was completed in 1900–1901. The architect in the beginning was Walter Cope, assisted by John Stewardson. A comprehensive rebuilding program would begin in 1976.

10. Hamilton Walk, the longest of these leafy ways, lived in the memory of every undergraduate who ever felt the need of a withdrawn hour.

11. John Bartram had been America's first noted botanist. He began to develop this garden about 1731, bringing to it many rare and exotic plants from other

ited, I naturally took in only gradually; for instance, I learned rather late that the site of the Centennial Exposition of 1876 was not far away.[12]

The university had not always been in the wilds of West Philadelphia,[13] where even now some of its neighbors were of doubtful respectability. There was, for instance, Blockley, the enormous and shamefully crowded insane asylum, just over the fence from the Biological Gardens, its gloomy pile always visible; and there was a fringe of stockyards, wholesale markets, and factories between us and the river. In this a soccer field made only a small gap—and one, at that, crossed by the Pennsylvania Railroad's tracks. Also there were some small hotels down by the Thirty-fourth Street station, favorite places of assignation for students who possessed complaisant enamoratas.[14] The ugly and prosaic Gray's Ferry bridge across the river, unknown to most of us—although I discovered it accidentally, as I also discovered the history of Woodlands and Bartram's Gardens —was at the very crossing which, when it had been first a ferry, then a floating log bridge, had been the official entry place into the nation's capital in the days of revolution and of constitution making. Here the Philadelphia City Troop had met Washington on his way to New York to assume the presidency of the new republic.

The gray chill of Philadelphia winters may have depressed more mature people, but spring came early, and, anyway, it was always

---

countries. His son and son-in-law carried on after his death and eventually the garden became a public institution. The house was beautifully proportioned Georgian, and in the hallway was the first Franklin stove I had ever seen. It had been given to Bartram by Franklin himself.

Woodlands also had an interesting colonial house, built about 1770 by William Hamilton, grandson of Andrew Hamilton, who designed Independence Hall. The garden was not far from being an arboretum, too. It still had the ginko trees and the Lombardy poplars brought from abroad by Hamilton. Its south slope above the Schuylkill was a pleasant spot in spite of being a graveyard crowded with ugly monuments.

12. The Centennial had been a notable event in Philadelphia's history, as well as the nation's. It was the first exhibition of both Bell's telephone and Edison's electric light. Some of its structures still stand in Fairmount Park.

13. It had been moved from Ninth Street when College Hall was completed in 1871. Even so late as this, it had been a small, unimportant, and lethargic classical college. Only the Medical School had preshadowed the later and greater university.

14. It was reported among my generation that the name of our pious elderly provost was forged on the register there (with wife) at least once a night.

present in undergraduate spirits. We had a certain immunity to the ugliness of the neighborhood; we selected from our surroundings the congenial elements. It seemed to us a thoroughly satisfying place. Our affection for all of it was immoderate.

The slim young gent in the high linen collar, well-made suit, and carefully polished shoes—that was I. The more compact but no less carefully dressed lad alongside—that was Leslie Hansen. The late September atmosphere (of 1911) was heavy with the last of the summer's heat and the dormitories were alive with returning students or new ones like myself. We emerged—Leslie and I—from the doorway of Lippincott House, hands in pockets, carefree and with the afternoon and evening ahead. We had arrived from Buffalo that morning, transported our effects from the West Philadelphia station to our third-floor room overlooking the quad, unpacked, hung a few pictures, wrestled and roughhoused a little to see how our fittings would stand the strain, got acquainted with our immediate neighbors, and were now on the town.

Tomorrow I should have to appear in my green freshman cap. There would be organized, interclass scraps, and registration formalities would have to be got through. But I was accepted; I was in; this new world was my own. We sauntered, two young men, like hundreds of other pairs of young men, down the slate-slab walks to the dormitory entrance under Memorial tower.[15] As we went, Leslie told me tales of dormitory life. I had heard most of them before, but it was much more vivid to hear them on the spot. Here was the room whose occupant had gathered up over the course of weeks dozens of water bottles, filched wash bowls and chamber pots, and even numerous mattresses, all to be smashed or burned as contributions to the grandest rowbottom ever known in the precincts. And just above us was the fabulous room where the great Rowbottom himself had lived. When did one of these magnificent celebrations occur? There was no

---

15. Memorial for the university's Spanish-American War veterans.

predicting, said my mentor, an experienced junior; if there were any regularity about them, they could be prevented. Besides, who could predict when the spirit of rebellion and the sheer animal energy of a thousand young men would challenge authority.[16] Penalty? Ah, yes. The destroyed chamber pots, the burned mattresses, the lost doormats, and the hacked furniture would all be charged pro-rata against guilty and innocent alike, a kind of injustice to the good young men that lent the proceedings an added gusto for the bad ones.

For my benefit, as we were joined by other friends of Leslie, there were added to the saga tales of disciplining for freshmen. Really obnoxious ones, it seemed, might be dunked in the frog pond over in the Biological Gardens, but there were lesser punishments for lesser offenses. There was a good deal of exaggeration about this. Merely running over the histories of past occasions was satisfying to the upperclassmen, who could lord it over a freshman. The truth was, as I knew and they knew, that hazing was rapidly disappearing. It might linger in the rural colleges for a while; but any outbreaks of the old sort on a big campus were not very likely. Just because he was a first-year man, a student need not expect to suffer very serious humiliations unless he grossly offended his preceptors, and that I was unlikely to do. I was, in fact, eager to be a conforming member of this new community.

This was different—and better—than high school life. This, indeed, was what I had always, it seemed to me, wanted. We dodged the streetcars on Woodland Avenue and stopped to exchange gossip with others in front of Beeston's.[17] But the occasion required more than soft drinks, so we headed for the Normandie and its beer.[18]

---

16. Rutting riots they were called by the sourish authorities.

17. Three Beeston brothers were proprietors for many years of a student supply shop at the corner of Woodland Avenue and Thirty-seventh Street. They overcharged, but they never sold shoddy goods; they allowed us to run unwise accounts, but they seldom pressed us for payment; they were innocent of any interest in the university except in its profitability to themselves, but they asked no particular fondness of us in exchange for familiarity, and we gave none. They were part nuisance and part convenience, but they were so much part of the place that we could hardly imagine its going on without them. Two decades later, I was enormously gratified when I received a congratulatory letter on becoming assistant secretary of agriculture from the only survivor among the brothers.

18. The Normandie was an ultrarespectable West Philadelphia apartment hotel. In its basement was a gloomy rathskeller and, since it was the nearest beer

This evening turned out to be not a very wild one after all, and in that it was characteristic. We were not really children any more, and our notions of a good time had certain elements of sense. We liked companionship—so the Normandie was good. We liked to be entertained—so we went to Keiths, where there was still vaudeville, but first we ate a big—but cheap—dinner at Bahl's restaurant, which in those days was at Eighteenth and Market Streets.[19]

It would be a marvel of memory if I recalled the entertainment on that particular evening, and I do not; but we felt, I do recall, that our fifty cents had been well spent. Afterwards we went to the St. James, where students also congregated, and drank Külmbacher. A little later we drifted up Walnut Street to the Bellevue-Stratford and visited the bar and elegant drinking room in the basement. There was a good deal of fraternizing and boisterous talk. Not long after midnight, we were on our way westward on the Woodland Avenue streetcar. Old and rickety, it groaned and complained even when its load was light, but it returned us to the dorms with sufficient dispatch and dignity, as it was to do so many times in the future.

Next morning, not too late, Leslie and I looked at each other from our single beds in opposite corners. The coming year, we agreed, ought to be pleasant. We had hardly finished laying away the previous evening in appropriate mothballs of conversation when call-

---

dispensary, inhabitants of the dormitories and the fraternity houses used it constantly. There was always company there; the draft beer was good and inexpensive; there were free Lititz pretzels and cheddar cheeses. Moderate celebrations were not frowned on, but I recall no real rowdyism except perhaps on nights after the big games; even then it never got out of hand. It would be different when I came back after the war, with prohibition in effect. Students then would be mixing poisonous spirits with their near-beer, and the effects would be revolting.

19. Bahl's deserves to be celebrated in Pennsylvania annals for having fed so bountifully and so excellently many generations of students. It had no special interest in students, of course, and was not even very near the campus; but that was where students invariably went to escape boarding house fare. There were a few tables, but most of the customers ate at long, wide plank counters scrubbed almost to whiteness. From clams to strawberry shortcake, the food was very nearly perfect. And many a student learned there that kidneys, livers, and other animal organs are quite as edible as chops and steaks. There was always a shaker bottle of sherry for the pumpkin pie, and terrapin, game, and fish were always available. To dine on oysters, fowl, vegetables of the season, cooked with respect, and to end with hot mince pie and coffee with genuine bouquet—all for perhaps a dollar—that was one of the excellencies of those days. I found, sadly, visiting Philadelphia in the thirties that Bahl's had disappeared—too good for the times, no doubt.

ers from down the hall began to come in. They, too, had been out on various expeditions that had to be told about. But not George Copeland! Leslie already knew him, but I first met George—thin and dark and a little unhappy-seeming—when he stopped in that morning with comment on the current doings but not much involvement in them. He had been home the evening before, walking in the Bi-Gardens and reading Greek philosophy, while we had been going the rounds. His comments on our activities were not sympathetic; he was used to silliness but felt no compulsion to be silly, too. Somehow I knew that George would be good for me. And actually, before the month was out, he had me going to an evening seminar of Professor W. R. Newbold's, where I learned more about the Athenian way of life and especially the way the Athenians thought about it, and had me accepted as a full-fledged member of the Zelosophic Society, one of the university undergraduate literary groups. I was at least to share my time with some of the more serious students.

That day I went to my first lecture in elementary economics and knew at once, as I listened to Scott Nearing and studied the mimeographed outline of the readings and subjects for discussion, that this would be meaningful for me. There was no philosophy among the formal Wharton courses, but, as George had taught me, I could find it. For my freshman work, apart from economics and government— the accounting, the language I had to go in with, and the rest of it —I felt the old unwillingness to do more than to make sure of a passing grade. For my freshman government course, however, I felt the same attraction as for economics. Here was something more than the clichés of high school civics. The real problems of democracy had found their way into the teaching material; and James Young's lectures, suave as they were, still led into whole new reaches of debatable territory. I felt that I had to explore the politico-economic complex to complete some requirement not of the university but of my own. That night I stayed in our room with the first little pile of books on Nearing's list of required readings. There was as much politics as economics and as much social philosophy as either.

Not that same day but the next, I had another pleasant experience. I went to my first English composition class and was told I could go on to a more advanced one. A first look at a few paragraphs of my writing told the instructor that I belonged further along. The shift was made at once, and I came into contact with a teacher whose friendliness and understanding were of that unusual sort undergraduates remain grateful for all their subsequent lives. George William McClelland, who, not surprisingly to me, in later years became president of the university, was then in his first year of English teaching; being new, he had the onerous chore of teaching composition. He said, and evidently meant it, that his compensation was the privilege of working with a few of us who showed promise.

By some chance, there has survived from among the many books, papers, and mementos of my life—most of which have, naturally enough, been lost in my preoccupation with immediate tasks— a red-and-blue scrapbook going all the way back to that freshman fall in Philadelphia. In it there are several photographs of Leslie and myself (he was an amateur photographer), many theater and opera programs, course registration cards, and an extensive coverage of then current poetic literature, revealing that my main literary preoccupation was still with verse. I deduce this from two notes folded between the now-yellowed pages, written in longhand, and signed by George William McClelland. They are, I should say, extraordinarily kind and thoughtful, coming to a lowly freshman from an overworked instructor who every week must have had hundreds of compositions to get through, and who felt obliged to be as critical as he might be.

The first of these notes had to do with my labor over a story— what story I cannot at all recall. It said:

My dear Mr. Tugwell:

Drop in some afternoon when you find it convenient and I will tell you my revised opinion of your story. I have gone over it since you left and have concluded that while the tale is well told there is a fundamental weakness in the tale itself. It is a page from life but is incomplete in that it really does not suggest the ending. You may quarrel with me over that—but we'll leave further explanation until I see you.

Meanwhile I repeat that you have succeeded admirably in much of the phrasing—in fact I think the workmanship is finer than the conclusion which hardly concludes. Give Jean a chance.

Sincerely yours,
George Wm. McClelland

The next note refers to an event some months later. It was the climax and in a way the reward for all those long and faithful efforts

I had made to learn something of the art of writing. Remember, I was a freshman in a sophomore writing class:

> My dear Mr. Tugwell:
>
> Will it be possible for you to turn in your 235 work completed by Thursday of next week or Friday at the latest? I have decided to enter you for the Sophomore Composition prize if you have no objections and shall need to hand over to Professor Schelling your entire output for the year. The story ought to be included if you can finish it—and be sure to give me the other short story, parts of which Dr. Weygandt praised so highly.
>
> Each instructor is permitted to submit the themes of three men (two preferred) and I have decided upon you, Mr. Copeland, and Mr. Williams. Don't disappoint me.
>
> Sincerely yours,
> George Wm. McClelland
>
> Mr. Rexford G. Tugwell
> 449 Lippincott

George Copeland and I! The other was Winthrop Williams with whom—on the *Daily Pennsylvanian* and on the *Red and Blue*—I was to have a three-year competition. But George Copeland! By then I was a fraternity man, moderately popular, commanding a fine new set of friends (among whom were some of the most popular of the university's athletes), and accepted in several circles as an all-around good fellow. George was a sophomore who had never even been approached by a fraternity and whose other friends were all greasy-grinds. His life was circumscribed by an anemic weakness; in fact, a few years later he would die of tuberculosis, hardly started in life. Now George was to lose the prize he probably valued above any honor the university might award. He could not win it. Williams was a better workman; my stuff had a liveliness, even if undisciplined, that his could never achieve. If it was not I who won, it would be Williams, so it would be of no use for me to withdraw. I had come to feel a great affection for George, and his feeling for me was that often felt by a physically unattractive but mentally superior person for one more roundly developed. If I could have managed it, I would have maneuvered that prize into his possession.

What happened was that Williams and I divided the prize, as we were to go on dividing honors of that sort, and George was not even mentioned. I shall never forget his mingled sorrow at his own failure and pride in my success when the announcement was posted. He told me privately that Williams deserved no part of it, a thing I was willing to believe, and I finally persuaded him to join in a night of celebration, beginning with a champagne dinner at the L'Aiglon. He barely touched the wine, but for him, he was quite gay. The prize money lasted several days, but George's share in its proceeds of pleasure was pitifully small.

Relations with my instructor friend reached such an intimacy in my sophomore year that we decided to travel together during spring vacation. Tired of Philadelphia's smoke and slush, we went to New York, then down the coast by steamer to Florida—a trip to measure many others by in later years, full of fine new experience and easy companionship. On this trip George revealed a secret admiration for Julia Sanderson, whose current musical we would see in New York. My preference for Hazel Dawn of the Pink Lady showed, perhaps, a less sophisticated taste.

We sailed up the St. John and down again, went to St. Augustine for a few days, saw our first poinsettias, palms, and hibiscus, then came home to Philadelphia's glooms.

I was still a freshman, however, and much greener than I pretended. The Pennsylvania environment emphasized my callowness; it induced, indeed, a lingering sense of inadequacy that lasted throughout the year. It was pretty carefully, and even successfully, concealed, but not from myself. Actually George McClelland recognized that such competence as I had was one I had worked for. From the very first he showed a respect for my efforts so unprecedented in my experience as to give me new determination. I had never been easily discouraged—quite the contrary—but I thought of my literary efforts as a secret alcoholic must think of his vice. I had shared them with hardly anyone, since most of my friends would have thought such an addiction bizarre. Now I was close to a time of change, when a strictly literary life would no longer seem so attractive. It was too bad, really, that this first actual encouragement arrived so late. I made the most of it, I think. That I was writing stories shows I had not quite given up the idea of becoming a writer. But looking over some of my undergraduate copies of the *Red and Blue,* I suspect that I worked off some accumulated manuscripts when I became an editor. Either that or I was more immature than seems credible.

Sometime during my freshman year, however, it began to be quite clear that other purposes were more important to me and that writing would be a means rather than an end. That change of view ought not to be stated too categorically, because the truth is that I never, at least until now, ceased cultivating it as something in itself worthwhile. The capture of ideas, the trying of words and phrases, the building of sentences and paragraphs was something I labored at with enthusiasm all this year; but I had a subject matter in the introduction I was having to social studies that gave me something else to work for. These two interests were kept well apart. I would not be surprised to learn that George McClelland and Scott Nearing never actually met. Perhaps there was no reason why two of the principal influences of a freshman should not have remained quite unconnected, each unconscious of the other's contribution. I was, after all, an unusual case. Not many young men do divide their interests between social studies and literature. In fact, in most universities— certainly in those where I subsequently served—it would not be possible to spread oneself so widely. In graduate work, especially, it would be quite impossible because of the demands within each discipline. This is another reason why I still feel that Pennsylvania was a fortunate choice for me. I was not only allowed this idiosyncrasy; actually Patten and Schelling,[20] the heads, respectively, of the economics and English departments, encouraged it. I had other difficulties with Schelling, as I shall note, but not ones originating in my devotion to the social studies.

My literary preoccupation had its headquarters in College Hall, and history and language also took me there; my social studies courses were in Logan Hall. Besides these, I went to the chemistry building for an elementary course in chemistry, taught by the provost himself, and deadly dull I found it, too. To Leslie's disgust—he was studying to be a chemical engineer—I dropped it after the first term. Houston Hall and the dorms were where most of my nonworking hours were spent. That would change presently when Delta Upsilon, after appropriate rushing, invited me to join. I was

---

20. Felix Emmanuel Schelling, Centennial Professor of English Language and Literature from 1893 until his retirement, and for most of those years chairman of the department.

not sought after among the fraternities to such an extent that the pursuit enlarged my ego, but still it was with fair persistence. I had such a preference, however, for Delta Upsilon that my choice was always apparent. I cannot recall all the reasons for this; probably the most important was the number of western New Yorkers who were already members. I did also like its nonsecrecy and the general air of helpfulness I found there. Roy Mercer had a good deal to do with this.[21] He was the big man in the house then, although the group in general was a well-regarded one on the campus. Roy was a new kind of person to me, and his friendship gave me certain sensations of distinction. He had a magnificent physique, a kind heart, and a clear mind. Scarcely less a hero to those of us who were a little younger was Lewis Walton,[22] who became captain of the crew, and who, like Roy, had the Quaker qualities of helpfulness and quietude. My own class included several New Yorkers, of whom Orval Wales of Binghamton became a special friend. A year later when Frank Forster followed me to the university, I should have him, too; then in his senior year, to my enormous satisfaction, Leslie would be asked to join.

While I was new, I took my part in the poster and bowl fights and came out a little battered but basically unhurt. After one poster fight, I had, to Leslie's terror, one of my attacks of asthma. I knew by now that I could quiet them, even if only slowly, with sedatives, but they still usually went on for several hours. This one inspired George Copeland to a bit of doggerel. I evidently had an appropriate lack of commiseration among my friends, and this was doubtless good for me. George's squib, which I found on an odd bit of paper in my scrapbook, went like this:

> Under the spreading Lippincott roof
> The frosh his bellows blows

---

21. Eugene LeRoy Mercer, captain of the football and track teams and all-American fullback in 1914; afterward football coach and then director of Athletics and professor of Physical Education. He succeeded R. Tait McKenzie who was director in my time and famous, as well, as a sculptor of athletes. I still think of Roy as perhaps the most admirable whole man I ever met. He died in 1957 after a full and useful life.

22. Of the famous Walton family, so many years the source of headmasters for the George School. Lewis himself was studying architecture and later was to have a distinguished career in and about Chicago.

The Frosh a sickly man is he
With asthma in his nose.

Which shows, of course, that George knew very little, if anything, about asthma, unless he felt that poetic license justified the confusion of bronchial with nasal passages. But it also shows that I was not actually sickly, apart from these allergic attacks, for his verse was obviously not written in any spirit of sympathy, as it would have been if he had been worried. I was, in fact, a normal, and none-too-studious freshman.[23] Later on for the *Red and Blue,* I wrote a story based on one of these class fracases called "The Man in the Yellow Pants," which still does not read too badly, and it shows respect for university

---

23. Pasted in my scrapbook is the account in the *Daily Pennsylvanian* of that first poster fight. It shows that something, at least, was left of the old kind of "college spirit" now so long vanished:

> Freshmen were victorious in the annual poster fight last night when they succeeded in completely removing the Sophomore poster from the back door of College Hall despite the determined effort of the Sophs to prevent them. The victory was largely due to the superior numbers of the Freshmen who were 250 strong, while the Sophomores only numbered 125.
>
> The Sophomore poster was pasted on the back door of College Hall a little after sundown. By ten o'clock there were one hundred and twenty-five second year men standing on the stone steps, with arms locked, ready to keep the Freshmen from tearing their poster down.
>
> The drawing on the poster this year is of a baby, tagged "1915," reaching out for a milk bottle tagged "1914 dope."
>
> The poster follows:
>
>> For we, the class of 1914, will wean you from your childish habits and puerilities.
>>
>> Some traditions and duties ye shall fulfill as good servants, other signs of newness we shall now warn against, viz:
>>
>> Knock only at the gates of learning on the side door of College Hall, as you will be forcibly ejected if you attempt to enter by the front door—the portal of the academically elect.
>>
>> Lower your leg draperies to the height of decency and wear not offending haberdashery of the colors red and blue.
>>
>> Inform not the public of your preparatory school valor by wearing any insignia or ornamentation, for the glory of Pennsylvania is what you are striving for.
>>
>> Gratify not your desire to seem big by the conspicuous smoking of the noxious weed on the campus.
>>
>> Sucklings! Ye have heard the just and proper commands; the Solomonic words of wisdom, and the true summing-up of your despicable characters.
>>
>> Wherefore, Take Heed. Class of 1914.
>
> Before the fight last night many of the fraternities gave receptions to Freshmen. The houses were used as headquarters for the fighters and they were supplied with old clothes and shower baths.

traditions. By Christmas of this freshman year, I was as fully immersed in undergraduate doings as it was physically possible to be. I had acquired not only new friends in the fraternity, but also a whole circle of acquaintances among dormitory inhabitants and others from my classes. I was working for the university's publications and had become an enthusiastic football fan. This last interest was purely spectatorial; I knew I could never aspire to be a practicing athlete. I had again gotten advice about it and had been severely warned. There was an old friend of my father's and mother's—Dr. Rae Sheppard Dorsett—who was now a practicing physician in Philadelphia; he and his schoolteacher wife and their two adopted children made me welcome, as an old Chautauquan, in their comfortable Girard Avenue home. From him I had a good deal of counsel concerning my health. I could, he said, lead an almost normal life, but I could never risk overdoing. Not much was known about allergies, as he said, but it was known that tension and strain had a good deal to do with the exaggeration of symptoms; as far as was feasible, I should lead a restrained existence.[24]

Neither then nor afterward would my circumstances permit such a proscription to be carried out except as to athletics. At least it was a kind of caution, and perhaps I did not try my system so badly as I might have done without it. But as a matter of fact, I never had worked harder than I did as a freshman, and I never would work harder again. I was busy from morning until late at night, often very late indeed. Mornings there were classes; about noon began meetings concerning various undergraduate activities, perhaps an assignment for the *Daily Pennsylvanian* (for presently I began work as an active editorial candidate), perhaps committee meetings or fraternity work, perhaps immersion in study or writing; in the evening, if it was not one of "recreation" with its own exhausting qualities, I worked in the library or in our room. It was

---

24. The habit Leslie and I had of tussling on the slightest provocation without loss of temper or emotional disturbance would often bring on an asthmatic attack. Leslie got used to them after a while and developed a theory that I ought to get the best of them by physical training. This was the first of my experiences with those who believed my allergic attacks to be psychosomatic. On occasion I have been tempted to experiments of various kinds to determine if it could be true. The answer is, as I can testify after eighty-some years, that the condition is a physical one.

an unusual night when midnight or just before did not find a group of us, finished with our work, at Beeston's or at Landrigan's White House Cafe, just up the Avenue.[25]

We went to bed physically exhausted after an hour or two devoted to a thorough review of the day with half-a-dozen of our dormitory friends. These night sessions were unpredictable. They might run off into discussions of philosophical differences, or they might involve elaborate and painstaking practical jokes. Such sessions were going on all over the dormitories, and this was the favorite hour for some stentorian-voiced inmate to lean out of his window and start the shrieking clamor of the Yea Rowbottom! Yea-a-a- ROWBOT- TOM! Thus started, perhaps a hundred alarm clocks on window sills would ring together, our heavier-voiced neighbors would disinter their megaphones from places of concealment, and at the worst, water bottles would begin to crash and furniture to fall on the walk below in a strange destructive downpour. Above all the smashing and clang- ing, Yeaaaa Rowbottom! would rise and spread. Such outbreaks might last a few moments or go on for an hour or two. All of us got from them a kind of satisfaction that would seldom again be so full.

There were variations on this Rowbottom theme, both crude and clever, but always of a sort to appeal to the restrained hoodlum- ism of even the best-raised lads. I recall a contribution Leslie and I made to the gradually building dormitory saga—one still recounted there years later. It was the product of inspired improvisation as the best of such inventions are apt to be. At the height of one such commotion, with perhaps fifty loud and impassioned megaphoned speeches pouring into the triangle, with crockery crashing and cow- bells clanging, we lined up a half-dozen of our freshmen neighbors in the hallway where the pay telephone was. Leslie called the nearest fire station, while I, acting as production director, evoked from my chorus, groans, cries, and varieties of other offstage sounds. These, against the background of bedlamic noises from outside, produced what was intended to seem at the other end of the line a frightful holocaust. At any rate, in a matter of minutes it produced at the dormitory gates the massed personnel of three fire companies. They

---

25. This latter, belying its name, was what was known then as a "quick and dirty," and was certainly anything but white.

had galloped in from different directions with a most satisfactory clangor. As we had a right to do, we and a hundred others slammed the heavy cast-iron portals and jabbered through them at the enraged firemen and their associated cops.[26] No authority from outside could, either by law or arrangement (I never knew which), penetrate our dormitory fastness. Our own authorities were supposed to keep order, a mandate they were manifestly unable to carry out on such occasions. There was an investigation and some indignant complaints about our spectacular escapade, but we went unpunished, though measures were taken to make such a *tour de force* less feasible in the future. At any rate we had a moment of fame carried off with what we hoped was appropriate modesty.

So my freshman existence was a busy one, and if a sense of insufficiency plagued me from time to time, it was mostly buried in crowded daily doings. Not the least of these this year, and indeed on into all my undergraduate life, was my exploration of a literature of revolt and reconstruction I had already discovered for myself. I now made further expeditions into that country, quite unlike the sporadic forays I had made while at school at Masten Park. One book led to another; one movement suggested relationships with others; one personality touched others of whose existence I had been wholly unaware. Beginning with the readings Nearing required us to write about during each term, I branched out into the minority history of America and accounts of the leaders of people's movements and their struggles to establish economic and political democracy. This mass of knowledge—the labor and agrarian movements, racial discrimination, municipal corruption, careers of "the robber barons," exploitation of the rest of the country by Wall Street, public utility scandals, the stock watering and trust building of the 1870s and eighties, the railroad

---

26. I may mention also the much-admired contribution of a bass-voiced sophomore in Foerderer House, who memorized all the stations between Philadelphia and Reading and called them backward and forward without hesitation through a huge jointed megaphone. We thought that an accomplishment of a high order.

scandals, the means by which big business had induced state and even national governments to serve its interests—I understood to be my special business to learn about. Gradually, too, I advanced into the alternatives: the political and economic reconstruction suggested by the Populists, the Grangers, and the Farmers Alliance, coming to a climax in Bryan's campaigns, especially his first in 1896; the progressive alternatives of Robert La Follette and his co-workers;[27] the socialists of various sorts—the Old-World traditions of orthodox Marxism and of Christian socialism, as well as the Fabian doctrine and the American variations of Eugene V. Debs and Morris Hillquit; also Henry George's Single Tax. Then there were the revolutionary proposals of those who had concluded that nothing could be done with the present system: the Communists, the Syndicalists, even the Anarchists. I was fascinated by the IWW, that romantic band of martyrs whose intentions were so violent yet so vague.

This was all extraneous to Nearing's freshman course, which was no more than an orthodox development of economics, with some modification under Patten's influence, such as the emphasis on consumption theory, which he had worked over so carefully in the years just past. To this theory I devoted myself, finding that I could, as we said, "get by" without extraordinary effort in other subjects. Economics as it was being developed by academicians—except, of course, Patten—was curiously uninfluenced by the German professors under whom so many of them had studied. They had gone to Germany—to Berlin, Leipzig, Halle, Heidelberg, Dresden—often for several graduate years, become doctors of philosophy, come back to the United States, and begun teaching out of English textbooks, as though they had never been exposed to another tradition. Moreover, their own textbooks, as they wrote them, were obviously merely modified versions of the English classics: Smith, Ricardo, Malthus, McCulloch, the Mills, Jevons, and Marshall.

There were reasons for this—not that they occurred to me as an undergraduate—having to do with the language, with the older American habit of copying from the English, common in the New

---

27. Cf. La Follette's *Autobiography* (Madison: University of Wisconsin Press, 1963), Claude G. Bowers's *Beveridge and the Progressive Era* (New York: Literary Guild, 1932), Louis Filler's *Crusaders for American Liberalism*, new ed. (Yellow Springs, Ohio: Antioch Press, 1964), and Richard Hofstadter's *Age of Reform* (New York: Knopf, 1955).

England colleges where economics had been taught for several generations, and with general American deference, as well as the support furnished by classical theory for the capitalist system. Professors of economics already had a reputation for radicalism by 1911, but it was a kind of orthodox radicalism, falling considerably short of fundamental questioning. Academic indignation was something like ministerial disapproval in the Protestant churches: it was confined to sins recognized even by the sinners. Businessmen who became monopolistic, who engaged in unfair trade practices, who, for lack of regulation, exploited labor and consumers, knew well enough that they were being wicked. By their own standards, they could not logically object to reproaches. They might not like being singled out as ill-doers, but they could not defend their behavior. So long, therefore, as economists were only against the sins in the laissez-faire book, they were well within their recognized rights. They might become obstreperous reformers, even, without seriously departing from orthodoxy; indeed, in so acting, they would be its defenders.

It was when they became "socialists" (the favorite curse word then), when they questioned whether a business system was justified at all by its works, that they departed dangerously from the accepted faith and were likely to be cast out by their own profession and to incur the displeasure of businessmen. Scott Nearing, because he afterward became the central figure in one famous academic freedom case, is an interesting example. I had the luck not only to hear him lecture, but to be in one of his quiz sections.[28] Almost at once I began to understand that an important issue was coming up having to do with the fabric of our university society and the limitations on our theoretical freedom. I did not have it properly oriented; at the time it seemed to me merely a matter of being for or against the exploited groups in the community. I suspect that Nearing was not too clear about it either, or perhaps it would be better to say he was *too* clear and quite mistaken. If he had a fault (although when I worked with him my admiration and regard were such that I was reluctant to grant that he had faults at all), it was that distinctions were too sharp. There was

---

28. The system then in each major course, was to have, a lecture or two each week; there were also meetings of small groups once or twice a week to discuss the lectures and such readings as had been assigned. These were directed mostly by younger "quiz-masters," but the course director himself usually took a section or two and held briefing sessions with his assistants. Later on, in this way, I began my teaching career with Nearing.

too much good and bad and not enough in between. He was, in other words, insufficiently realistic, not willing to compromise. Lincoln Steffens, who was interested in the same problems, saw them so much in the in-between shades that he could never make up his mind what really was right or wrong.[29]

I mention Steffens because I had had considerable admiration for him. I was never directly under his personal influence as I was now under Nearing's; nevertheless, his books and articles had been for me a rather puzzling body of work. He had left me frustrated and indecisive: he found the bad men good and the good men bad all through the system. This was all very well for a beginning, but it was not much more than a clever observation. It did not explain the paradox. My own doubts had a tendency to clear up with Nearing's teaching, and the few following years would be among the easiest of my life in that way. The incipient radicalism of the high school student turned to a kind of hopeful social morality. I knew which side I had to be on, and I knew why. I knew that institutions had to be improved, and I thought I knew something of how it must be done.[30]

---

29. I ought to say about Nearing, however, that he never personalized evil. He never thought men were wicked even when they were obviously and quite personally persecuting him. He always blamed the system, the institutions. He believed that to change the system would be to reform men.

30. The kind of social philosophy I was developing under the tutelage of Nearing, reinforced by other instruction, is perhaps best defined in a little book called *The Super Race* (New York: Huebsch), which Nearing published in 1912. It illustrates the reformist aims of that time. Also it illustrates, what I now feel to have been extremely important for me, the close mutual relationships in the Wharton School of 1910–20 of all the social studies. Nearing's thesis was that it was quite possible to develop a Super Race through (1) eugenics—the science of race culture; (2) social adjustment—the science of molding institutions; and (3) education—the science of individual development.

There were in our sociology program a whole series of biologically based courses looking to racial and social improvement. And a good deal of attention was given to the mechanism of heredity. We studied Mendel, Weissmann, Darwin, Huxley, Galton, and Spencer, as well as contemporary figures, going as far as mere readers could who were interested not as researchers but in conclusions for a philosophy.

Nearing's concept of the Super Race was the logical outcome of the economics of reform, the sociology of race improvement, and of governmental institutions devoted to social welfare. How we felt at that time is expressed in one of his closing paragraphs:

> With a boundless wealth of natural resources; bulwarked by the stock of the dominant races; with abundant leisure; granting freedom and individuality to women; foregoing war; cognizant of the principles of race making, social adjustment and education, the American nation is thrown into the foreground as the land for development of the Super

This conviction would determine my decision to become an economics instructor and to study our economic and political system. I would not by then be a literal follower of Nearing, but I would have the same intentions. Most students took the Nearing criticism of the economic system as something a good deal less than a questioning of its values. Even some of the most conservative had a momentary feeling that something ought to be done about child labor, about the denial of collective bargaining to labor unions, about the poverty among the disadvantaged, and about the privileges of the few. He had that effect. He and others like him must have been influential in softening up a whole generation. When it came into positions of power, it would give way on many of these issues. The war that was to come so soon would be far more disturbing to those of us who had accepted the need for reforms than to others who had not. We would see it as the beginning of a world reaction to colonial imperialism. Others would regard it as merely a challenge by the suddenly upstart Germans who were determined to dominate the accepted system.

Not even the German-trained professors anticipated the war. Some of them, indeed, were more amazed than ordinary folk at its outbreak. Certainly our freshman world in 1911–12 held no intimation of what was so soon to come. We were learning a trade. Most of my friends were intending to comply with Wharton's adjurations to mercantile youth. They would become good businessmen. A few others, myself included, meant to become something else. That something else might involve public service or it might be an academic career. At that point we were far vaguer than the others who knew exactly what they wanted, the ones who were going into business.

Race. The American people have within their grasp the torch of social progress. Can they develop a race of men who shall set a standard for the world-men of physical and mental power, efficient, broadly sympathetic, actuated by the highest ideals, striving toward a vision of human nobleness?

It was out of this philosophy that I later wrote the verses that would be so often quoted, containing the line "I shall roll up my sleeves, make America over." Making America over was what I thought we were supposed to do. Quoting these lines of mine would be intended as ridicule, meant to show what a set of impractical dreamers we were. It would be a long time from 1912 to 1934. By then no one would hope to do more than establish minimum standards of living; ten years after that, intentions would have declined to the faint hope for mere survival.

I must note that my copy of this long-forgotten little book was presented to my mother by Nearing with an inscription that said: "Since you are doing so much for the Super Race I thought that this book about it might interest you."

They wanted to make money, to become substantial and influential, to become, in fact, managers and directors. There was also an in-between group: those who would be experts in a dozen categories—accounting, insurance, finance, business law, and so on—and might decide to join the civil service or to go to work for one of the big corporations where the duties of an expert, at least in the lower levels, were not easily distinguishable from many of those in government. To the larger middle group this choice was an indifferent one.

Reactions to Nearing's teaching were varied. Since it had a hard core of satisfyingly difficult theory, much of the students' efforts had to go into learning the elements of production, consumption, exchange, and distribution.[31] Production did not detain us long; neither did consumption, although its theory had been greatly extended, as I have noted, in strictly orthodox terms, by Patten. Much of the attention necessarily went to the elaboration of value theory and its effect on the exchange of goods and services. But there was, at the latter end, long consideration of the distributive shares and their adequacy. This was where the quarrels of those days centered. No one suggested more than modifications of the orthodox theory. Even the more radical accepted that system; their radicalism consisted of showing that businessmen were violating the canons of the theory they accepted.

The economists, in concentrating on this kind of criticism, were within a perfectly good American tradition. The agrarian and labor movements and the political revolts so representatively illustrated in Hiram Johnson of California and Robert La Follette of Wisconsin were orthodox in the same sense as the economists. The monopolists or those who engaged in unfair trade practices, those who exploited labor beyond the going rules, and those who cheated consumers were making it impossible for the system to operate beneficiently, as it might be expected to do if there were freedom and strict adherence to accepted standards. Selfishness was, to this extent, not enlightened, a matter the orthodox found it difficult to explain. But the general opinion at that time was that if individuals failed to act according to formula, they ought to be made to conform. Enlightened standards of self-interest ought to be strictly enforced. This involved suppress-

---

31. Land, labor, capital, and management were the productive factors. The distributive shares corresponded with the elements of production: land received rent, labor received wages, capital received interest, and management received profits. These were the classical categories.

ing monopolies, regulating hours of labor and working conditions, and supervising the quality of goods and the performance of services.

It was believed that if there were freedom within well-enforced rules, the propensity of men to compete would ensure the fixing of fair wages and prices in the market place; workers, consumers, and merchants alike would be treated fairly. Exploitation would be impossible. Some critics suspected that escaping from this theoretically free competition was a primary and, indeed, natural activity among all businesses and that *the enforcement of freedom* was a contradiction in terms. But Nearing held to the orthodox theory. In my freshman year the exegesis of fundamentals was still emphasized more than the criticism of departure from them. This was changing; the criticism was getting sharper year by year.

There was ample reason. These were the later years of McKinley-Roosevelt-Taft Republicanism. William Jennings Bryan's defeat by William McKinley, who was managed by Mark Hanna, began the complaisance concerning completely free enterprise that was only slightly modified even during the loud-talking regime of Theodore Roosevelt.[32] This complaisance returned when William Howard Taft succeeded Roosevelt. Since 1900 the government in Washington had very nearly been reduced to puppetlike motions controlled by the lobbyists for big business. This happened in spite of earnest protests not only by La Follette, but by George Norris, Albert Cummins, William Kenyon, Albert Beveridge, and others, mostly Westerners, who were known as insurgents.

It was somewhat different in the state capitals or in the seats of municipal government. It was, in fact, worse, because it was more open and cynical. The period had begun in an atmosphere of moral abdication. The excitement of the Spanish-American War and the agitation by the agrarians, culminating in Bryan's campaigns in 1896 and 1900, seemed to bore the electorate. People had sunk back after these efforts into a long lethargy, interrupted by severe depressions and once in a while the election of a Progressive to some office. Then,

---

32. Roosevelt spoke harshly of the "malefactors of great wealth" but made such a distinction between "good" and "bad" trusts that the force of his diatribes was lost. As far as theoretical laissez-faire was concerned, goodness or badness was irrelevant; the control of prices and the consequent exploitation of competitors, consumers, and workers was what really mattered. Whether it was arrived at legitimately or illegitimately, the effect was the same. But T. Roosevelt never looked at the business system realistically, or perhaps it was politically convenient not to. At any rate his maledictions served mostly to stir public opinion.

of course, there had been the customary war and postwar boom. The catastrophic economic events of 1907 resulted in no more than a momentary awakening. The weight of the depression had been borne by those least able to bear it, and its causes had not been generally appreciated. There had been sporadic revolts among those who were called on to suffer, but strikes had been ruthlessly broken, and even local third-party movements had been contained. In the United States Senate was a group of dissatisfied protestants, but there were also Nelson Aldrich, Orville Platt, Henry Cabot Lodge, and Boies Penrose to prevent any damage to business.

It had been a period, nevertheless, when approaches to a wide public had been found by the muckrakers,[33] as well as the growing group of Progressives. It had been a period, too, when reformers had gathered surprising followings, although none had had a national success. Material accumulated by the journalists in the preceding decade was now being enlarged and systematized by my Wharton School professors. Like others in other universities, they were investigating more extensively and were closer to causes than Steffens and his colleagues. They used a good deal of their research for teaching purposes, too, although a freshman naturally would not be exposed to much of it. But from 1903, when the first Steffens and Tarbell articles appeared in *McClure's,* the journalists had found an audience whose size caused consternation among conservatives.[34] For once,

---

33. It is interesting that this term, which later came to be worn as a badge of honor by Steffens, Ray Stannard Baker, Ida Tarbell, David G. Phillips, Charles E. Russell, Upton Sinclair, and others, was fastened on them with intended scorn by T. Roosevelt himself in a speech in 1906. It was, in effect, an attack on all those who were then exposing corruption. He recalled the Man with the Muckrake in Bunyan's *Pilgrim's Progress* who "could look no way but downward . . . who was offered the celestial crown for his muckrake, but would neither look up nor regard the crown he was offered, but continued to rake the muck on the floor."

34. Accounts of the fascinating muckraking period can be found in a number of personal records, for instance, those of Steffens, Baker, Tarbell, and Russell, all of whom wrote autobiographies. So, in fact, did McClure, the entrepreneur for this kind of literature. Later assessments can be found in histories like that of Samuel Eliot Morison and Henry Steele Commager: *The Growth of the American Republic* (New York and London: Oxford University Press, 1930); in Mark Sullivan's *Our Times* (New York: Scribner, 1926–35); in Lloyd Morris's *Postscript to Yesterday* (New York: Random House, 1947); Louis Filler's *Crusaders for American Liberalism;* and C. C. Regier's *The Era of the Muckrakers* (Gloucester, Mass.: P. Smith, 1957). And the effect of combined general complaisance and sporadic reform on political thought can be traced in C. E. Merriam's *American Political Ideas* (New York: Macmillan, 1923); Edward R. Lewis's *A History of American Political Thought from the Civil War*

epithets had no effect.[35] Even Roosevelt's "muckraker" became an honorable appellation. In one city after another, reform movements were organized and led by colorful characters, none of whom had a desire to make fundamental changes or felt that any were necessary, but whose battles against corruption at least made loud commotions.[36] Among the most notable of these, in the tradition of John Peter Altgeld, were Tom L. Johnson in Cleveland, Henry T. Hunt in Cincinnati, and Brand Whitlock in Toledo,[37] Joseph W. Folk in

---

to the World War (New York: Macmillan, 1937); and V. L. Parrington's *Main Currents in American Thought* (New York: Harcourt, Brace, 1954–58), as well as in more general histories of the time.

35. "Communist," "Socialist," "Anarchist" were indifferently used, just as they had been in the eighties by Collis Huntington when his railroad piracies had been checked, and as they would be later on in the era of McCarthyism.

36. These municipal movements were not actually brought about by the writers. For instance, Joseph W. Folk in Missouri was in full operation when Steffens first visited St. Louis. But the muckrakers undoubtedly helped to make reform easier. National audiences followed "The Shame of Minneapolis," "The Shamelessness of St. Louis," "Philadelphia, Corrupt and Contented," and all the rest. So with Steffens's articles about the state capitals. The remarkable thing is that within a short time the movement disappeared altogether, not quite as though it had never been, because it lived on in some people's minds, but at any rate from the national scene. What was left were such movements as the National Municipal League, the Civil Reform Association, the National Planning Association, and the like.

37. The most self-conscious of these was Whitlock, whose real ambitions were literary and who regarded his political activities more as education than as a career. This can be seen from reading *The Letters and Journal of Brand Whitlock* (edited by Allan Nevins [New York: Appleton-Century, 1936]). In spite of—or perhaps because of—being primarily a literary man (see *Forty Years of It* [New York: Appleton, 1914], *The Turn of the Balance* [Indianapolis: Bobbs-Merrill, 1907]), he never penetrated very deeply the causes of the conditions he deplored. His ideas of reform stopped at home rule for cities, penal reorganization, and similar superficial changes. His gradual progress, after becoming Wilson's Minister to Belgium, was, in spite of his wartime experience, toward a kind of disillusioned conservatism. He found that he liked the formalities of diplomatic life and gradually became more and more an esthete. He had once been called a socialist for believing in the municipal ownership of utilities, but the Russian revolution offended his sense of propriety and caused him to confide to his diary that socialism was a revolting and dangerous enemy of civilization. He became so withdrawn a litterateur that when he was displaced by Harding in 1912, he retired to the Riviera. Thenceforth he lived a secluded, even if busy, life. His *La Fayette* (New York: Appleton, 1929) was written in Cannes. He, like so many others, was lost to the main current of American life when the mild reforms he had fought for had been accomplished. He was incapable of visualizing new goals and of mobilizing his energies in the interest of new accomplishments. He died without ever returning to the Midwest.

St. Louis, Francis J. Heney in San Francisco, and Rudolph Blankenburg in Philadelphia.[38]

There had been some battles more notable than those of the municipal reformers—that, for instance, of La Follette, who, because of his Wisconsin fame and his leadership in the Senate, was by now a national figure. He was more prominent as a progressive leader than were Albert Beveridge, for instance, or Hiram Johnson, who had had somewhat similar careers. It was during this freshman year of mine that La Follette made his first bid for the presidency. A year before (in December 1910) as spokesman for the Insurgents, he had issued a manifesto for a Progressive Republican league. Roosevelt, back from his African trip (in June 1910), had begun to expound his "New Nationalism" and had, in fact (in August), made a speech at Ossawatomie underlining his growing differences with his protégé Taft: "I stand for the square deal. . . . I mean not merely that I stand for fair play under the present rules of the game, but that I stand for having those rules changed so as to work for more substantial equality of opportunity and of reward for equally good service. . . . we must drive special interests out of politics."

Roosevelt and Taft were not quite yet political enemies, but Gifford Pinchot and James R. Garfield, conservationists who had been ousted by Taft in the notorious Ballinger quarrel, as well as other Progressives, had Roosevelt's ear.[39] In spite of Taft's attempt to keep up friendly relations, Roosevelt was pulling away. He had, however, assured La Follette that he would not be a candidate for the presidency, whereupon in the fall of 1911, La Follette had begun to

---

38. Cf. C. F. Jenkins, "The Blankenburg Administration in Philadelphia: A Symposium," *The National Municipal Review* 5 (1916): 211–25. Morris Llewellyn Cooke, friend of Frederick W. Taylor and of several Wharton professors, was Commissioner of Public Works in the Blankenburg cabinet, and occasionally he talked to our classes. Clyde King, Ward Pierson, and others of our faculty collaborated in the investigation of municipal corruption and inefficiency for several years; numbers of us who were students of economics and government assisted in such ways as we could. Some discomfort was caused for the United Gas Improvement (U.G.I.), the Philadelphia Rapid Transit (P.R.T.), and others of Philadelphia's vulnerable interests, most of which had directors or lawyers who were also trustees of the university. The consequences of this conflict will be discussed later on.

39. Following at a distance the controversy between Richard Ballinger and Pinchot, I came to my first active realization of the attempts to exploit the public domain by cattle- and sheepmen in the West and by the timber companies who were busily slaughtering the forests.

campaign in earnest as the acknowledged leader of the Progressives with what looked like an excellent chance of displacing Taft. But in February 1912 in the middle of a speech in Philadelphia, he had a mysterious seizure. He became almost incoherent, wandered widely from his text, and seemed to be dazed, raising at once the question of whether or not he was permanently deranged.[40] This dramatic occurrence was the closest I had yet come to events of political importance, and I was greatly excited. La Follette's challenge seemed to be in a fine American tradition, and I had hoped for his success.[41] After this Philadelphia tragedy it became quite obvious that Roosevelt was going to make use of the Progressive movement for his own purposes. La Follette could not recover from the enormous exaggeration of the incident in the reactionary press. I lost interest in Progressive Republicanism because of its obvious perversion and began to watch hopefully the career of Woodrow Wilson, who was governor of New Jersey and seemed a possible Democratic nominee.

The reaction from the long dominance of government by "the interests" was by now very strong and very widespread. This was the

---

40. This incident bulks very large in my memory. It seemed a real disaster to all young Progressives. It led directly to T. Roosevelt's inheritance of the movement and therefore to its betrayal. If La Follette had been the candidate in 1912, subsequent developments might have been quite different. The La Follette speech was at a newspaper publishers' dinner. He was tired from a long speechmaking tour and worried about a family illness. He had a manuscript but soon began to depart from it, attacking the publishers and, in raucous language, the "money power." It was not his ordinary exposition but an intemperate diatribe, recognized by his hearers as abnormal. Many, in embarrassment, left. He shook his fist at them and said, "There go some of those I'm hitting." The chairman called him to order, saying that personal abuse would not be permitted. He continued. Thus he began to wander, repeating passages and losing all coherence. Finally the hall had almost emptied, but he talked on for an hour afterward, wandering and pathetic, then fell forward on the table.

Pinchot and others like him had already been trying to go over to Roosevelt anyway; in Chicago, Medill McCormick seized the occasion to proclaim that La Follette was through.

Even the *New York Tribune* had some pity: "The haste with which most of the insurgent leaders are seeking to clamp the lid down on Senator La Follette's candidacy must excite the compassion of those who believe that there should be at least some moderate standard of honor among politicians. . . ." But the Roosevelt Progressives were merciless. They saw their chance and seized it with cynical energy. Soon Roosevelt's "hat was in the ring," and the movement became less Progressive than merely Rooseveltian.

41. His picture is the only one of any public man I find in my freshman memento book, together with clippings describing the disastrous speech.

reason for Roosevelt's sudden adherence to the Progressive cause. Aside from political chances he had taken for the conservation cause, he had guarded his Republican credentials with great care.[42] Now, however, inflated by his reception abroad and by the deterioration of the Taft administration, he saw a chance to capitalize on the formidable Progressive revolt from Republicanism.[43] That this would be at the same time a betrayal of his loyal successor, Taft, and of La Follette and the Progressive cause gave him no visible qualms. He was a true political adventurer. It was obvious that if the Democrats should choose one of their old guard as a candidate, the Progressives might well win. The dislike I felt for Roosevelt added value to my Democratic inheritance. I was going to cast a presidential vote for the first time in 1912, and I began to hope that it would be for Wilson.

Another interest of great importance to me was developing along with these new political and economic ones: the amelioration of social conditions represented by professional social work, by the organization of charity, and by the settlement house movement. Hull House in Chicago was the most famous of these last, though there were others in all large cities. I was beginning to have a better understanding of what my sociology teachers called "the social debtor classes." We were, in 1911–12, on the verge of real attempts to correct serious social injustices. It was in 1911 that Wayne McVeagh called on President Taft to "stop widening and begin narrowing the gulf between the rich and the poor" by the use of the federal taxing power. And this was only a representative statement of the attitude support-

---

42. The Country Life Conference, held at the White House in his administration was the first real demonstration of the political importance of conservation. Its influence was a continuing one, and it would grow into a massive movement during the next generation.

43. A Democratic congressional majority had been returned in 1910, and Champ Clark had emerged as Speaker of the House and the most prominent of the regular Democrats. This was the year Franklin D. Roosevelt first ran as a Democrat and was elected to the New York State Senate.

ing Wilson's reforms. An important one of these was the graduated income tax.[44] And perhaps another important one was the amendment providing for the direct election of United States senators.[45] In states and municipalities there were numerous other electoral reforms.

Such efforts represented no genuinely fundamental changes; mostly, in fact, they were inheritances from earlier movements. They were embodied in the third party manifesto of 1912, but they could also be found in Democratic pronouncements. They went back, most of them, to the agrarian demands of the eighties and nineties, and many of them could be found in the Populist platform of 1892. They were merely delayed items of a change that ought to have been brought about some decades earlier to have been really useful. The delay had worsened the many injustices in a system marked by the extravagances of Newport, Palm Beach, and Fifth Avenue and tolerance of the slums and sweatshops of New York's lower East Side. These conditions were duplicated in Buffalo and Philadelphia, as I well knew, and elsewhere, as I was learning. Many of those who were favored by this system were incredibly complacent and thickskinned, but this was not a universal rule. There were others who at one stage or another became convicted of sin, and tried, sometimes desperately, to free their consciences by charity. This happened fairly frequently. There had, in fact, been so much private giving that a movement had been organized to direct philanthropy in such ways as to do the most good for those who were helpless. Since 1873 there had been a National Conference of Charities and Corrections. In 1882 the Charity Organization Society was founded in New York, and by now there was one in nearly every large city. There was also, a growing number of foundations managed by trustees. The Carnegie, Russell Sage, Rockefeller, and

---

44. A constitutional amendment had been made necessary by Supreme Court interpretations. The Congress passed a resolution for this purpose in 1909, and it was ratified by the necessary number of states by 1913, whereupon an income tax law was passed and signed by Wilson.

45. Instead of by the state legislatures. A resolution for this purpose was passed by the Congress in 1912 and ratified by 1913. This was only one of the several electoral reforms of that time: others were the establishment of direct primaries, proportional representation, the initiative and referendum, the recall of officials, and in municipalities new forms of government, such as the commission, the city manager plan, and the like. All these I was studying in my political science courses. Some were tried locally; none affected the federal electoral processes.

Fels organizations were examples of these. Reorganization of efforts to study the causes of poverty, to understand juvenile delinquency, to mitigate racial prejudice, and to grant women legal rights, all went along with the major effort to better the situation of workers who suffered so many disadvantages in our "free economy."

This kind of knowledge and understanding was almost wholly new to me. It came not only through my undergraduate sociology courses,[46] but also through the books I was first introduced to in that supplementary list for Nearing's economics course. Nearing divided the list into two categories: one group was expository accounts of social and economic problems, with, perhaps, suggestions for their solutions; and the other was fictional treatments of injustice or exploitation that were having an effect on public opinion. Sometimes, as in the books of W. A. White, it was hard to distinguish fact from fiction, but since it was truly representative in any case, such classifications did not much matter.[47]

---

46. Notably those of Professors Carl Kelsey and J. P. Lichtenberger.

47. Scott Nearing, as this account was begun, still thought of himself as an educator, although he had long been involuntarily separated from the teaching profession. I had lost touch with him for more than thirty years when the attempt to recall my Wharton School experiences brought him so vividly to mind that I began inquiring about his activities. He had lived for a long time on a Vermont farm and had spent his winters journeying about to various campuses where groups of students organized meetings to hear him speak. He was still writing, too, although publication for him was restricted to an audience interested in privately printed pamphlets and a newsletter he sent to those who subscribed. All this had escaped me.

In 1952 I wrote to ask whether he could help me in reconstructing the readings for the economics course in 1911. I received the following reply. I was deeply affected by its optimism and courage; I was ashamed not to have known of his persecution.

San Bernardino, Calif.
12/20/52

Thanks for your letter of December 5, which reached me here.

Helen and I left home (Cape Rosier, Maine) on a six-month tour, designed to enlighten as many people as possible on the current trends in U.S.A. and elsewhere. We were led to do this by the increased efforts of the oligarchy to prevent the transmission of information which the oligarchy considers unorthodox or subversive.

To this end we bought a used Plymouth suburban, loaded in all of the printed matter the springs would carry, and set out on Oct. 9. Thus far we have driven more than 7,000 miles, having held about 75 meetings in 71 days, have contacted many individuals outside the meetings, have given away much printed matter and sold about $1000 worth of pamphlets and books.

On the whole our reception has been more cordial than we had expected. We find

I must add that in 1972 Nearing published *The Making of a Radical,* an account of his experiences. It was a mark of welcome change that passages from it were published in the *Pennsylvania Gazette,* a magazine for the alumni. It was an account the university had no reason to be proud of, but in doing this the *Gazette* made amends for another generation's departures from decent behavior. Somewhat later the president, Martin Meyerson, and the faculty went further. They made Nearing an honorary Professor Emeritus. His promotion had taken sixty years.

From the list of readings each student was asked to read any three in each term, making six in all, and to write reviews of them. It was part of the quiz master's task to read and comment on these. This assignment was not regarded with the same seriousness by all students, and most of them read no more than was required; however, for some, an introduction to such books and the opportunity to discuss them with instructors were regarded as among the most rewarding of all freshman activities. What I wrote about some of these books first brought me to Nearing's notice. He sent for me more than

---

a small but growing Resistance to war, exploitation, discrimination and injustice and a determination to end these social maladjustments by setting up a more orderly and stable economy and polity. As yet this group has no detailed program, that will come later. For the present these people are seeking, though some of them are ready for affirmative social action.

Optimism. The outlook was never better. Who would have hoped that Asia, Africa and parts of Latin America and Europe would be on the socialist construction job so soon after the European collapse in 1936–45. Under old conditions this step might have taken centuries. Technology has made it possible in a couple of decades—and with few semblances of a dark age in between.

Economics 161. In 1917, when the Federal Snoopers rifled my house and loaded all of my papers into a truck, I stopped keeping records. At the moment I have virtually none —not even a file of my own writings. Wharton School records went with the others.

Now, more than ever, I feel that all men and women who love order, beauty and justice, and who serve the truth as they see it, must be prepared for action—ready to take what comes, with the barest minimum of belongings or entanglements. Only so will we be able to meet the onslaught of ignorance, bigotry and fanaticism which the Vatican and the Truman administration have conjured up by their incessant invocation of fear, hate and the spirit of vengeance.

When I mentioned optimism, I should have qualified my statement by a reference to the ferocity of the U.S.A. oligarchy.

Yes, after 20 years in Vermont on a self-determined project, we sold out last winter and moved to Maine. Cape Rosier is the Post Office.

Stop in if you ever get up that way.

Hail to the great times which lie ahead!

Scott

once and, sitting me down in the bare and orderly but crowded office on the third floor of Logan Hall, probed the apparently unusual attitudes he had discovered.[48] Those for me were exciting explorations. In all the categories of social interest mentioned here Nearing had information and connections. It was not long before he invited me—as he often did his students—out for an evening at his suburban house. There I learned what a family was like whose interests were mainly intellectual. I learned that scholarly affairs need not be merely retreats for stolen moments; they could be ordinary daily occupations. For Nellie (Seeds) Nearing, Scott's wife, no less than he, was caught up in the general movement of those times for change and reform. She was, I learned, a graduate of Bryn Mawr and was in the process of taking her Ph.D. degree at the University of Pennsylvania. They had one boy of their own and one who had been adopted. They were lively boys, and I came to know them well.[49]

Scott's specialty (by now I was calling him Scott) was facts. All our discussions revolved about them. This, too, was something new to me. It was his own conviction that it was necessary to buttress criticisms by careful research and that this was, after all, not hard to do. It was this that was causing the widespread disapproval of reactionary Philadelphians, for if one Establishment attitude was more marked than any other, it was the desire to escape from unpleasant reality. All the less defensible results of free enterprise had to be concealed and ignored. Probers beneath the gloss so carefully protected by press and pulpit were naturally regarded with abhorrence. Even a freshman could know that Scott's promotion had been retarded, that a certain number of Wharton alumni wanted to be rid of him, and that his teaching was regarded as an affront to the tradition so well represented by the university's trustees and administrators.[50]

---

48. As I remember, the economics offices were shared by six or seven instructors. Nearing never had a private office during his years of service at the university. Later on, I should have a desk near his and learn what it was like to try to work under such conditions.

49. John, their own child, after all the notoriety of the next few years, would, on Scott's advice, drop the Nearing part of his name. As John Scott he would become a foreign correspondent. Years later, returning from Europe during World War II, he would stop over with me at La Fortaleza in San Juan.

50. Edgar Fahs Smith, the provost, was a distinguished chemist in a not very creative way, but in all matters of the mind, he was a reactionary of the most mulish

I am not able to separate certainly the events of 1911–12 from those of the three succeeding years. During all this time I was spreading out. I was devoted to several quite different, though not necessarily conflicting, activities. At some time in the future, I hoped to be able to bring all these into one scheme. For the present that was impossible. I was trying to live as an economic dissident in what was essentially a conservative, even a reactionary, environment in spite of some liberalism among my instructors. I believed in and wanted to work for change, and yet I had a well-developed appreciation of tradition. I wanted to be of public service, yet I saw the need for a profession.

That these divergent pulls involved some strain I do not need to insist. Gradually, as the undergraduate years unrolled, it would become clearer what I had to do, but only slowly did I became aware that all my closest interests could be brought together in academic life. Not too strangely, I think, I was held back from such a conclusion by seeing the disfavor my friend Scott had to contend with.

Actually, of course, I enjoyed the many pleasures available to my generation and was not too troubled by divergent desires. I went from one thing to another, packing experiences into appropriate compartments. If occasionally I was surprised at what had happened since I opened the door for the last insertion, it was a surprise I could handle. Everything was under control. I was well integrated, really, or at least well enough integrated so that everything made some sense and there was much enjoyment. When summer came, I felt I was making genuine progress at last. I looked forward happily to my sophomore year.

In that year came an awareness of the grand pageant of the American past and its relationship to what seemed to be just ahead in the future. We who were yet unconscious of it were destined to participate in global conflict, in the assumption by our nation of premier power, and the emergence of mankind into years of exposure to colossal risks. I myself would come to such participation in future events with something deeper than mere patriotic sentiment. In fact,

---

sort—even in religion. One of the worst experiences of my undergraduate days was a revival campaign under his sponsorship at the university by that mountebank of fundamentalism Billy Sunday. The provost wanted all of us to be "saved," and he exposed himself to the ridicule of the whole campus in his efforts to foster enthusiasm for an evangelical crusade.

because of my unusual university education, the base from which I would move would be world-wide and inclusive, if nothing else. This sense of largeness and depth I owed to geography, to history, to Kelsey's kind of sociology, to Patten's geopolitics and geointellectualism, and to a basic acquaintance with political theory and public law.

My courses in law were lively. I always found a way to schedule one or two every year, and from them I learned how men had found ways to compromise their differences and live with less frequent recourse to violence. This branched out into the making of government, and I was taught in a series of courses in constitutional law under Leo S. Rowe and Clyde King how our institutions had been conceived and shaped. We read the documents, studied the cases, and argued the issues as predecessor generations had seen them. As a result of this, I became for the first time consciously American. Heretofore, I had never considered seriously, or even at all, my own relationship to my country. Now as I saw how its institutions had unfolded in the conflicts among contending interests and in the reasoning of Adams, Jefferson, Hamilton, Madison, Marshall, and the other great executives and justices, I had a new pride in our traditions, which extended itself to an almost equally prideful regard for all things British. I began to recall my relationship in blood and my nearness, even in time, to the England of the common law, of people's sovereignty, of civil rights, and of the literature that now seemed such a faithful reflection of my origins.

It is a wicked exaggeration to say, as I hear it said sometimes, that what happens in the classroom is of little importance in the educational process, and that students, after all, must fight their own way through the accumulated mass of knowledge to the areas on the periphery where there are still advances to be made. At least in my case what happened in the classroom was critical. I had my share of uninspired instructors, but I also had a succession of teachers to whom I sat with attention and benefit. As I look back, the incidents of the classroom, though I cannot always separate them clearly from one another, and cannot always give them a time, are still quite as vivid and, in perspective, much more important, than the other items of undergraduate life. I can see my teachers behind their desks and in their offices, recall their personalities, their ways of expounding the subjects they had mastered; even their foibles and weaknesses seem to have contributed, somehow, to the whole experience of education.

Not all my freshman instructors were younger men of the faculty: J. Russell Smith in geography, Ward Pierson in commercial law, and James T. Young in government would be called elders. Since 1904, Young had been director, as the Wharton School's maturity had been reluctantly conceded, and Smith had already begun to publish the long series of texts that familiarized a whole generation of youngsters with their world. Smith's lectures were not, I discovered, so interesting to all my classmates as they were to me. Most of the young men were more concerned with the methodology of administration than in the reasons commerce flowed as it did and why cities and industries were where they were. This I learned in various ways, for example, by noting that the later tennis champion Bill Tilden (whose name, also beginning with T, placed him next to me in a row far up toward the ceiling where it was stuffy) thought of Smith's lecture hour as a convenient period for catching up on sleep. He woke up with a start with remarkable regularity after forty-five minutes and spent the last five minutes copying my notes. Somewhere before graduation he fell by the wayside. It was in Smith's lecture, too, that some rascal who sat by the center aisle discovered (or, more likely, rediscovered) the art of rolling nickels down the steep stairway. A coin started skillfully at the top would sometimes roll all the way to the pit, falling off each of some twenty flights with a most satisfactory clink. These comments Professor Smith was good natured enough not to resent overmuch. But they never happened to Dean Young. He had a suave manner, but the steel was visible just under the surface, and no one had the temerity to try him very far.

Ward Pierson won our hearts with a story he told in his opening lecture to illustrate the complicated nature of property rights. It began with an elaborate description of a woman of easy virtue proceeding down a public street in a shiny, red-wheeled buggy, parasol atilt, and feathered hat fluffing in the breeze. The question was whether, being engaged in the unlawful pursuit of soliciting, she was entitled to damages when her vehicle was smashed in a runaway caused by her horses' fright at a gesticulating policeman. It was a nice point, and he made the most of it to an obviously appreciative audience. Even at this distance I can sense the good will he gained. Ward Pierson, although he was over fifty when he enlisted, was killed in action a few years later, and we all regretted his loss. He treated us like men of the world. He was at heart a boulevardier as well as a professor, and we did not think the two incompatible. I can imagine that he went into battle as gaily as he always came into the lecture room, a big, handsome figure, with a flower in his buttonhole and a wicked gleam in his eye.

But the procession of collegiate years, even if they did not sober us overmuch, started me, at least, on the way toward an increasing comprehension of that vast onward movement of civilization toward the unknown. It was beyond possibility that my generation should do more than make a start, but nothing seems really impossible to youth. In those years I first began to put things into patterns, and pattern-making finally became for me a long-time preoccupation. I have said that Simon Patten contributed most to that: he did it by considering wholes, using the same methods and with no more paraphernalia of analysis than others of my teachers used in considering lesser social organisms, movements, and forces. He calmly assumed that we would follow him into the most subtle analyses of human achievement, and if we were often bewildered, he ignored it. I described in a biographical essay written about him after his death how this preoccupation with the civilized past came about, or, perhaps I should say, I tried to explain as much as I could of the mysterious greatness in the man.[51] He was called an economist, and, in fact, he had in the past written even more subtly than his American contemporaries—Clark, Richard Ely, Edwin Seligman, John R. Commons, Herbert J. Davenport, J. H. Hollander, or Frank A. Fetter—in the tradition of classical economics, and he had taught courses with this material as texts. In my time (I did not study with him until I was a junior) he was preoccupied with cultural matters.

My economic theory I learned mostly from Roswell McCrea and, later on, Ernest Minor Patterson; from Patten I learned to look for something grander, something regarded as arcane then. He taught me the importance of looking for uniformities, laws, explanations of the inner forces moving behind the façade of events. He was trying to penetrate the mysteries of civilization, no less. We were privileged to follow if and as we could. I, and a few others—in these later days his classes were small—did follow earnestly and with a sense of immense consequence. I had never had that experience before. I should never have it again quite so intensely.

Patten was reaching for generalizations I would appreciate only

---

51. "The Life and Work of Simon Nelson Patten," *Journal of Political Economy* 31 (1923): 153–208.

long afterward. One of these was the conclusion that our pluralistic system—laissez-faire in industry, checks and balances in government, and so on—must be shaped into a unity if its inherent conflicts, beginning to be so serious, were not to destroy us. He thought that the Germans had the key to that unity in philosophy, in economics, and perhaps in politics. He saw the conflict, now so ominously coming up over the horizon, as one between the living wholeness of the German conception and the dying divisiveness of English pluralism. But he anticipated, or hoped for, a peaceful absorption into our democracy of the Germanic conception of integration.[52]

Patten's was an organic conception of man's evolution. The inevitable course of human development seemed to him obvious. The demarcations were becoming apparent. There was the world, now becoming technologically unified, and there was man, learning how to proceed toward his destiny. For a great society, a unified organism, to come into being, it was only necessary to establish institutions calculated to sort out of the rich resources of human nature the cooperative and creative elements, meanwhile discouraging the competitive and destructive ones. This was so reasonable a program that a well-nourished and well-educated people could not fail to accept it and carry it out. I have described in another place how, one day (but this was, I think, in my first graduate year) I had met him in a rejoicing mood on the street and heard from him the news of the Einsteinian theory unifying the basic laws of science.[53] "And," Patten had said, "as economists will discover, the basic elements of

---

52. I shall come back to Patten. I must, because I believe his to have been the most profound mind of his generation. I was too immature to understand him then, or even when I undertook to write a memoir about him a few years later. He afterward published several articles in *The Annals* and *The Monist* in 1917, 1919, and 1920; these are the fairest representation of his coordinative powers. I shall need to analyze these later on and try to suggest their implications. Like de Vries, for instance, he may well be rediscovered in later years when lesser minds have begun to catch up; Professor Lightner Witmer has suggested to me that this might well happen. Perhaps I should say that Nearing, too, wrote a small book mostly about Patten (*Educational Frontiers*, privately printed, 1925). It spoke of him mostly as a teacher. Nearing got no closer than I to understanding.

53. *The Special Theory of Relativity* was published in 1905, but in 1916 the *General Theory of Relativity* was announced. This concept integrated the universal law of gravitation with the earlier synthesis of space and time of which matter and energy were phenomena. Cf. my *Chronicle of Jeopardy, 1945–55* (Chicago: University of Chicago Press, 1955).

economics as well!" Understandably, the war was to be a tragic interlude for him. It would interrupt progress toward unity and perhaps lead to destruction because of the pluralism it enforced.

No one could really believe in a cataclysmic finale for all human hopes in such an atmosphere of optimism and progress as prevailed in those prewar years. Specifically, it was impossible for a student in the Wharton School, where so much affluence and justified expectation of increase was to be seen. Nevertheless, I could not avoid being impressed by the emphasis of my professors on the divisiveness in American life. In Patten's view these separatist forces were being, or would be, caught up in an overwhelming tide running toward the same integration he had found in Germany. He found the evidence for this view in the technology gradually taking shape out of pure science, both physical and natural. This had now manifested itself in many methodologies: in cost accounting and scientific management, in serialization in factories, in the trend toward consolidation of business, and in numerous others. To most of my other teachers, it seemed that interests profiting from the uncertainties of division and competition were dangerously strong and growing stronger; they appeared to be planting themselves in American institutions so firmly that they might never be eradicated. The integrating forces were, by comparison, not nearly so strong.

I had the impression that most of my teachers were growing desperate in their opposition to degenerative forces they inwardly believed to be so powerful that they might prevail in spite of all efforts to expose or to reform them. Profits, prosperity, and the corruptions of commerce were rising in an irresistible flood. Little professorial exposures of the ghastly skeleton underneath the silky surfaces of upper-class luxury would be lost in a general atmosphere of acquiescence. Some of them—Clyde King, for instance—spoke darkly of that distant time when all consumers would have been squeezed beyond toleration and when, perhaps, their reaction would be something like a revolution. Others who attacked the evils measurable by the ordinary moral yardsticks were simply frightened. What they went in fear of they were not quite certain. Something had gone very wrong, but they were not able to say where or when it had occurred or what was likely to come of it.

Carl Kelsey, for instance, carried us through courses on race problems and taught us in what degraded ways the "social debtor classes" had to live and what the philanthropists and social workers were doing about it. There was often indignation in his voice. He was a fine, just, upright man, and because of this, we were made uneasy by the revelations of misery, maladjustment, and even downright hunger and cold. All his cures were palliatives, and he recognized it. King was shriller. His disclosures of financial rigging in public utility organization, of baseness in municipal management (more specifications on the Steffens theme), and of the subservience of officialdom to pressure, ended, however, in simple indignation. This was not a lasting emotion. It wore off. Reiteration led to expectation of more instances, and indignation grew less in each instance.

I, at least, got used to thinking that the system of business was a turbulent, cruel struggle, and that no rules were recognized unless they were ruthlessly enforced by a higher power. Even then they could and would be evaded with some frequency and usually with impunity. I no longer thought of joining in that game. It seemed incompatible with any aspiration I could conceive except merely that of making money.

This problem became more real as time passed. In my junior year, I became aware that Nearing was in trouble and thus was awakened to the dilemma of the American liberal patriot. For that was as good a way as any of describing his attitude. There was nothing wrong with Scott or with anything he did unless simple honesty was a fault. There are people who can be honest provocatively, of course, and I can now see that he was one of these. But there was so much background to his case, there were so many similar incidents, that it became symbolic.

Scott's trouble became a cause to all his colleagues, even those who taught purely business subjects—the Huebners, Conway, Mead, MacFarland, Budd, and Hess—and who probably shared few of his convictions about the economic system. It thus drew them together into a cohesive family: theirs was the closest academic association, except for the group I should later serve with at Columbia, that I should ever know. When Scott left us in the spring of 1915, I was a member of the group, perhaps its youngest. The loving cup passed around at our final dinner together at the shabby old Lenape Club had tears mixed with its wine. The *Blutbruderschaft* was real, but it did not extend to sharing in a common revolt. By that time I was a good deal further along, and much would have happened in the meantime.

The short account of Patten's life and work I have mentioned would be written less than a decade after he had finished as a teacher and while my memories of him were still vivid. It would reflect my still immature attempt to understand him. The years I write about now were those immediately preceding World War I—1913–17—when I was finishing as an undergraduate and becoming a graduate student and instructor. In this period Patten was incomparably the most influential of my teachers. One paragraph of my essay telling of him in the classroom is especially relevant here:

> Patten talked with only a line or two of notes scrawled on cheap, rough paper in his large cramped hand. His fingers seemed more accustomed to the plow than to the pen. But he never glanced at his notes as he talked. He seemed rather to be communing with unseen auditors in a rather impersonal and yet familiar way. He came to his place behind the desk awkwardly, his large gaunt frame crumpling into the chair and onto the desk, seeming, when the process was complete, to consist of angular bunches of well-worn cloth dominated by a long-jawed face. His hands with their long, bony fingers and their rough skin, moved uncertainly about until suddenly the right hand rose with the forefinger pointing out, shaking, creating a silent prelude of appreciable length. The finger rose until it pointed outward from the right eye, alongside the enormous nose. Only then the flood of quiet, stirring words began, carrying his young hearers' minds with his, back along the sweep of ages, probing the movement of races across the earth, the coming and going and living of the driven hordes of ancient man. When he stopped, it was an abrupt and climactic ending. His words still seemed to permeate the air. It was only after coolness had set in that we realized what had happened. He had not explained in the usual way how civilizations grew or moved, depending for each step of reasoning upon the evidence of formal anthropology or history. It was nothing so easy as that. He had been reaching back into those dim times and selecting social forces which seemed really to account for what had happened. It was rather explanation than description. He rejected much evidence and passed over others' speculations, working back into the neglected crevasses of history, searching out the forces, at the

ultimate beginnings of motivation. Invariably—as always in his teaching—he first raised the difficulties into sight, turning them over and over, then swooped down upon them as though he would crush out of them the very juice of truth. When he had finished there was no difficulty: simply a light, shining luminously upon the place where difficulty had been. This light shone, however, only for the more earnest, more mature students who had already come to question orthodox explanations of social forces. Others were respectful, very much impressed, but confused and disturbed.[54]

Even when I was still a junior and had my first course with him, I felt the impact of his intelligence and knew that he was the teacher for whom I had been searching. Nearing was by now a friend. I respected him, but his, as I have said, was a factual more than a creative mind. It is true that he was the first to make "earned" and "unearned" major categories in national income studies; that he was one of the first, in fact, to study the yield and the sources of our wealth as a whole.[55] But otherwise he was one of those dissenters from business practice who leaned hard on economic orthodoxy to sustain his criticisms. Even that did not seem sufficient. He would later be driven to orthodox Marxism; he would thus have an alternate system to compare with laissez-faire, but it would be no nearer reality than classical economics.[56] And it was precisely these fundamentals I was learning, under Patten's tutelage, to question, not as to their logic, which was unexceptionable, but as to their usefulness. I ought not to pretend that I saw this distinction more than dimly then. In the mixed intellectual and social affairs of undergraduate life, I was not always

---

54. Tugwell, "Simon Nelson Patten," 193–94. My recollection has to do with Patten discoursing on the history of civilization, not on his quite original theories of economics.

55. In his *Income* (New York: Macmillan, 1915). But by then he was the author not only of a widely used textbook of elementary economics (with Frank Watson, entitled *Economics* [New York: Macmillan, 1908]) but also of several other books such as *Social Sanity, Financing the Wage-Earner's Family* (New York: B. W. Huebsch, 1913) and *Social Adjustment* (New York: Macmillan, 1911). He turned them out at the rate of more than one a year. He was still doing it fifty years later. He would send me his *Economics for the Power Age* (East Palatka, Fla.: World Events Committee) in 1952; and finally his autobiographical *The Making of a Radical* (New York: Harper and Row, 1972).

56. His acceptance of Marxism, however, was temporary. He was not one to tolerate the necessary intellectual confinement.

careless of fundamentals, but I did not often re-examine them with the seriousness those years required.

As the nations moved toward the final incidents foreshadowing war, I no more than others understood the nature of the coming crisis or its relation to Western civilization. That our world was now engaged in an unconscious struggle for unity, Patten was certain. I should understand later that he had always been trying to convey a conviction that a convulsion was imminent; although we had some intimation of this even then, we were too intrigued with the events of everyday life to accept his warnings. Then too we were engaged in that protest against the outrageous injustices of the business system we felt it our special duty to carry on. We felt that our existence was being justified by such good works.[57]

The geographic centers of my life continued to be in Logan and College Halls and in the library. In the one I was progressing into social theory and constitutional law; in the other I was absorbing history and exploring with undiminished enthusiasm the various realms of literature. Edward P. Cheyney and William E. Lingelbach were the historians of most importance; Clarence G. Child, Felix E. Schelling, and Cornelius Weygandt were the principal impresarios of letters and literature, though there was a memorable introduction to the European novel through J. P. W. Crawford.[58]

Besides this I pursued a course in the history of drama with

---

57. Much of what I say is illustrated in *All Our Years* (New York: Viking, 1948), the autobiography of Robert Morss Lovett, one of the truest of these liberals. He was some two decades my elder, and his service at the University of Chicago was before my time there; but our ways would cross on numerous occasions. Reading his own account of his life, it can be seen that the chances he took were considerable, and that the causes he served always involved risks. I have the feeling now, however, that if all of them had succeeded, our affairs would not be so very much improved. Still, what can a man of conscience and sensitivity do when he is confronted with consequences of a system to which, if he makes no protest, he must seem to consent. He must, of course, resist. He may know that what is needed is a grand-scale counteroffensive and still not see how such a campaign can be organized. Most of those who, like Lovett, spent lifetimes between 1850 and 1950 in a struggle for social betterment, were really engaged in guerrilla actions behind the enemy lines. In the camps of such irregulars, grand strategy is very little considered. It is not relevant to anything they can achieve.

58. I had read French and German authors in translation, but to the Italians and Spanish (except Cervantes) I had, until then, been a complete stranger. And I believe I had read, of Slavic literature, only a novel or two of Tolstoy.

Arthur H. Quinn and made some excursions into other specialized fields. Weygandt I regarded as my principal guide. His interests were wide, but, in general, modern. The seventeenth and eighteenth centuries were left to others. With him I read the British novelists and poets, explored the Irish Renaissance, and surveyed the contemporary Americans. He had not yet taken to writing books, as he later would, and the whole experience of his life was poured, in a rewarding mixture, into his lectures.[59] Weygandt reached back a good way even then, or so it seemed to us. He had begun as a reporter on the old *Philadelphia Record* and had been a favorite among students for many years. He was an enthusiastic amateur ornithologist and a collector of Pennsylvania Dutch memorabilia. He also drew on the neighborly lore of his summer home in New Hampshire. Literature to him was, as he said repeatedly, a "reading of life." He was a freely flowing spring of experience.[60]

It was all personal, however; in social matters he was as innocent as a child, and, like a child, completely reactionary. That is to say, he found individuals and their small circles of friends fascinating; he mined them for human interest, but he could not bear the thought of change unless it looked backward toward isolated home and village life and more marked differences. This was first apparent in his treatment of Shaw, Galsworthy, and Wells, who were too important as storytellers to be ignored, but whose orientation toward purposive

---

59. His autobiography, *The Edge of Evening,* would be published in 1945. Some of his other characteristic books, aside from his bow to scholarship in *A Century of the English Novel* (New York: Century, 1925), were: *The Wissahickon Hills, Philadelphia Folks, The Dutch Country,* and *The Plenty of Pennsylvania.* Some of his lectures were gathered into *Tuesdays at Ten* (Philadelphia: University of Pennsylvania Press, 1928), the most reminiscent of them all for his students. He would go on teaching until his retirement in 1942.

60. Several lectures I recall with pleasure had to do with Walt Whitman, mostly about the eccentric old man with long hair and whiskers who had lived in Camden across the Delaware, had ridden the ferries and wandered the streets by the river. Weygandt had often seen him in his newspaper days. But even his wide tolerance could not stretch to the approval of Walt's wild verse.

Perhaps I may go on to tell of a letter he read to us one day from the farmer who looked after his place in New Hampshire. It was a report about conditions, and it contained a few words I have never forgotten:

> The apples are in red bud and the
> plums went white last Sunday. . . .

Robert Frost himself never wrote better lines.

exposition he deplored. Mostly I managed to ignore this prejudice of his and drank freely from the fountain of his delight with life.[61]

In my junior year I acquired, merely, I suppose, by becoming a familiar, the privilege of roaming at large in the library stacks; finally I was allowed the use of one of the small seminar rooms high up under the roof, where I might pile my books, store my papers, and work as I pleased through many uninterrupted hours. Seminars met infrequently, and I was seldom disturbed. I acquired a taste for the quietude of libraries, with only the rustling sounds of scholarship around, the smell of old books in the air, and the kindness of all librarians toward scholars to depend on.

My other activities as a junior, however, were compressed into small allowances by the major task of running the *Daily Pennsylvanian*. I doubt now, and I had some moments of doubt even then, whether this was for me a paying enterprise.[62] I had enthusiasm enough at first, and unquestionably I made this one of the most intense efforts of my life. I suspect this may not be so unusual as it seems; even the most placid-appearing existence may have that kind of intensity concealed by an opaque surface. To begin with, there was the frantic competition to become a lowly member of the editorial board, but then there began the long strain of further contest for selection as managing editor.

I have before me the *Daily Pennsylvanian* for Friday, April 26, 1912. At the head of the editorial column there appeared this paragraph:

> *The Pennsylvanian* takes pleasure in announcing the election for the ensuing year of Ralph Edward Edenharter as Editor-in-Chief; Ed-

---

61. When, a little later, his books began to come out, I was amazed to discover how badly Weygandt wrote. In some dismay, I read one after another, concluding finally that his genius was oral and that it was unable to come through into print. There are passages in every book he wrote that a sophomore in our undergraduate courses in composition would have been afraid to perpetrate. There is some of that unquenchable gusto with which he repeated good stories and appraised their authors, but in print his personality was dimmed and his enthusiasm dampened.

62. I found it interesting in later years to discover that a similar immersion in college journalism would raise no such doubts in Roosevelt's mind. About ten years before this he had given most of two years to the *Harvard Crimson* with no expressed doubts whatever about the usefulness of such an effort. In after years we discussed it. He still thought it had been the best thing he had done at Harvard.

mund Hoffman, Jr. as Business Manager; Malcolm R. Lovell as Assistant Managing Editor; W. L. Saunders as Assistant Circulation Manager; J. F. Van Vechten as Assistant Business Manager; H. B. Dunham and C. A. Brown as Second Assistant Business Managers; and J. M. Austin, R. G. Tugwell and H. I. Murray as Associate Editors.

Thus Jim Austin, Had Murray, and I had survived from the score or more who had entered the competition in September. It was not regarded as any great honor, but we were praised for it in our respective fraternity houses, and to us it seemed ample reward for hard work and neglect of academic duties. None of us, in consequence, would have very creditable grades, and we would have sacrificed a good many other interests. I think now that these were not too important; I doubt, even so, that the *Pennsylvanian* was worth it. This might not have been so true if we had gone on to become journalists, but none of us did. The junior year really took it out of us. As a sophomore I had regularly spent an eight-hour day in work on the paper. I was then elected managing editor. But a sudden accession of sense made me drop it all after that. Actually I served as managing editor only from early May until the end of term. When we came back in autumn, I had made up my mind that I would finish work for my degree in one more year and get on with academic affairs. I did not give up the managing editorship of *Red and Blue,* and I kept up other collegiate interests. But I was through with the *Daily.*

Dropping out of journalism was also, to a certain extent, actuated by the continuing competition with Winthrop Williams, which suddenly did not seem worthwhile. He had been elected to the editorial board late, but he had shown so much real talent and had been willing to put in so many hours, that when the sophomore elections came along, it was really a toss-up whether he or I should become managing editor. The outgoing board settled it by creating a news editor in place of the former assistant managing editor and giving that job to Williams with the explanation that henceforth the positions were to be thought of as equal.[63] What I faced was a year of tense competition for the editor-in-chiefship if I kept on. Perhaps I was a quitter to drop out, but at this distance it seems to me one of the more sensible decisions of my collegiate days. Williams made a fine editor-in-chief, and I got on with my studies.

Editorship, however, had given me a certain position in campus

---

63. In the *Daily Pennsylvanian* of May 3, 1913.

affairs. Achievement of this sort certainly did not rank with athletic honors; but it was the nearest other approach to consequence afforded by collegiate activities, except, perhaps, an appearance in one of the annual musical shows of the Mask and Wig Club. I began, at any rate, to be appointed to those committees all undergraduates long to be members of—for class dinners and dances and other similar affairs; and, a little belatedly, I was elected to the Junior Society, Phi Kappa Beta.[64]

This affiliation gave rise to an incident I still recall with amusement. Phi Kappa Beta is obviously a use of Greek letters intended to parody Phi Beta Kappa, an irony emphasized not only by the elaborate fooling of initiation, but by the society's symbol. This was a key, worn by members as their more serious brethren and their elders among the professors wore their badges of scholarship. It featured a pretzel and the bung of a beer barrel, together with appropriate subsidiary symbols. One day, coming out from the city by subway-surface car, I stood hanging to a strap directly in front of Professor Schelling, so that the key on my vest must have flaunted itself directly before his eyes for a quarter of an hour. I finally noticed him. He had given up the perusal of his paper and was unaccountably but unmistakably glaring at me. At Thirty-fourth Street he rose, and as I stood aside respectfully, he pointed at my key and said in a loud voice: "Young man, do you have to advertise your deficiencies?"[65]

I am afraid that was the kind of essentially pompous and unhumorous man Schelling was. I was to see a good deal of him. Apart from his respect for and cooperation with Patten, I have little to say in gratitude. In a course on the seventeenth-century lyric, I discovered that although he was lecturing from a penciled manuscript, he was really reading from the introduction to his book on the subject printed some twenty years before. This kind of professorial cheating was just not allowable. On another occasion, I had been called to his office for what turned out to be caustic criticism of a paper I had written on Shakespeare's lyrics, when, as I approached the open door, I heard him

---

64. But I was not elected to Sphinx, the senior honor society, in my senior year.

65. This Phi Kappa Beta business must have tormented Phi Beta Kappa members a good deal. Editors, of course, always thought the reversed initials after a name were a mistake, and in this way conferred scholastic honors on some of the strongest backs and weakest heads of my generation at Pennsylvania.

say loudly, "Mr. Pound, you are either a genius or an idiot, and I am inclined to think the latter!" As I stepped aside, Ezra Pound came out. He, too, was an unconforming reader of seventeenth-century poetry. Schelling wanted no imaginative students or even ones who were dissenters from received opinion. He preached the law, and the good students accepted it; the others he treated with contumely in academic fashion. His most special scorn, as might be imagined, was reserved for those who were unorthodox about authorship of the Shakespearean plays. On that subject, he enlarged to absolute boredom even for the interested. He usually ended these diatribes by denouncing those who would change the spelling of the venerated author's name. "From the name of one so incomparable," he would say, "it is unthinkable that we should delete a letter." This might show devotion, but also, we thought, it showed how literal was the Schelling scholarship.

Roy Mercer and Lew Walton both graduated in my junior year, the one in medicine, the other in architecture. But this was not until I had had a year in the fraternity house. It was then at 3610 Walnut Street, not a very desirable location, and not a very desirable house either, but it contained youth and friendship, as well as any dwelling could have done. Our chapter was even then raising funds for a new house, and within the next few years it would be built. After the war, I should have a graduate year there, but for my contemporaries, the dark old quarters on Walnut Street would hold all our fraternal memories.

I roomed at the fraternity with Roy Mercer and Anthony Hildreth. Tony, who was from a manufacturing town in New England, had all the unstable temperament and attractiveness of the Irish; he and I had both more time and more inclination for frivolities than Roy, whose studies required prodigies of memorizing, though not much thinking, so far as I could see. He was a Quaker as well. My other Quaker friends, who were numerous (naturally, in Philadelphia), found their youthful impulses less limited by their upbringing than Roy.[66] Anyway, he was a good influence on both Tony and me.

We had another friend living with us, too, whose life was very much part of our own. That was Punch, an English bull terrier, who had adopted all the fraternity, but the three of us in particular. He slept on one of our beds every night. He gave us the kind of priceless affection I have had from so many dogs, but also he kept us enter-

---

66. Perhaps also his George School years had reinforced his natural serenity and his confident clarity of purpose.

tained by his weaknesses. He was handsome, pure white, and very vain. He not only carried on numerous and complicated amours but seemed actually to love a fight. Several times he followed other fraternities' pets all the way to their houses and attacked them there. This caused a good deal of indignation, culminating when he nearly killed the Psi Upsilon's collie in the living room of their house. Several of us were required to rescue him from the brothers' wrath, and it seemed for a while as though the insult might be the cause of interfraternity conflict as well. We promised through Roy, as ambassador, to chastize the miscreant, and so were allowed to take him away. He was still obviously unrepentant, however, and we knew reform was not to be hoped for. He outstayed all three of us, but some time after we had gone and he was getting on toward dog senility, he merely disappeared one day. He was a good and valiant friend; we all mourned his going. We agreed that he had doubtless been arrogant once too often with a younger dog, but we did not like to think of his smooth white body lying somewhere in an alley or a gutter.

In my junior year, I went back to the dormitories to live in Franklin House with Frank Forster. There we had quarters approximating those I had often read about at the English universities; but we, of course, had better sanitary facilities. Each of us had a bedroom, and we shared a big living room. My father sent down a large roll-top desk, and we picked up enough other furniture, rugs, and pictures to have genuine comfort. The difficulty with this, of course, was that our amenities attracted many visitors. To this we had no objection, but it certainly was a serious handicap to study. Jack Lansill,[67] Wade Judge, Edward Russell, Stewart Foley, and several others might as well have lived with us, they were there so often. A game of *vingt-et-un*, I remember, went on all year; we kept a continuous score. Sometimes our debts to each other soared astronomically, but we had appropriate faith in averages, and the year-end settlement, although carried out with acrimony and complicated negotiation, was not actually so burdensome to the losers as to be really important.

Wade Judge and Edward Russell (Unc to us) came from upstate

---

67. John Scott Lansill, who had been a classmate of Frank's at Masten Park. I afterward saw something of him in New York, and he would later take charge of the Suburban Resettlement Division of the Resettlement Administration for me. It would be he, more than anyone else, who would be responsible for planning and building the Greenbelt towns. But also he would give me friendship and support beyond repayment.

Pennsylvania. Wade's father was a country merchant, and Wade expected to inherit the business (as he did). Unc likewise expected to inherit a business, but its nature furnished the material for such jokesters as Roch Harmon. It was a monument business. Roch's contention was that Unc had attained his solid 225 pounds by carrying tombstones on his shoulder around the Pennsylvania countryside making deliveries. Unc was a dependable guard on the football team and had a certain dignity in consequence. He did not calmly suffer humiliation from 130-pounders. Roch always saw a way clear to an exit before he offered his characteristic comment. The climactic incident, however, occurred in our room at Franklin House.

Unc naturally felt that his weight and position entitled him to be heard on numerous subjects, and it was in view of this weakness that we laid a trap for him. Jack Lansill had an ancient .45-caliber revolver. We loaded it with blanks, and then in an evening roundtable session we turned the talk to firearms and hunting. The buildup went on for some time, and Unc was encouraged to dilate freely on his prowess in the upstate woods. At the very climax of a bear story, just as Unc drew bead with his imaginary Winchester, Roch fired the .45 several times just behind his chair. It was Roch's contention for weeks after that if the door had not been open, Unc would have gone through it anyway, leaving a complete cutout of the kind seen in movie cartoons. And it was certainly true that in a remarkably short time that 225 pounds removed itself to the triangle outside. Unc said, of course, that he jumped instinctively and was only going home for his own gun. So we had the material for another collegiate saga to go on and on gathering patina as it aged.

Stewart Foley, who adopted Frank and me, lived next door in Foerderer House in solitary grandeur. He considered himself a bohemian and tried to perform accordingly. He lacked something of the physical attractiveness a genuine Casanova ought to have, but he did his best with what he had. He also wanted to be thought of as a littérateur and, having a sardonic sense of humor, played a solemn joke on all of us. It went on for a whole year. He submitted verse of creditable construction and sometimes of genuine quality, and we accepted it for *Red and Blue*. We thought it, moreover, the best undergraduate verse we had ever seen. It should have been. It had been produced by distinguished poets. It was, of course, in their minor strain and published obscurely, so that those of us who were students of English had that much excuse for having been taken in. But actually Foley, the joker, was gone from the campus before our ignorance came home to us. We kept the secret in a small circle, and I think the real authors never knew that their efforts had been pirated.

From Jack Lansill we never had anything but pure delight. He was an enormous boy even then—some six-foot-three and two hundred pounds—and he was still young. He was not a practicing athlete, but he had all the other talents anyone could imagine; all, however, were possessed in subdued and happy degree. And he had no bothersome temperament. His chief attraction was his endless and capricious fancy. He was capable of invention piled on invention in such delicate and complicated designs that all his hearers were speechless in wonder and admiration. We listened to his tales by the hour. They were sometimes obscene in a kind of inoffensively happy taste, but they were always fascinating. They contained not a word of fact or truth, although they were usually supposed to be personal adventure; if they had possessed the least verisimilitude, it would have spoiled the whole atmosphere he sought to create. The only writers I know of with such a gift are E. B. White and Robert Nathan. But Jack never wrote. Spoken words were his genius—laughing, trembling, fanciful words, making evanescent structures too impermanent for the relative rigidities of writing. We never heard enough of them.

Frank and I, with our big room in Franklin House, were more or less at the center of this group. It included perhaps a dozen intimates I have not mentioned here: Tom Keator, Orval Wales, and Walter Baughman from upstate New York; the Raudnitz brothers from New York City; several Buffalo boys, including Hamilton Wende, Fred Silverthorne, Howard McCall, and George Rand, Jr.; and others from Philadelphia—Don Kent, Clem Webster, Walter Antrim, and Ray Young. With but few exceptions, those we knew best would become bankers or manufacturers. There would be a few architects, lawyers, and doctors, but most would "go into business." They would be, again, with one or two exceptions, successful. We knew then who the failures would be. They were, as a matter of fact, already failures. They showed it by exaggerated devotion to those activities the rest of us knew enough to take or leave alone.

One of these characters was so well known at Roseland, one of our favorite public dance halls, that habitués generally thought him a son or nephew of the proprietor. In sheer boredom, although he seemed unable to keep away from the place, he invented an amusing recreation that we joined him in on occasional Saturday nights. This consisted of making a pool, each of us contributing a dollar. The winner was he who had danced a whole round with the ugliest girl of the evening, as decided in a postmidnight conference. When some twenty young men with money in their pockets devoted a whole evening to the least, rather than the most, attractive of the girls, it overturned the customary conventions in most pleasing ways. The whole environment became unreal; there was a run on wallflowers; the belles got a rest. We experienced a subdued hilarity among ourselves that, although not understood by outsiders, communicated itself to everyone present. The tired mechanical tunes of the orchestra turned airy and lively, and sometimes the ugly girls really seemed like Cinderellas. Incidentally, and this perhaps proves something, I recall no occasion when easy agreement was not reached as to the winner of the pool. About the ugliest girl there was never any question.

For the most part, however, our wasters were tolerated nuisances. We had to help them pass examinations; we had to listen as they recounted their monotonous swaggerings; and we had to watch while the degenerative processes went on. We learned from it without suffering vicariously overmuch. We were not callous, but we were busy. Of the group—the few exceptions aside—most succeeded in business to the millionaire or presidential level; others became prominent in their professions. Almost none had merely mediocre careers.

The junior year, with all its amusements, was for me enough of undergraduate life. At the end of it, I had accumulated enough credits for graduation. Most of them, because I had taken marks lightly and had crowded my program, were undistinguished credits; but they counted. I did not take my degree then: I wanted to graduate with my own class. But I withdrew from candidacy for the editorship of the *Red and Blue*. In the spring I was called into Dean McCrea's office and, with Scott present, was asked if I would like to become a teacher.[68] It was no grand prize I was being offered. I should be one of Scott's four or five quizmasters during the next year without any further commitment,[69] but I accepted on the spot without a moment's

---

68. Roswell C. McCrea became the Wharton School's first full dean in 1912; he would go to Columbia in 1916 to become the first dean there of the School of Business. He was professor of Economics as well as dean, and I had studied theory with him. Besides general advanced courses, I had had special ones centering on John Stuart Mill and later classicists. It was he of whom Scott once remarked that he would give anything to possess as much knowledge of theory as McCrea—except the time it would take to learn it. He died in 1951.

69. At a salary, as I recall very well, of $600 for the year.

hesitation. This, I knew, was what I wanted.

And, besides, I wanted to get married. Florence Arnold, the adored being of my later high school days in Buffalo, had decided in my favor as against my competitors. A salary for the year of six hundred dollars was not much, but my father would help out without missing the contribution, so prosperous had his business become. Anyway two could really live for the price of one when the one was me, alone in Philadelphia. I rented a row house at Forty-ninth Street and Warrington Avenue in West Philadelphia, and my senior year was one of combined teaching and study.

We were married in June of 1914 by Dr. Case of the Delaware Avenue Baptist Church in Buffalo. It was a nice wedding, given a slightly zany turn by my mother who, when I repeated after Dr. Case the customary "with all my worldly goods I thee endow," snorted audibly. She was right, we were undeniably starting on the proverbial shoestring. But my father gave us a new Buick, I think the first model with a self-starter, and with that Buick and fifty dollars we went on a honeymoon. It began at the Roycroft Inn in East Aurora and lasted two weeks at Bemus Point on Chautauqua lake. The Scofields loaned us a new house they had built as an investment. We coasted over the hills; we stayed for a day or two with the Dennisons in Sinclairville, scene of boyhood adventures now so far in the past; and we visited Scott, who was lecturing at Chautauqua.

For several years, Scott had been a favorite with the regular Chautauquans. He was, in fact, a superb teacher, clear, concise, and friendly. Until now his kind of moral radicalism had been quite all right; intelligent Americans were used to criticism of their institutions when it proceeded from obvious concern for reform. Chautauqua was not a place where businessmen congregated. The lecturegoers were teachers, preachers, housewives, and others with some interest in—if not much knowledge of—public affairs. Teachers were used to pointing out, in those days, how many schoolhouses could be built for the price of a battleship; preachers had stock sermons on foreign missions whose burden was good will toward all men. These mild and superficial dissents from nationalism and imperial competition had never before been tested. But an international crisis was coming up now, and, Scott told me with a wry smile, that in an assembly dominated by preachers and actually organized for the advancement of Sunday School teaching, he, not a professing Christian at all, was by now the only defender of such an obvious Christian principle as pacifism.

Wilson's first term was almost two years old, and the European war had not yet begun. The crisis there was deepening, however, and sides were being taken in the United States. Already the preacher-teacher class in America had decided on its affiliation, and if principles interfered with it, so much the worse for principles. Scott would actually go on appearing at Chautauqua until we got into the war in 1917. That would be two years after his discharge from the university, showing how comparatively tolerant Chautauqua was. His incorrigible pacifism, rather than his economic opinions, would bring about his separation from the institution.

That June the Chautauqua hills were dreaming behemoths crouching all around the valleys, their backs clothed with the silks, satins, and tinsels of devil's paintbrush, buttercups, and mustard. The streams were marked by billowy willows, and the water meadows and swamps were still full of blooming iris and trillium. Whole fields almost, as with winter snow, were white with Queen Anne's lace. And the woods were cool and damp even in midday heat. Without ever venturing more than twenty miles from Bemus Point, we journeyed widely through the backroads and lanes of the Chautauqua country. And I renewed in Sinclairville and No-God-Hollow many old acquaintances.

Back in Wilson, working again at the old familiar summer job, the coming of war took me by surprise. I had heard enough about its possibility, but for a generation, we in the United States had been hearing about one crisis after another, and we had got in the way of trusting that somehow each new one would be averted as all of them had been in the past. It was really more of a shock to hear of actual declarations of war and to read of armies marching than it would have been if this confidence in the beneficence of events had not spread so widely. The prevalent optimism was not quickly, easily, or completely extinguished. When a tired, pessimistic old man in England remarked sadly that the lights now going out in Europe would not be lit again in our generation, we put it down to exhaustion or maybe to incompetence. And we had not the slightest (perhaps just the very slightest) inner warning that all of us would be involved before the affair was over. Certainly we had no intimation that, in our time, war would never really end.

It might be that Patten had been telling me more than I had taken in. I was eager that fall to get back to Philadelphia, not only for my first classes as a teacher, but so that I could explore Europe's ordeal with my academic friends. That year Charles Reitzel and H. L. Baldensperger were my colleagues as quizmasters in the freshman economics course, and we spent many hours in our bare office exchanging such thoughts as each of us had. Many times, too, we went in company to Patten for clarification. We always got it. Our general conclusion was that there was behind it all a kind of crisis of events not apparent on the surface. Fundamentally Patten thought, and we agreed, that the British were defending an empire impossible to hold together in an age of advanced technology. Its continuation depended too much on economic and class differences among peoples: superiority among the British, inferiority among others. But technology could not be kept secret, and especially it could not be kept in England. The Germans had mastered it. They seemed to have a special genius for industrial organization, and it was outrunning and challenging that of the British, who had allowed their financiers and international bankers to slow down their productivity. The contest was between a once supreme but now inefficient and ramshackle empire and a vigorous and ruthless but efficient, challenging people.

Geopolitics came into it, too. We read Ratzel and Semple again. And we wondered if seapower would turn out to have its old effectiveness. It was not even certain that the British could hold the seas in this new contest; the Germans were reputed to have a formidable modern navy. We did not think, then, of Britain as an outpost of the American continent; that would have been too great a mental wrench. For we had not quite escaped from colonial psychology even yet. Many Americans were then identifying this inferior feeling for what it was and resenting it. We could see that apart from this, the fact of being fellow Anglo-Saxons might influence us to support the British, but if it did, we thought such sentiment ought to be regarded with suspicion. The vast power being generated in our own factories and fields, we, no more than other Americans, fully realized. Nor did we realize that ours would be the determining weight in the beginning contest of the European powers. We should have. Within the next two years this would become plain enough, but the truth is that we were provincial and did not understand what a little later seemed so obvious.

Patten's certainty that Germanism was in tune with modernism —a drawing into unity—and that the British pluralistic philosophy was one of disunity, class discrimination, laissez-faire, and exploitation, influenced us deeply. And it did not help Britain with us that she was allied with Czardom in Russia. The latent power of the vast Eurasian continent could not be organized and brought to bear by the incredibly corrupt and ineffective Russian bureaucracy. Even if it could, such a confirmation of divine right in the twentieth century would move civilization backward instead of forward.

Germany's struggle for unification, culminating in 1870, her solution of the federal problem, and the progress since the *Zollverein* and the unification, were familiar historical occurrences. We had heard them treated sympathetically by American historians as the most recent example of a people's struggle for union. Moreover Germany had gone further toward the establishing of social security than had any other nation. In that she was far ahead of Britain and was held out as the example we in America should follow. Social security was, in fact, an important objective of Progressives in the United States.[70]

---

70. What seems to have been forgotten, even by some historians, is that the Germany we knew in the United States was a land of *Gemütlichkeit*, of kindly family life, of boat trips on the Rhine or the Spree, of picnics in the Black Forest, of beer halls, and sentimental music. The iron Prussian discipline, the racism, the militarism, the cult of the State, of ruthlessness and hatred for France and England, were conveyed to us first in prewar propaganda.

In my mother's little library I found a copy of a widely read, typical account of German life, published for the Chautauqua Literary and Scientific Circle (with editions in 1908 and 1912), written by Mrs. Alfred Sidgwick, an English woman of German parentage. It stressed all the homely and ingratiating characteristics of life in Germany and presented its inhabitants as an essentially kindly and happy people. But in the preface to the edition of 1912, she felt impelled to say:

> There are many Germanys. The one we hear most about in England nowadays is armed to the teeth, set wholly on material advancement, in a dangerously warlike mood, hustling us without scruple from our place in the World's markets, a model of municipal government and enterprise, a land where vice, poverty, idleness and dirt are all unknown. We hear so much of this praiseworthy but most unamiable Wünderkind among nations, that we generally forget the Germany we know, the Germany still there for our affection and delight, the dear country of quaint fancies, of music, and of poetry. . . .

The English—and the Americans—were changing rapidly in response to the need for a justifying hatred.

In all these matters the Germans were more admirable than the British. And what could be more natural than a highly developed industrial society with a growing population resenting British confinement. Germany's commerce was allowed to move upon the seas only by unwilling concession. She was shut out, practically speaking, from the tropics, so necessary as a complement to northern industrialism. Africa and southeast Asia were closed to her by the Triple Entente. Her own Triple Alliance included two other recently unified countries: Austria and Italy. These were lesser powers in every way, but we had been taught to admire their struggle for federal union and their attempt to emulate the progress of Germany.

Then there was the more compelling philosophical reason for feeling that the German civilization represented a future struggling to be born. Germany was obviously moving toward collectivism and away from individualism, but this did not follow the predicted pattern of Marxian revolution leading to a Communist commonwealth. We regarded Marxism as a rigid and outworn dogma, based on preindustrial premises. The Germans, on the other hand, had grasped the technological imperatives. They progressed toward unification rather than division. Or so we thought.

We had no contact with policymaking or policymakers as young instructors; we were not even able to take part in the rising national debate over which side the United States ought to support. We tried. Charles Reitzel and I wrote several joint articles in which we stated the economic and philosophical issues as we saw them, but none was published. We watched with sorrow and concern as the nation moved toward an intervention we thought ought to be considered in more realistic terms. We were far from being anti-British. We knew where the common law, civil liberties—the whole Bill of Rights— came from; but that did not mean to us that contemporary British imperialists had a right to exploit all the dependent peoples of the earth and to choke off any progress threatening their prerogatives. We were afraid that this might be a result of the war if the United States intervened.

Under America's open observation, and with complete public knowledge of the way it was done, Germany's organizing capability was successfully transformed by propaganda into a ruthless statism likely to extinguish the liberties of Anglo-Saxondom; the kindly family father turned into a heartless militarist; a nation of progress was suddenly intent on destroying the world if it could not be conquered.

President Wilson did not take the lead in this conspiracy, but he let it happen without protest, and presently our neutrality became an empty fiction. But that would not be until after the election of 1916, won with the slogan, "He kept us out of war." Wilson changed gradually, along with the country.

It would be a mistake, however, to credit propaganda alone with America's rapid transition from the friend to the enemy of Germany. There was an underlying reason for the change. What we did not acknowledge, and would not, even when we had fought a war as her ally, was that Britain and we were, and for a long time had been, as Winston Churchill would put it in the midst of a later war, "mixed up together." It was inevitable that we should assist in the suppression of a new and challenging threat to the supremacy of Britain-America. We might have family differences with the British, but that we were members of the same family was inescapable. This unacknowledged oneness was resented so strongly by both peoples that it could not be appealed to; the best the propagandists could do was to stress a common danger. This they did very well, but, again, it was not done in realistic terms. It was not said that between us we refused to tolerate any threat to our joint supremacy. We had to picture the rising Germans as suppressors of liberty, outragers of consciences, and even, a little later, as the perpetrators of inhuman atrocities; of course, this was made easy by the German militarists themselves. As they came into control of their warring nation, they set it on courses impossible for Americans to approve even if the British had not been quick to enlarge on their offenses.

But we were not so naive that we accepted the German challenge to the British as the real cause of war. We saw well enough that an era of world disturbance had opened, but we did not at all measure its profundity. We could see that the hard shell of imperialism, as it had developed during the nineteenth century, was cracking as a result of swelling populations, the spread of industrialism (even to so-called backward regions), speeded-up transportation and communications, and all the other contemporary phenomena of change. The Germans were merely the first to challenge the old system and to break its shackles. Others would surely follow. As people became more literate, advanced their standard of living, and grasped the new industrial technique, their demand for political freedom would intensify. After having been the first to develop liberty and freedom, the British were in the unfortunate position now of denying it to others. This was indefensible; they ought to have made adjustments to new circumstances and new ideas more rapidly than they had. There were those in Britain who would have done so: Laborites and Socialists, of course, but it was the Tories who were in power, men who, like the Bourbons, neither forgot nor learned anything and who meant only to hold the empire together on the old terms and to extend it if they could. Patten was inclined to neglect the German imperialist movement or somehow not to think it so dangerous as that of the British.

The evolution of the commonwealth in future years and a new conception of colonialism would have to wait new and hard lessons far in the future. These changes would not begin until a war had been fought and the challenger suppressed. They would not gain the necessary momentum until after another war. Meanwhile Americans would be forced into a situation even less consistent with their traditional beliefs than that of the British. If the British had developed the ideas of liberty, we had made them our own and had enlarged their meaning. Independence and self-determination for peoples was in our blood, in spite of small departures in imperial moments, such as, for instance, that after the Spanish-American War. Now we were to support the British empire from which we ourselves had successfully seceded. None of it made any sense.

On the other hand there was nothing to show that the German militarists had any other intentions. Such colonialism as they had practiced had been a worse version of the British kind. To have substituted the imperialists in Germany for the ruling British Tories would have been to substitute tweedledum for tweedledee. The choice for America was too difficult. Neutrality seemed at first the only course, until, following Wilson's leadership, a majority chose for Britain. This, by that time, seemed to liberals of our sort more or less justified. Wilson had defined our aims in satisfactory terms. We were to make the world safe for democracy; we were not to bolster a crumbling empire. There were those who questioned whether it would work out that way. By that time I was, if not convinced, at least calmed down and not too unwilling to go along. That did not mean so much to me as it did to many of my contemporaries. My peculiar physical weaknesses made military service impossible. But, for what it was worth, I did, under Wilson's guidance, consent.

In the spring of 1915, after the university had closed and the students had left, Scott received notice of his dismissal:

My dear Mr. Nearing,

As the term of your appointment as assistant professor of economics for 1914–15 is about to expire, I am directed by the trustees of the University of Pennsylvania to inform you that it will not be renewed. With best wishes, I am

Yours sincerely,
Edgar F. Smith

There had been some argument among the trustees; one or two of them had had some question whether such an action was wise. None, it seemed, had felt any doubt that teachers were employees of the Board to be dismissed with or without cause. That his faculty and his dean had recommended Scott's reappointment was not thought by the trustees to be a commitment they must accept. It could be seen, after the fact, that the action had been well prepared. In the preceding year a by-law had been adopted by the Board stating that full professors were to be regarded as holding appointment indefinitely, but that all other officers of instruction were subsequently to have definite terms; unless they received notice of reappointment, their positions were to be considered terminated without further notice.

In the ensuing controversy, legality was made much of by the trustees, but it was ignored by others, and the issue was defined as a clear case of dismissal because of heterodox economic opinions. There were no students to protest during vacation, and the faculty was scattered; but discussion before the issue died down was fairly full. It did not result in Scott's reappointment. At the most it made the trustees more cautious for the future. But that they were unrepentant was shown clearly enough by their determination to retire Patten a year later at sixty-five, although the custom had theretofore been for service to continue until seventy.

The issues in the Nearing case were thoroughly explored by

Lightner Witmer of the Department of Psychology,[71] and afterward were gone into by the newly formed Association of University Professors.[72] But the matter was quite simple. Scott had wanted businessmen to perform in the enlightened way classical theory said they were supposed to do. He had agitated against child labor especially, but he had been generally "radical." Such trustees as Randal Morgan of the United Gas Improvement Co.; E. T. Stotesbury of J. P. Morgan and Co.; J. Levering Jones, corporation attorney; Louis Madeira of the Newton Coal Company; and George Wharton Pepper, noted lawyer, later senator, and leading Protestant Episcopal layman, were determined that he should be dismissed. Others, notably Wharton Barker and J. B. Lippincott, had dissented from the proposed action. In the ensuing discussion, another Philadelphian of noted ancestry, Effingham B. Morris, took a leading part in castigating the offending trustees.[73] There was thus some division of opinion, although the reactionary group prevailed.

As young teachers, we were interested in the conditions of our professional employment; but Scott was too close to us as teacher, and, almost, as elder brother, for us to regard the matter abstractly. Our loss was a personal one; our resentment was bitter. The feeling of mistreatment was the deeper because we were in a position to know Scott's qualities: the honesty and earnestness of his work, his dedication as a teacher. We thought he ought to have been rewarded rather than punished. We were quite certain about the real cause. We recalled a particular lecture of the last winter when the theory of consumption was reached in due course. On this occasion, Scott, seeking an example, had brought into the lecture hall and pinned to the bulletin board a double-page spread from the rotogravure edition of the *Philadelphia Public Ledger*. There, in picture and print, was his text. The account was one of a dinner given by Mrs. E. T. Stotesbury at her famous mansion as a contribution to the current social season. It had been a lavish, absurd, even an outrageous performance. He

---

71. In *The Nearing Case* (New York: Huebsch, 1915).

72. In the *Bulletin of the American Association of University Professors* 2 (3), part 2. Indeed the Nearing case was responsible for the rapid enlargement of the Association. There had, of course, been other serious violations of academic freedom. Cf. "A Nineteenth Century Academic Cause Celebre," *Bulletin*, Autumn, 1952.

73. Witmer, *The Nearing Case*.

placed it precisely in a world still tolerant of child labor, unemployment, slum dwellings by the hundred thousand, and, in that very winter, actual cold and hunger within the proverbial stone's throw of the Stotesbury mansion. In clear and unimpassioned language, Scott had pointed out the appropriate contrasts and had drawn the moral. He had known that Mrs. Stotesbury's son, J. H. R. Cromwell, was sitting before him as he talked. He had known, in fact, that Howard Baldensperger, Cromwell's instructor, had had an embarrassing exchange of classroom opinions with the young man. At the end of the lecture the students, who had been quite conscious of the risk Scott ran in presenting what he believed were relevant facts, had broken into prolonged applause. That applause may have stayed with him as some recompense in his exile; but we, his helpers, were sore and unhappy that a university professing dedication to the search for truth should stifle thus incontinently one of the truth's most earnest seekers.

There were other hidden causes. Scott had done a good deal of public speaking in the interest of the usual reforms being sought at that time, and much of his speaking had been done to church groups. He had often pointed out the ethical implications of Christ's teaching. It was hard for us not to feel that George Wharton Pepper, as the most prominent of Episcopal laymen, had been acting in the interest of his clients and associates rather than of Christian principles. The contrast between profession and practice was impossible to ignore.

Then there was the "best family" issue. The roster of the university's trustees contained many members of Philadelphia's old families. The sons of these families, as Witmer pointed out in his brief,[74] mostly went to Princeton or to Yale, seldom to Pennsylvania, and the family fortunes were not shared with the university any more than were the sons. Said Professor Witmer: "The aristocratic element of Philadelphia, which is loyal to the university, represents about one-quarter, or, generously, not more than one-third, of the city's ruling caste. The remaining two-thirds is indifferent and even hostile to the welfare of the institution." That a professor should be dismissed for offending a member of this caste, or that class interest should play any part in such a dismissal, seemed to us an inadmissible misuse of power.

---

74. Ibid., 100–101.

Our indignation had a tendency to widen as time passed. It went very deep and disturbed many otherwise well-rooted loyalties.

Naturally we wondered what we might do to register protest. In the end we did very little, except that within the next two years many of us would go elsewhere to work or teach. McCrea and J. Russell Smith went after Patten's release; the rest of us went then or later.[75] We knew well enough that this was no punishment for the trustees. They were glad to be rid of us. And Scott was very much opposed to our leaving. "You must stay," he said, "the University does not belong to the Trustees; it belongs to you, its teachers, and to its students. That the Trustees have an essentially undemocratic power and have used it irresponsibly does not warrant you in confirming them in it. They want you to leave. You must not accommodate them. You must think of your students and of the University's mission." But just the same, as opportunities offered, we went.

My chance came in the spring of 1917. By then Charles Reitzel had been lecturing in Scott's place for two years. The Wharton School had grown so that he had to give each lecture twice. The whole freshman class could no longer be gotten into any lecture room on the campus, and we had a half-dozen quizmasters. Patten had been succeeded by Ernest Minor Patterson, who would have a long and useful career at the university, but whose presence we at first resented. He became professor of Economics when, the truth was, no respectable economist would come to the Wharton School. He had been moved into Patten's chair from a minor post in the Department of Finance. The whole affair had been degrading and unsuitable. In spite of this bad start, Patterson gave the department a sound, if unimaginative administration, and the reactionaries would in time learn that he, too, was an unintimidated scholar.

I was now the father of a girl child, Tanis, of whom I was very proud. I had earned a master's degree, and I was well advanced toward the doctorate. But such matters had begun to seem small and unimportant now: for the United States, too, had gone to war in the spring.

The unimportance of personal decisions in the midst of such wholesale calamity undoubtedly made me careless. Besides, I wanted

---

75. McCrea and Smith went to Columbia; the rest of us were variously dispersed.

to get away from an institution I had such affection for, yet one where betrayal was tolerated. Still I ought to have stayed on. I was doing well as a teacher; I was within a year or two of my doctorate; I could not become a soldier. There was undoubtedly opportunity for me at the Wharton School. Yet my mood was such that when Carl Parker, who was a first-rate academic siren, came along, I was quite unable to resist.[76] Here was the opportunity for a clean break to a new environment far out in the West. Carl himself would perhaps be another leader under whom I could serve as I had with Scott and with Patten, loyally and creatively. When he asked me to go with him, I accepted.

---

76. Carlton Hubbell Parker, then moving from the University of California to be dean of the new School of Commerce at the University of Washington in Seattle, at the invitation of its president, Henry Suzzalo.

II

INTERLUDE

1917–1920

My offer of an instructorship at Columbia University came to me in April of 1920 from H. R. Seager of the economics department; it was the result of a recommendation by Patten. I was discouraged about an effort to get back into academic life, and the invitation was a kind of rescue. Patterson, by then head of the department at Pennsylvania, had advised me not to try further but to think of something quite different. This advice, given in all earnestness, and after having watched, for some months, my struggle to accommodate myself again, was naturally distressing. I had been tempted to give up, because he seemed so certain, but after talks with Seager and with Patten, I decided that Patterson's judgment might be mistaken. He had no proper measure of my recent difficulties, and possibly his judgment where I was concerned might not be trustworthy anyway. So I went to Columbia in a chastened but determined mood in the fall of 1920. Everyone, I suppose, has these crises, but mine seemed to me worse than most. One thing was certain. I could surmount it only by my own efforts. No one was going to help me.

To account for my discouragement, I had better tell something of the interval between my leaving Pennsylvania in the spring of 1917 and my going to Columbia in the fall of 1920. I have mixed feelings about it. If nothing else, it closed for me all other avenues to a career than academic work. At the end of it I knew that what I had wanted when I began to teach had been right for me. At a certain remove from university life, I had come closer to the understanding that what I wanted most to do could only be done in a university environment.

When Carlton Parker had appeared in Philadelphia in the winter of 1916–17, he had been in the midst of what had seemed to him an infinitely dramatic adventure.[1] He was making a kind of grand tour at the age of forty of intellectual leaders who might add to his understanding of human behavior in economic life. Nothing like it had ever before come to my notice, and, in fact, I had never known anyone like Carlton Parker. His wife, Cornelia, herself living in a state of perpetual excitement, afterward conveyed in her little book about their relationship something of his breathless search for new explanations of reaction to the confusions of modern experience. Her account now seems exaggerated; but actually it represented rather faithfully the way they lived. That so much agitation over intellectual matters could be sustained for so long seems incredible, but it was. And it was not only dissatisfied young people like myself who were infected with something of the Parker enthusiasm; the mature professors of psychiatry, psychology, sociology, anthropology, and even some few economists to whom he went for consultation found themselves, for the time he was with them, almost as excited as he.

For instance, one time he wrote to Cornelia that he had just spent thirteen hours with Thorstein Veblen: "It went wonderfully and I am tickled to death. . . . Gee, but it's some grand experience to go up against him!" At Yale he saw Keller: "He is a wonder and is going to do a lot for me in criticism." In New York, T. H. Morgan took him to his heart; so did Edward L. Thorndike and W. C. Mitchell: "The visit with Thorndike was worth the whole trip." John Dewey discussed with him the conflict between William McDougall and the Freudians. W. B. Cannon and E. B. Holt in Cambridge talked with him "for hours." From seven-thirty to eleven-thirty he "argued with Dr. A. A. Brill, who translated all of Freud!!! and it was simply wonderful." He went to see Dr. Bernard Glueck at Sing Sing and found him a "true wonder." When Thorndike asked him to dinner with the "four biggest psychiatrists in New York . . . made me simply yell, it did. . . . I can't tell you how much these talks are maturing my ideas about The Book. . . . There have come up a lot of odd problems touching the conflict, so called, between intelligence

---

1. A good deal of it is recounted in Cornelia Parker's *An American Idyll*, published a few years after her husband had died (Boston: Atlantic Monthly Press, 1919). *An American Idyll* was, indeed, one of the most widely read of postwar books, and Cornelia was able to capitalize on its popularity for some time. She became a well-known lecturer and writer in her own right, as, indeed, she was entitled to do. She was a vivid, an overflowing, personality. The references here are to her book or to the collection of Carlton's papers, *The Casual Laborer* (New York: Harcourt, Brace and Howe, 1920).

and instinct, and these I'm getting threshed out grandly."

He wrote also of a trip to Philadelphia. There he was "dined and entertained by various members of the Wharton School faculty." And later on he wrote again of "hurried, full days in Philadelphia with most successful talk before the University of Pennsylvania Political and Social Science Conference, and extreme kindness and hospitality from all the Wharton group."

This was my faculty. By the time he had come back for his second visit, after a month's interval, I was his slave. I was reading abnormal psychology, exploring man's instinctive machinery, and in general looking at the human equipment with wholly new eyes. I wondered how I had managed up to then, in spite of two courses in psychology, to miss all this revealing light. It seemed to me, in the new enthusiasm, that, for the first time, I understood why and how men behaved as they did. It was apparent to me at once what Carl was after. He had been dealing with labor—in fact, with migratory labor.[2] These lost human beings seethed with resentment; they were outcasts; they were mentally ill and physically malnourished. Where, in the economics texts was there anything to explain their situation or the explosions resulting from their maladjustments? Carl had a point there. The weakest foundation of economic theory was the assumption that human behavior was essentially rational. I saw that his was one way out of intolerable theoretical confines.

In spite of my enthusiasm, I should never find myself in such an elated state that I could write home as he did, one midnight: "I had

---

2. The problem of casual labor became Parker's specialty not only because of an initial interest, but because after the riots in the hop fields at Wheatland, California, in 1913, he had been appointed to carry out an investigation for the State Commission of Immigration and Housing. An account of that investigation appears in *The Casual Laborer*, 61 ff. What he found produced the indignation that quivers in every word of his report. The curiosity as to causation led to his long inquiry. His tale of the tragic Wheatland affair and the way he relates it to the general situation of the American migratory worker shows that he was already far advanced in his understanding of the situation. In one passage (p. 88), he said, for instance, that

> as a class migratory laborers are nothing more nor less than the finished products of their environment. They should therefore never be studied as isolated revolutionaries, but rather as, on the whole, tragic symptoms of a sick social order. Fortunately the psychologists have made it unnecessary to explain that there is nothing willful or personally reprehensible in these vagrants. Their histories show that starting with the long hours and dreary winters of farms they ran away from, through their character debasing experience with irregular industrial labor, on to the vicious economic life of the winter unemployed, their training predetermined but one outcome.

from 11:30 to 1:00 an absolute super-grand talk with Adolph Meyer and John Watson. He is a grand young southerner and simply knows his behavioristic psychology in a way to make one's hair stand up. We talked my plan clear out and they are enthusiastic!" Still I did feel that I had opened out a new and fruitful country. Now I began to think that I knew how to find the answers to many questions I had believed altogether unanswerable. Of course, I knew far less than I thought I did after a few months of such reading and discussion. As is always true, my first sense of achievement was succeeded by a growing awareness of depths below the surface. These deepened, and presently I was lost again in the unconscious. When I came to realize that I should never know psychology in a professional way, there still remained the contribution it had made to my political and economic understanding. If I did not know why men behaved as they did, I at least knew it was not because they were rational. And certainly I understood better not only workers and employers but also other kinds of people.[3]

---

3. In her introduction to *The Casual Laborer,* Cornelia Parker quoted from a page of odd manuscript, left, like so much of Carl's work, lying around unfinished. He seemed fated not to finish anything. Life was illuminated for him by flashes, but they were real flashes, as this one was:

> Union recognition, the closed shop, the sympathetic strike, are not pursued by the unionist because of any deep realization of the ethical or strategic significance of the issue, but because it is a means of expressing resentment at the stresses and strains of their position. This diverted energy becomes a relief activity, an activity tending, curiously, to reestablish the unionist's dignity in his own eyes. It is impossible for man to suffer economic and social humiliation without an important feeling of inferiority, of *Minderwürtigkeit.* A common cure for this, it has been observed, is a resort to some enterprise in pugnacity. In modern translation this means a strike of more or less violence, a riot, or at least some conflict with the law. . . . a rabid socialist, an I.W.W. (even today a pacifist), has dissociated himself more or less completely from the going norms of society, his subconscious completely in the saddle. His fixed idea is a mental complex supported by a strong emotion and runs back for its explaining cause to a life of extreme stress or privation or a neurasthenic disposition.
>
> The I.W.W. are recruited from the most degraded and unnaturally living of America's labor groups. Their inherited instincts are *in toto* either offered no opportunity for functioning, or are harshly repressed. They are without home security, have no sex life except the abnormal, they are hunted and scorned by society; normal leadership, emulation, constructiveness is unknown to them. And it is both psychically and physiologically a sound deduction that they will at all costs seek some relief activity. The one prerequisite for a permanent acquisition of crop-and-barn-burning as a habit for this migratory group is that the law and society should show itself properly and openly fearful. This, as events in California, Arizona and the Middle West show, is the very contribution of society. Deportation, bull-pens, imprisonment, is food for the sore dignity of the syndicalist. It is the psychological parallel to the newspaper publicity of the ego-crazed murderer. . . .

Carl was wringing some meaning from the sciences and therapies he was sampling. He flitted from flower to flower, sipping where the store was richest. What he wrote and what he said were never important except in their translated meaning for economic theory. To apply the accumulated knowledge of anthropology and the techniques of psychotherapy to labor-employer phenomena was, however, something quite new then, and the sense of a wider usefulness for the practitioners of individual therapy was extremely gratifying to them. He found them ready to explore his suggestions at any length.

This wider usefulness was most obvious in the fields of Carl's main interest: labor relations. Before 1917 the struggle between employer and employee had been growing steadily more vicious. After the setting up of conciliatory machinery at the beginning of the war, it would never be quite so brutal again. The spread of such ideas as Carl had got hold of and was purveying missionary fashion to all and sundry did bring about a more humane approach. Economists were, until then, in the habit of interpreting the class struggle in Marxian terms and accepting it as a war, and in a war it was natural to use force. The new analysis Carl, and, of course, others, brought to bear in these years exposed the futility of simple repression. Although what Carl said needed to be done was not very often accepted, or if it was, only in part carried out, dissatisfied laborers from then on were not so easily called revolutionaries and treated as outcasts to be beaten and starved into submission.

That this might be so dawned on me suddenly. It was one of those times—like the one when I first heard the beautiful phrase about the conservation of energy or when I first grasped the principle of evolution—when what is heard or read seems to bring a kind of order into a terrifying chaos. I was not particularly interested in labor relations—professionally, I mean—but for three years I had been engaged in introducing newcomers to economic theory. I had done it, as others had, by way of assigned work in economics texts.[4]

---

4. In the freshman year at the Wharton School we still taught from Scott Nearing's and Frank D. Watson's elementary text, *Economics* (New York: Macmillan, 1908); in the sophomore year we used Taussig's *Principles of Economics* (New York: Macmillan, 1911–12), and after that went to Marshall and Mill. Only intending graduate students survived ordinarily into the third year of theory. If they went still further, as graduate students, their theory courses were organized about the historical

I had, therefore, from repeated drill and endless discussion, a good grounding in the classics of economics. Also, by now I had been through it all: that is, I had not only taught the elements from the contemporary texts, but I had had the advanced courses as a graduate student. I understood the development from one phase to another of the theory now so rounded and complete. I was even then somewhat dissatisfied with its high polish and a little restless with the implied conclusion that when the market forces were given free play, the resulting prices, wages, and profits were not only equitable but inevitable. I did not believe any more that everything turned on that word "free," as did most economists. They said that if there were inequities, it was because the freedom postulated in the texts did not exist, and that what was needed was to restore it. I did not see how the forces I knew about could produce the kind of results any person of sense and sensibility would want even if they were free. Besides, of course, they were *not* free.

Carl took me into a lighted room. I began to be certain that the economic theory I had been teaching and learning was an abstraction of seriously limited use in the real world. I began to conclude that the economists' tour de force back in the time of Adam Smith, David Ricardo, Thomas Malthus, Nassau Senior, and John Stuart Mill had been inappropriate attempts to imitate the method of Isaac Newton and other physical scientists.[5] By making generalizations reducing

---

development of economic thought with Charles Gide's and Charles Rist's *History of Economic Theory* as the central text. It was, it will be seen, all within one logical system. What questioning there was of it was in its own terms.

5. But there were many economists still writing, some of them just beginning, to whom the Benthamic pleasure-pain principle seemed a sufficient, almost physical, support for their theory. They, like W. S. Jevons, for instance, who represented so complete a development of classical theory, believed that all economic action was determined by the quest for pleasure and the avoidance of pain. They believed, furthermore, that the amounts of pleasure and pain could be expressed in quantitative units. The total number of positive units (wants) determined market demand; the total number of negative units (the pain of producing or giving up something) determined market supply. The interaction of supply and demand determined values and prices.

Patten made a formidable attack on this when he said that it might be applicable in a scarcity economy (when pain was actually involved in giving up or producing something) but not in a surplus economy (when nature is generous and productive work a pleasure). His distinction between pleasure and pain economies was made in Benthamic terms but obviously for the purpose of breaking down their validity.

much scattered data to understandable norms, they, too, had hoped to establish laws. These could then be relied on in further reasoning. The trouble was that Newton's laws had been real in the sense of being derived from and related to a body of data. The economists' laws had been largely imaginary, very often set up to rationalize public policies they wished to defend. They had been accepted even by Marx, but he had used them to show that the only alternative to their acceptance was a communist revolution. After the revolution a new set of socialist laws would take over.

Suddenly all this seemed to me questionable; much later I should come to a time when it would seem dangerous. But people like Carl, who were moved by human dilemmas, either had to find a way out of the theoretical logic or else give up. The psychological considerations Carl wanted to bring to the wage bargain and to the other issues in labor disputes were not part of the freedom postulated in the economic logic. Indeed the economists had always had troubled consciences about this. If wages were interfered with and set too high, the theory said that the employer would be unable to sell his product; the costs would be prohibitive. It could be argued, and often had been, that it was against the workers' own interest to advance wages at the expense of profits or interest. Carl did not probe this dilemma very deeply; indeed he never saw his way through it. What he did see was that he was quite safe in ridiculing the assumption that all economic processes were carried out in a mood of enlightened but selfish calculation. And it was true that the theory was fatally dependent on it.

There would follow a decade of fruitful discussion about these issues. For its beginning and its illumination, if not for any important contributions to it, Carl must be given at least some credit. He would, in fact, succeed in disturbing the more complacent elders—he was something of a sensation wherever he went—at the meeting of the American Economics Association a year later.[6] Because his address there indicates better than any other written memorabilia what he had been saying when he was in Philadelphia and I was attracted to him, I shall repeat here something of what it contained. The attack on the postulates of economics was direct. For instance, he began by saying:

---

6. The paper he read at the meeting, "Motives in Economic Life," is reprinted in *The Casual Laborer.*

The first quarter of this century is breaking up in a riot of economic irrationalism. . . . We look hopefully to see patriotism flow pure and strong from an industrial stratum whose occasional phenomena are Lawrence, McKees Rock, Patterson, Colorado Fuel and Iron, the Durst hop ranch in California, Everett in Washington, Butte in Montana, and Bisbee in Arizona. . . . Our conventional economics analyzes no phase of industrialism nor the wage relationship, nor citizenship in pecuniary society, in a manner to offer a key to such distressing problems. Human nature riots through our economic structure with ridicule and destruction, and we economists look on helpless and aghast.

He went on to say something about the richness of the data already available in the work of ". . . Veblen, Thorndike, Hollingworth, Dewey, James, Watson, Holt, Thomas, Hall, Jastrow, Patrick, Hobhouse, MacDougall, Hart, Shand, Wallas, Lippmann, Freud, Jung, Prince, Southard, Glueck, Brill, Bailey, Patten, Cannon and Crile. Each one of these has contributed criticism touching the springs of human activity of which no economic theorist can afford to plead innocence." Yet, he said, economists still use the careless a priori deductions touching human nature. They are still dominant in our orthodox texts. And this launched him into a tirade using such phrases as "astounding indifference," "crass ignorance," and "delinquency." He quoted MacDougall: "It would be a libel not altogether devoid of truth to say that the classical political economy was a tissue of false conclusion drawn from false psychological assumption!"

There followed a summary of man's instinctive equipment and a lucid discussion of his inherited nature. Man's nature, he argued, was obviously unsuited to the industrial environment, and ended by saying that:

the dynamic psychology of today describes the present civilization as a repressive environment. For a great number of its inhabitants, a sufficient self-expression is denied. There is, for those who care to see, a deep and growing unrest and pessimism. With the increase in knowledge is coming a new realization of the irrational direction of economic evolution. The economists, however, view economic inequality and life-degradation as objects, in truth, outside the science. Our value concept must be the yardstick to measure just how fully things and institutions contribute to a full psychological life. The domination of society by one economic class has for its chief evil the thwarting of the instinct-life of the subordinate class and the perversion of the upper class. The extent and characteristics of this evil are only to be estimated when we know the innate potentialities and inherited propensities of man. The ordering of this knowledge and its application to the changeable economic structure is the task before the trained economists today.

This paper, as may be imagined, caused a sensation. If any other individual had said these things, the economists might have ostracized their author. But not Carl! He not only provoked an intelligent discussion, but thereafter, to my knowledge, received offers of professorships from no fewer than five eastern universities. He had that kind of personality, and that, I suppose, is what induced me to accept his invitation to join him in Seattle. If we all worked together, he said, his new college could be made a new and better Wharton School.

The fresh (to me) theorizing about men's minds in the various circumstances of their lives supplemented very usefully the really considerable study I had behind me of biology and economic change. For although I had not grasped the causes, I did have a good deal of information. I had read extensively in the history of labor. I knew about the spectacular incidents in the struggles of unions for recognition and of workers for decent standards of life. I had studied race relations and knew something of political behavior. I had at my disposal what there was to be contributed by scientific management and some acquaintance with Taylor's conclusions as well. The exploration of instinct, motive, and emotion I had heretofore touched only in a routine introduction to psychology, but this had cleared the way for the range of explanation I now could see ahead. I was especially attracted by studies of primitive man. Scholars like Franz Boas, Alexander Goldenweiser, Robert Lowie, and Alfred Kroeber were pointing out how little the human equipment had changed in historical times and what problems of adjustment were involved in accommodation to the complex modern world. Primitive man's satisfaction in identification with the group was less and less available to the modern man. He had become relatively tieless and lonely.

Carl's migratory workers were only more striking and pitiful illustrations of the essentially bereft nature of homeless men and migratory families. That their protest should register in strange and antisocial ways was to be expected. They were ill and malnourished, made so by circumstances beyond their control. Means had to be devised for better adjustment, for the satisfaction of normal wants and desires. Most well-to-do citizens regarded these others as revolutionaries, as "reds"; violence would be used to suppress them in the social

counterpart of those measures once used on the insane in Bedlam—
and in our neighboring Blockley. Carl implied that civilization might
well simply dissolve in a welter of rage and recrimination. The new
understanding of individual and social behavior had not come too
soon; the question was whether it would spread widely and quickly
enough to prevent a debacle. Scott's super race began to seem a very
distant and doubtful possibility.

Later generations will find it difficult to understand the impact
of these ideas as they entered into more general currency among
academicians. Imagine the situation: We were entering the war that
spring, the first of repeated worldwide cataclysms destined to succeed
each other closely throughout the lifetimes of those who were then
still young. Coming to its climax was a series of attritions on time and
space, represented then by wireless communication and airplanes.
These were primitive then, but soon would develop into an approxi-
mation of instantaneous communication and time-destroying flight.
We were just beginning to experience the consequences of the new
technology.

I was, perhaps belatedly, discovering how all this was affecting
those who by and large were caught by it unaware. Young men and
women who are now learning to take not some homestead, village,
or city, but the world, for their home, and to whom its furthest
reaches are as familiar as the borders of a county or city were to me,
find it hard to appreciate the emotional adjustments forced on my
generation between 1915 and 1930. Nor can they appreciate, of
course, the rude lessons furnished by successive wars and depressions.
The intellectual struggles of the nineteenth century had been bitter
enough, if the conflict between science and the religious establishment can be said to have been intellectual, but they had been nothing,
nothing at all, compared with those we could see impending as the
inevitable adjustment was made to the new knowledge. For it demanded the unification of the world, the collectivization of enterprise, and a common government of mankind. There would be no
escaping it. The commitment was already made, but it would be

feared, hated, and resisted, and those who had chosen careers as social technicians could look forward to continuous struggle and often vilification. The displeasure of the disturbed would be visited upon all honest inventors and adjustors from now on.

I knew all this then, not in its full implications, but quite certainly nevertheless. Presumably I thought that escape from Philadelphia, where the disturbed were powerful, to Seattle and the University of Washington, where I could at least find shelter in Carl's shadow, would be a momentary personal relief. I knew nothing about the Northwest except from geographic study, but I had an idea that so new a country must have a peculiar willingness to accept nonconventional ideas. There must be a flexibility Philadelphia did not have, sunk as it was in its long tradition of conservatism. How wrong I was!

Mistaken as I was in these anticipations, they did influence me in the serious business of cutting the old ties at the Wharton School and going west. The experience did shake me and brought about certain of those crises young people must undergo if they are to mature. I should be grateful for that. Most of all, however, I should be grateful for the translation to the new circle of friends in Seattle. There was not only Carl, but Will Ogburn,[7] whose life would be curiously juxtaposed with mine so many times in future years, Edward Guthrie, Stevenson Smith,[8] and several older teachers, notably Professors William Savery, J. Allen Smith, Frederick M. Padelford, and Vernon L. Parrington, who seemed curiously stranded in Seattle. They were distinguished scholars, though the University of Washington was still far from being a distinguished educational institution. Such elders are found everywhere, I later learned, often in the most incongruous circumstances, pursuing their research among the infantilisms of athletics and general undergraduate nonsense. To have them at Washington almost made the place an educational institution.

---

7. William Fielding Ogburn, who came to the University of Washington from Reed College in Portland. He would go to Columbia in 1919 to be professor of Sociology until 1929 and later would become Avery Distinguished Service Professor at Chicago. His contributions to social science and his services to the public would make him one of the most useful men of my generation. I learned to depend on him for advice and consolation; he was a never-failing source of both. When he died in 1960, we were planning to do a joint book on social theory in our retirement.

8. Both of whom were then instructors but who would become professors at the University of Washington.

It was not then so large as it later became, and anyway, it was wartime and games were suspended. So education had an inning, modified by the preliminary military training of students.

Most of all I was grateful for the association with Carl and Will. Later on I discovered Ferdinand Silcox, and perhaps I learned from him more than from any of the others. He was not, and never would be, a professional teacher; he was a forester. Still he had a remarkable facility for translating experience into useful rules, and if anyone knew more about work and workers than Carl Parker, it was Ferdinand Silcox. Had I not learned from the two of them, I should indeed have been a dullard.

The translation from Philadelphia to Seattle among the disturbances of war's beginning was not easy. Our household goods were started off after a struggle, and the Warrington Avenue bird cage in Philadelphia was abandoned without regret. It had been the scene of a good deal of futile conspiring for what we younger teachers had believed to be the good of the university. Authority had gotten a good deal the best of us. Charlie Reitzel and I were about the last of the old crowd to go, and with us went the Patten and Nearing spirit. E. M. Patterson was now in charge. He might have a bold mind—indeed, he did have—but he was cautious about what young men he kept around and about the direction of Wharton policy. Clyde King was still teaching political science. He breathed a little fire occasionally and worried the trustees, it was said, but on the whole, the great days were over. Reform was finished in City Hall; most of the Wharton School was given over to the teaching of military housekeeping; and I felt myself lucky, for the moment, to have the western venture in prospect.

When in future years I should recall life on Warrington Avenue, I mostly remembered, besides this conspiring, the early days of my eldest daughter, each of which seemed a new miracle to me, and the conditioning of a lonely and difficult old man to a certain measure of domestic affection. For Patten had learned that he could come to us informally and be as nearly at home as he ever had been. His only other centers in those first years of exile from the university (he lived through seven of them) were, I think, the University Club downtown and the Baptist Church on Walnut Street where he remained all his life a loyal member.[9]

---

9. One of his characteristic, but seemingly bizarre, ventures was his attempt to reform the hymn book. The idea was to set new words to the old music, or at

My family preceded me to Wilson by several weeks, leaving me to finish my work at the Wharton School and attend to the packing. My farewell to Philadelphia was a lonely one. Charlie Reitzel and I took a final look around at the old classrooms and the bull-pit lecture halls, paid a final visit to Patten at the University Club, where, as was his custom, he had us to breakfast. He was going off alone, as he had been doing for years now, to Brown's Mills in the Jersey pine barrens instead of to Vermont as had been his custom. He was all for my western venture but predicted prophetically that I would be back. "Back to what?" I asked a little bitterly. But he would not have it that way.

"You take too short a view," he said. "The things we stand for have by now got a life of their own; they will prevail." And on that note we parted. But he was more deeply hurt by the war than he wanted us to see. To him it seemed like a civil war. He believed so deeply in the Germanic aspiration toward a more highly organized life and distrusted so thoroughly the intellectual and upper-class Britons that he could not believe anything good would come of the conflict. The Germans will be beaten, he predicted, and it will be the best of them who will suffer. The Germanic genius for organization and unity is what the British businessmen resent; they will see that it is strangled.

I stopped in Allentown on the way home where Frank Forster, Jack Lansill, and some other friends were training. They had chosen the ambulance service as the best way to satisfy authority. I made tentative efforts toward joining them; the ambulance driving seemed to me, too, better than other services for an amateur. I was given the same answers I had been given when I thought of going to officers' training camp. No one wanted a confirmed asthmatic. My wheezing

---

least to tunes within the old tradition. For the retribution, blood, and apocalyptic threats in the Hebrew manner, he thought it would be useful to substitute sentiments of sympathy, kindness, aspiration, and benevolence. Frank Watson, who was something of a musician, worked with him, and Scott, who believed in this kind of thing, too, did what he could. But none of them had any lyric facility, and although they did publish a hymn book and succeeded in getting it used to a certain extent, it never really caught on. It soon disappeared from circulation.

These *Advent Songs* (New York: Huebsch, 1916) were subtitled *A Revision of Old Hymns to Meet Modern Needs*. He tried a wider revision later on. The first of these was called *Songs of America* (New York: Huebsch, 1917); the second was called *Folk Lore: A Union of Religious, Patriotic and Social Sentiment* (New York: Huebsch, 1919).

did not prevent us from having a few nights of celebration, which were given a special quality by the certainty of long separation. Also I had an acute sense of the risks they must expect unless our generals were smarter than the British ones who were allowing men to be slaughtered by the million in Belgium and northern France without appreciable reason or result. But finally I tooled my small Buick up the northgoing roads alone, bearing west. I felt a lot less exhilarated than I ought to have done, facing a new life I myself had chosen.

Until late in August we stayed in Wilson with intervals in Buffalo and one trip to Chautauqua. All summer I was beset by dread, a new emotion to me. Seattle seemed a long way off. And my mother, always ready to believe the worst, predicted that the climate would lay me low, that I should be in hot water as an Eastern radical, and that we should starve on the salary I was to get. She enlarged on these probabilities at such length that finally I began, if not to worry about these putative disasters, at least to value what I was leaving more highly than I might otherwise have done. In this I was justified, as it turned out, for none of it would ever be the same again. When I came back to Wilson after the war, it would be to a new home—a reconstructed one, but not the one I was used to. Not even Chautauqua would be the same. Already Sinclairville was deserted by the families I had known as a boy. When I visited there again, it would be as a stranger. Bemus Point would have become something very different from the old leisurely resort, and the Chautauqua Assembly would finally be dominated by musical appreciation and other amateur arts and would have lost its character as a place for systematic instruction in the elements of natural and social science.

This was Scott's last summer at Chautauqua. Our visit there would be the last time I should see him for several years. Our few meetings in the future would be almost as casual and perhaps even less intimate than this. We should never have the opportunity to work together again, though we talked about it and hoped it might happen. He enjoyed Chautauqua; he liked the opportunity to shift the American middle class a little off base, to convict the complacent of smugness, and to show them what their land might be like if they wanted it so. Also he felt that those who went there were good people. He had, up to now, been tolerated in this one-man educational enterprise. Scott had been regarded as a man of good will who ought at least to be given a hearing. There were few who seriously suggested repression. Our university trustees had represented a peculiar concentration of frightened interests, but most of America was not like that. It was soon to become so; and Scott would retreat to forums not frequented by the middle class—and only a few, indeed, of the workers.

The countryside I knew so well seemed especially rich and beautiful that summer. Nothing had arrested the return of the Chautauqua hills to grass and trees. The old houses were a little shabbier, and the barns sagged a little more in the middle. The thorn trees had marched farther down toward the valleys, and even the herds of cattle were sparser. But along Lake Chautauqua there were now concrete roads, and in a few minutes the journey could be made from Bemus Point to Jamestown or up to Mayville and down the other side of the lake to the assembly grounds. Dust still followed me over the Ellery heights from Sinclairville to the lake, and the old ferry still operated between Bemus Point and Stow. Elsewhere improvements made things better. Even the retrogression of the hill farms was a return toward accommodation with nature. Along Lake Erie the vineyards were heavy with grapes as the summer advanced. And down in Niagara County the fruit hung thick in the well-trimmed trees as the wheat turned toward the harvest. So it was, the newspapers said, all over the land; there would be enough to eat for soldier and civilian alike. The farmers wondered desperately who would take the place of the boys now being gathered into training camps, and my father was furious at the wages he had to pay for labor suddenly turned arrogant and careless.

His business, however, was developing in the way he wanted, and he himself was more and more dominating everything within sight. He had bought the home factory in Wilson from the parent company, he was putting together a string of country banks, and he had even begun, after a few years of experimentation in Puerto Rico, to manufacture citrus products in Florida. He was one of the first to master the technique of preserving grapefruit and grapefruit juice. This last gave him something interesting to do when he and my mother went south for the winter. He seemed to be endlessly successful.

He did not object very much to my western adventure. I think by now he had decided that I was unmanageable. He was generous. If ever I had a few bills it was difficult to meet, he simply paid them without discussion. But if he wondered why an only son should show no more desire to join in his profitable and expanding enterprises, he said very little about it. I think now that he had a shrewder sense than

I of what it would be like to have me around. His genius was for individual enterprise. He could delegate nothing; he could not work with anyone. He had partners in two of his ventures beginning about that time, but they were passive and let him manage things. He resisted organization. And that would in the end prove to be his limitation, as it would be that of so many of his generation.

The recent Wharton School graduates were already coming into competition with their rule-of-thumb elders, and the next decades would belong to them. In the postwar scramble, my father would fail because he could neither engineer nor become a part of the consolidation and expansion of corporate enterprise in his industry. The depression would catch him in the same vulnerable position as did the war: as an individual with large risks outstanding. He would prosper during the war just now coming on; the depression would make him poor. But who in 1917 could foresee depression? Everything was ahum. Those in charge of business were optimistic, and why not? They had had several years of profitable markets abroad, and now army contracts were beginning to be spread around. Since Wilson had defined the Germans as wicked, it was quite all right to prosper from expanded production. There was nothing to be done but simply drive ahead, and this was what Americans were best at. My father was too busy doing that, along with the others, to make any difficulty about my choices for myself.

It was a troubled year for my generation and especially for those of us who were morally concerned. We were no longer very young. Most of us had set ourselves for careers we thought attractive, but they no longer seemed to have success guaranteed at the end, even if we were persistent. Furthermore, most of us were having them interrupted in one way or another. Those who were not going for soldiers were being jostled by the adjustments to the increased tempo being felt everywhere. There was not much satisfaction in fish being caught in these troubled waters either, because there was a certain guilty feeling in being a young civilian in wartime, and no excuse could quite smother it. But perhaps most disturbing of all was that the old world we had known, the old ways we had pursued, the old culture we were used to—all were being changed, broken up. The direction of our lives was shifting uncertainly. A torrent of events tossed us about like small boats in the rapids of a stream.

It was even worse for me than for most others. I had sustained the shock of what I regarded as abused loyalty to the university and a parting under strained circumstances, as well as the shifting under my feet of the civilization I had hitherto felt was evolving toward a super nation, a super race, and world understanding. Universal brotherhood, supported by immensely increased productivity, now seemed to have been an infantile dream. Hatred had come to take the place of anticipated mutual trust. Destruction was suddenly the aim of our technology, not progress and welfare. The readjustments were painful. I could no longer feel myself a part of a vast constructive enterprise leading to a better world.

It was a puzzled young man who gazed out the windows of the Canadian Pacific as its transcontinental express carried us through the bush of Ontario out over the prairie seas toward the West. The descent into the damps of Vancouver, the transfer to an overnight steamer, the awakening to a thick Puget Sound fog, the translation to the happy-go-lucky Parker household, and the immediate problem of my teaching shook me out of my lethargy.

In the excitement of change, I had not examined too carefully what my duties were to be. I found that Carl, with characteristic insouciance, had put me in charge of the Department of Marketing in the new college. It was true that I had had (under G. G. Huebner) the appropriate courses at the Wharton School. I had my notes and I knew the books. I had even done some survey work under Clyde King's direction in Pennsylvania, Delaware, and Maryland. So I was not wholly unprepared. The difficulty was that I had very little interest in the subject, and I was reluctant to undertake the drudgery of teaching two simultaneous full-time courses. I wanted to spend my time on the new psychology, reading its literature and discussing it with Carl and Will Ogburn. Still I had the teacher's faithfulness to his commitment. So I put everything else aside for the moment and began to lay out my year. In the first weeks, the only interruption was the necessity for finding a place to live. This was happily settled by discovering on the slope of a hill down on Twenty-first Avenue at Fifty-fifth Street a new little house so nearly perfect, even if almost miniature, that moving into it was a genuine satisfaction.

That done, my course outlines finished, and the classes well begun, I began to conclude that I had made a mistake. I disliked the prospect of each separate class meeting, and I resentfully gave up each hour spent in preparation.

With some notable palliatives, such as my pleasure in the company of the generous and interesting folk on the campus and the few excursions I was to make in survey work for Carl in some of his many efforts at labor adjustment, the rest of that academic year was unhappy. I had to work hard and long to do my duty by my classes, and it was work I was more and more convinced I ought not to be doing. Not that it ought not to be done by someone, but not by me. When Carl sent me off to do an odd job in the lumber camps, in the shipyards, or at the fish docks, the intrinsic interest in these new experiences was spoiled by the knowledge that to do them I was neglecting my academic duty. For I had no substitute and no assistant. I hated slovenly teaching, but I was falling into the way of it in spite of myself. That constantly tormented me. The other part was interesting, although what good we were doing was unclear.

We had hardly started on our academic year when the War Labor Board, or a good part of it, came to Seattle and sat for hearings. This was meat for Carl. He had already done some jobs for them and was, indeed, their counselor on all the problems of our area. There were real problems: warfare in the woods, in the shipyards, on the sound, and on the fruit and produce farms all up and down the valley. The workers' grievances were old ones: wages not rising with the cost of living; primitive working conditions; and employer opposition to collective bargaining. The employers' idea of settling labor troubles, as I heard Carl tell them once to their faces in the Seattle Club, was to pick up a two-by-four and—backed by a few husky foremen—go to look for "agitators."

The workers' responses to grievance plus suppression were typical. They formed revolutionary groups. There never had been such a flowering of the "Wobblies" (the International Workers of the World). The war effort was obviously going to be seriously impeded if labor's willingness to participate could not be materially improved. The situation in the Northwest was only a more exaggerated form of nationwide trouble. It had become so prevalent that the Labor Board had been set up to inquire, and then to remove causes if it could. They came early to Seattle because violence had broken out repeatedly, and because lumber, food, and ships were all so important to the war economy. It was in preparation for their coming that Carl sent us out to gather facts. These expeditions took me for the first time into the Douglas fir forests and the camps of the loggers. It was by then the season of mist and gloom around Puget Sound, when all vistas were obscured. The trees dripped and the damp chill struck inward.

The camps usually accommodated some sixty to more than a hundred men, who slept in wooden, tiered bunks on filthy blankets in their woolen underclothes. The barracks were flimsily built and had no recreational facilities. They were heated by great iron chunk-burning stoves, red hot toward night when the men came, wet and tired, out of the woods. Lines hung about the stove held drying socks and lumberjack shirts; the heavy boots were stacked about it, too. The miasma can be imagined. Add to this that most of the loggers were loners, many were foreigners, and not a few were tormented by chronic ailments that made their heavy labor almost insupportable. The conditions breeding revolt were not difficult even for an observer like myself to understand.

Aside from indicating the easy conclusion about the causes of unrest, with the obvious supporting factual material presented at the hearings, we met the members of the board individually and informally. We had several evenings at Carl's house and one at mine. This was my first acquaintance with one member who would mean something in my life for many years—Felix Frankfurter, who was then professor of Law at Harvard University. I also met Ferdinand Silcox, who had come over from Missoula in Montana where he was a regional forester. Silcox was well known in the Northwest, and even nationally, for his handling of the many casual laborers who were engaged every year to fight forest fires—more of them than in later years, because then they had only hand tools for the job. He had appealed to the men's patriotism, no less. Appearing at Wobbly headquarters, he would ask the loafing casuals whether they wouldn't go out and save their own forests.[10] This proposal evidently took their breath away, and before they had recovered their equilibrium, they had been out in the woods hard at work.

---

10. I later had the privilege of drawing Silcox back into the service, this time as chief, when I was an undersecretary of agriculture. He served with distinction for several years and died in office. I wrote a short memorial in the *New Republic,* March 1940.

When the board members left, Silcox was borrowed from the Forest Service to be mediator for the Northwest Region, and I saw a good deal of him all that winter. It was then that I learned from a practicing master not only some of the arts of association, but a new loyalty to the future expressed through the conservation of resources. All real foresters, I learned, as I got to know them, have that mystic tie with their living charges, the trees; but not all had such a feeling for men. Most of them, in fact, regarded men as useful only when they helped trees to grow safely and come to their natural harvest. This was to be expected. Most of the powerful men they knew were predators; so were many of those who were not powerful, but who regarded a few unauthorized sheep or cattle on the range or a few stolen logs as matters between themselves and their God. Foresters who intervened were nuisances. So foresters were apt to be cynical about people and were often defensive and clannish even when they were not, as they so often were, on lonely duties.

But not Silcox. Silcox was incorrigibly social, another man of words like Carl. He loved to talk. His audience mattered not at all. I heard him hold forth to loggers in their camps, to employers in their clubs, to meetings of experts, to his own foresters, to the secretary of agriculture and, yes, to the president himself. And it was all the same talk: charming, determined, illuminating, oriented to the public service, but understanding about human frailty. He was an operating conciliator such as never was; and such a forester as there would not soon be again.

One incident, among many, stands out especially in my memory. Silcox took me with him when he went one day down to one of the shipyards on a hunch. He had been hearing a good deal from Washington about "reds" in the shipyards, and especially since one of the hastily built Victory ships had opened her seams in mid-Pacific and sunk. The subversive workers, said Washington, were deliberately not driving their rivets tight. Silcox thought it over and finally equipped himself with a pressure gauge and several witnesses, including myself. At the shipyard he gathered the superintendent and several foremen, so that a small crowd of us followed him from one air hammer to another as he applied his gauge and noted the pressure. In not one was there even half the pressure required by government contract. No amount of patriotism would have driven tight rivets in that yard. So, concluded Silcox, it's not the "reds," is it? It's rotten management! Silcox made good use of that demonstration. He was still beating employers over the head with it when I left the following spring, and I imagine he kept it up until the war was over.

In spite of the activity around the sound in wartime, we seemed very far away from the center of the world's current activities. The European struggles of that year were only faintly reflected in the xenophobic and prejudiced Seattle press. The local papers pictured the war in Europe as considerably less important than the war going on in the shipyards and in the forests. Newspapers everywhere were going to incredible lengths to prove that American workers who thought wages ought to go up along with profits were disloyal. This pounding insistence that labor should sacrifice while business prospered gave an otherwise understandable situation its fantastic quality. Labor's grievances were chronic low pay, intolerable living conditions, and public hostility, with real wages falling as the cost of living rose, and with the newspapers screaming day after day at the reds and revolutionaries. The sabotage they were being accused of actually began to be used by workers here and there. Agitators, who were blamed anyway, thought they might as well agitate openly and continuously. The unions grew as they never had before, and their leadership, pushed from underneath and in competition with the IWW, really became militant.

The lessons I learned in the dark and misty days of that winter were indelible ones. It seemed to me that out here in the western country, still possessed of the physical characteristics of its pioneer days, the issues were more sharply drawn than in the East. The economists' generalization that all the factors of production must combine and cooperate and that a just return to each would result from the free play of competitive forces was here, if anywhere, on trial. And with what result? As far as I could see, it centered in a nasty struggle to stifle freedom itself. Each wanted to exploit the processes of production and wanted to do it by taking away the liberty of all others involved in the process. Employers wanted workers to accept the wages and working conditions convenient for them; workers wanted the whole product of industry and wanted to work as little as possible to get it. Neither scrupled to sacrifice the national interest even in wartime, just as in normal times they regarded consumers as inconvenient economic nuisances. They did not say this, of course. None of them were honest except the IWW, which was about half underground at the time, not sure whether it would emerge. The Wobblies talked about the war as, in normal times, they talked about "free enterprise" and "service to the public," without in the least intending their words as anything but a cover for withholding and sabotage.

If I had not before been a convinced collectivist, that winter would have made me one. Men must have a higher goal than profits, than loafing on socially necessary jobs, than exploiting each other. War was destructive in Europe; it was just as destructive around Puget Sound. Washington—that distant bureaucracy—was hostile and uninterested in anything but allowing those who held war contracts to have their way so that lumber, ships, and agricultural produce would flow toward those who needed them to prepare for war. And all the mitigating agencies, the liberal, the understanding, the sympathetic people, were laid under the compulsions of noncombatants in wartime.

We gathered occasionally, those of us who were fresh from the books explaining such things, at Carl's, at Will's, at Ed Guthrie's, or at my house. Silcox often came, too. We probed and analyzed. And gradually I came to the conclusion that there was only one way out. That way was socialization, collectivization. Call it by any name, but arrange matters so that destructive conflict was stifled and men were given something common to achieve.

Seattle had only been settled since the fifties of the nineteenth century. It was now becoming a city of a quarter-million. It sprawled over the hills between the sound and Lake Washington, its row houses and scraggly business districts still interspersed with lonely, sparse clumps of Douglas fir—all dying, because firs can only live close to other firs. Settlement in the 1850s had hardly been more than a token occupation. Not until 1870 had there been a thousand people living on the present site, but in 1900 the population of 80,000 was spreading, camp fashion, quite unplanned. Everything except the downtown district still reflected the forest culture in 1917. Even the university library was housed in one of the old timber buildings of the Alaska-Yukon-Pacific Exposition of 1909; its façade was distinguished by pillars of Douglas fir with the bark still on. It was not much of a library, but the fir trunks were impressive.

It was impossible to live, even for a few months, in the Northwest and not be conscious of the forests. The misty winters, the mountain valleys saturated with moisture, making it possible for growth to go on all year, had nurtured these largest (except for their sister redwoods in Oregon and California) of living organisms. The western slopes of the Sierras and the whole of the Olympic peninsula had, as late as 1900, been completely forested. The trees grew to more than two hundred feet and, what seemed to an easterner, to an incredible girth: sometimes eight or ten feet in diameter and quite ordinarily five or six feet. The forest was cathedral-like, made so by the majestically rising trunks, bare of foliage almost to the top, and the carpet of needles underneath, without much undergrowth. There had been some kind of holocaust about six hundred years in the past, as could be told from the tree rings, probably a fire started by lightning in an unusually dry season. This made for uniformity of size over an enormous area.

Quite without regard for the past or the future, but with a single-minded intent to exploit, this priceless heritage was being used up. The cutting was being done in such ways that growth could hardly start again for a generation, since fires were inevitable among the dried debris of broken trunks and lopped limbs during dry seasons. Whole districts had been cut over, and the mountainsides and valleys most accessible to rail or road were now a burned-over wilderness, useless for any human purpose. A former forest area cut over by commercial logging operators and burned is about as desolate a sight as will be found on earth. The Forest Service's conscience was communicating itself to others, and there was a certain resentment against such waste, just as there was against the quite similar ruin of millions of square miles of western range lands by ruthless cattlemen. The sustained-yield principle was at least understood. But talk of free enterprise still confused the issue, and conservation was making slow progress.

The movement's progress appeared, in fact, to be too slow to save more than a remnant of the big trees. Soon most of the cattle and sheep ranges seemed likely to be fit only for abandonment to the slow cycle of succession. Not for hundreds, perhaps thousands, of years, even with careful tending, could the West be given back the riches now being stolen by irresponsible exploitation.

Seattle, Bellingham, Everett, Tacoma, Hoquiam—all the sound cities had been founded on lumber. When the lumber went, the cities might go, too, unless farming and fishing proved more adequate supports than appeared likely. So some chambers of commerce had moments of doubt in the general spreading of mushy optimism among the lumber operators. But the interludes of sense were few, and the spirit of gain-getting was strong. Public policy regarding natural resource exploitation was revised with such distressing reluctance that it seemed the Northwest must within an appreciable time begin a general decline.

The situation was made worse by the war. In those days spruce was an important raw material for planes, and spruces habitually grew in clumps of fir. The firs had to be cut to get at the spruce, and there were occasions when they were treated as weeds and burned or left to rot. Then wooden ships began to be built. These were regarded as supplementary to the steel ships so feverishly being riveted together in Seattle and Tacoma yards. But since steel was limited and the forests still stood, there was an expansion of cutting for this purpose, contributing further to the devastation of the forests.

The art of wooden ship building had almost been lost. Only a few oldsters in Vancouver and Seattle remembered how to shape, join, and caulk the timbers. These men were naturally in great demand, and there were never enough. A good many inexperienced workers represented themselves as experts, and a good many poorly built ships were launched. It seemed unlikely that any product so independent as a ship could sail the seas when it had been constructed in such a slovenly way. Some of them did, however, and were useful in their own degree.

It seemed to me that resources were being used up extravagantly. The Northwest was approaching economic suicide; as for Seattle, it had already lost all form and cohesion. It could not furnish ordinary municipal services to its sprawled-out communities. It seemed to be turning into a shack town of unprecedented size and squalor. Aside from these observations on the region and its probable fate, I came to question the importance I had been attributing to the new psychology. In my enthusiasm I had followed Carl into his analysis not only of management-labor relations but also of many other social maladjustments. I was more than a little inclined to go back to the solid ground of geographic and environmental causation. Carl's analyses failed to disclose any realities not recognized before. He failed, as well, to assess properly the part environmental factors played in the radicalizing of the workers.

It did not really advance us very far to express in new terms the resentment of homeless and badly paid men, or to say that inadequate working conditions, long hours, and the like, led to unrest. The techniques of psychoanalysis were simply no substitute for the correction of deplorable conditions. The transfer to social organisms of the methods invented for individual analysis had some validity. But there seemed to me a danger (and Carl was falling into it) of substituting palliatives for necessary reconstruction. Later on I should grow to feel that much of the improvement in economic theory traceable to the new learning in psychology would have to be diminished in any general reckoning by the escape it furnished from realism in labor relations. Even here it had its uses, of course, but it would often in the future be used as an excuse for neglect. It was too easy to say that strikes arose from such emotions as inferiority and resentment or from the irresponsible elements in the workers' primitive inheritance. It was still true that for millions of workers wages needed to be raised and protected, and working conditions had to be improved. These were the sources of the revolt Carl spoke of as psychological.

In communities such as those of the Northwest, all these genuine grievances were intensified, especially during the unprepared-for influx of war workers. It was no answer to say that the newcomers were better off than they had been where they came from, else they would not have come. Saying this only emphasized the deficiencies elsewhere, and it overlooked current changes for the worse as the cost of living increased, as overcrowding intensified, and as the pitch of patriotic hostility to labor rose. The workers were not only at a disadvantage in bargaining with their employers but also helpless before the profiteers and patriots. Some escaped—or tried to—to the beach slums on the sound or around Lakes Union or Washington; many more were crowded into boarding houses where the beds were never allowed to cool. For the skilled laborers and foremen, the little boxlike houses marched, row on row, over more hills and down more valleys. Trees had disappeared. There was a good deal of raw earth; sewage and water systems crawled only slowly after the marching houses; there were never enough schools; and, to get anywhere, it took longer and longer on worse and worse transportation facilities.

It was in this confusion caused by private enterprise that I, motorless for the first time since adolescence, had my first thoughts about cities as social organisms. I even did some reading in Ebenezer Howard and others of the English Garden City School, and I learned something more of municipal management and the gas-and-water socialism of the Fabians in Britain. Seattle seemed hardly to belong to the same genus as Frankfurt or Manchester, to say nothing of the Garden Cities. It was true that a movement toward municipal ownership had already begun. A genuine counteropinion to oppose the shouters for private ownership of utilities would eventually develop, but it was not anything like a majority opinion, and no results could yet be seen.

Yet the Northwest, now being so ruthlessly gutted, had been, and still was, a mystically appealing land. Set as it was toward the north, with its details softened so many months of the year by gentle slanting rains, the forests gave it a mystery and depth impressive even to the casual visitor. The snow-covered Sierras toward the east and the white piles of the Olympics across the sound were felt, even when not seen, as boundaries to a closed domain. And most magical of all were the rare days when the great mountain, seventy-five miles to the southeast of our campus, disclosed its shining mass: Rainier seemed to draw up the darkness toward her peak until it hung alone above the veiled slopes. I saw the mountain only a few times during my months in Seattle. Once or twice I saw heads turn and heard exclamations. And, turning myself, I saw the mists resolve into the solidity of vast snowy heaps built up into the mighty mountain, its whiteness stained with blues and reds.

The everlasting dampness made everything green, healed quickly the savage man-made scars of building, and, in the fertile soil of the valley, grew flowers and vegetables in quantities and of a quality unknown to visitors from drier and poorer lands. Then there were the sound and the lakes. Taken together, they made a city of waters. The harbor's vastness was on a continental scale. All the navies of all the world—and the merchant fleets as well—could anchor here. And since Seattle was, by geography, the home port for the Alaskan North and the Orient, the shipping was various and romantic. Also these northern waters all the way to Alaska were one great fish farm where some of the finest varieties came up the rivers annually to be caught.

It was a fact that only man was vile. He acknowledged no discipline; he obeyed no laws; he violated the most elementary rules of nature. Not he, of course, but his descendants would suffer, and because the penalties could be deferred, he found it possible to contend that they would never be exacted. Within a few years Seattle would fall into the final social paradox. There would be a general strike. It sounds like a contradiction in terms, like a fantasy, but it would happen. One who knew Seattle could only be surprised that it did not end in disintegration.

There came a day in early March when I found myself walking up and down Seventeenth Street in the rain, which had not really stopped coming down for weeks, and looking upward at the open windows of the ugly overgrown bungalow where the Parkers lived. Carl was down with pneumonia. Presently he died, as pneumonia victims did in those days, smothered to death with pus in the lungs. His bright spirit was overcome; his husky voice was still. I had no further interest here, I told myself, and presently rescue came. Felix Frankfurter had recommended me for a civilian job in Paris with the American University Union. I went away without regret.

Translation to Paris was not easy in the spring of 1918. I was something more than a month on the way, stopping for two weeks in New York to straighten out my papers, and also making a trip to Washington before they were in order. These were by no means my first visits to New York or Washington. New York had become quite familiar during my student years; it was, after all, only an hour-and-a-half from Philadelphia. But I had never before explored Greenwich Village, always having been with a student crowd more interested in Broadway or in some sporting event than in literary or artistic matters. This time I stayed at the already ancient Brevoort on lower Fifth Avenue; and, not having much to do but wait for officials to move, I looked up a few old friends and explored the lower part of town. Most of the people I knew were either getting ready to enter the service or already in, but there were some few with whom I could pass the hours. It was not the kind of time to be visiting art galleries or discussing the subjects ordinarily important to academics. There was, as there had been in Seattle, an extraordinary concentration on everyday affairs. Civilians had suddenly become armchair diplomats, and there were many who fancied themselves to be amateur strategists. The war could not be said to be going very well. Russia was through; American weight could not yet be felt; and the French and British were about exhausted. The dark days seemed to grow darker. The possibility that the huge German armies, transferred from the eastern front, might break through to Paris and perhaps overrun all France became a probability. New York suddenly grew close to Europe.

I felt the humiliation of going to France as a civilian to do a service job. Everyone else naturally thought me lucky. Going to Paris was itself a priceless privilege. I should have a chance to see history being made even if I might not be too active a participant. This was true enough. Mine would have been more like a journey toward home if I had been going to London. Nevertheless Paris was a true center. What had happened there was part of my heritage; what had been decided there had changed my life. I should have been wooden indeed not to have regarded my visit as a privilege. I had not much idea what my duties would be, but I knew that they would require me to be in the very heart of the city.

Yet the war was too immediate, and Paris was now too much in peril for such an opportunity to seem very valuable. To go there now was not so much to visit the city of light, the seat of Gallic learning, as to enter a beleaguered headquarters, abandoned by as many of its peacetime inhabitants as could get away (among them, of course, the literary and artistic folk), and given over mostly to the uses of war. All this I was told in my sketchy briefing before I boarded the old *Niagara.* So it was not with any expectation of pleasurable cultural experience that I set off, but rather with a grim hope of being useful, even if not to any immoderate degree. I was to help run a kind of combined club and service station for university men who would be temporarily in Paris, a war enterprise of the American University Union in Europe.

The *Niagara* was an antique. Her old engines clanked; she was rusty from stem to stern; she was dirty and slow; also she was packed with humanity. Most of my fellow passengers were Red Cross or YMCA workers, but there was a platoon of troops somewhere below and several detached officers on not very urgent missions. We made a good trip of it in spite of submarine scares and the compulsory wearing of life belts. There were a certain number of Holy Joes among the YMCA people, but the Red Cross seemed to have recruited a good number of westerners and men from the sporting world, mostly over fifty, and they refused to be subdued to the evangelical level. The food was good because it was French; there was *vin ordinaire* on the table. After we got well acquainted and sorted out, it became a lively crossing. Going over on the same service as myself to be secretary of one of the university missions was a certain old grad of one of the eastern universities who seemed to have spent his entire life in the barrooms of Manhattan, and, in the course of his career, he had accumulated a stock of obscene but really comic stories. He formed a circle of serious drinkers and raconteurs whose guffaws issued from the smoking room starting around 11:30—as soon as the first tippling of the morning had had its lubricating effect. It was all very jolly, and since the *Niagara* took more than two weeks to make her landfall at Bordeaux, we had time to settle into a lively family party. The old grad's consumption of gin-and-milk—a beverage peculiarly repulsive to me—was something wonderful to behold. The others gradually learned to shift from rye and bourbon to cognac, a necessary accommodation to the hardships involved in welfare work for the soldiers.

There were a few perfect days toward the end as we rolled slowly in toward the coast of southern France, days when the sea under pale blue skies was frosted here and there by a lazily breaking wave. It was possible then to sit most of the day far up on the boat deck where the draft from the funnels blended with the hum of the gears far below and where there were overtones from the wind in the rigging. Even so old a craft as the *Niagara* took on a certain brave and self-sufficient carriage in the vast, beautiful sea, riding it with certainty, a perfect work of man at peace with nature. Then we could forget that wolves prowled beneath that urbane blue and that human works like the *Niagara* were potential victims of other human works like the U-boats.

But nothing happened. The elderly YMCA'ers had done their best to sight a dozen periscopes and start a half-dozen panics. But the careless French sailors had been so obviously amused as to make hysteria hard to sustain. We had only one lifeboat drill all the way across, a neglect that amazed the fearsome among us so greatly that they held a meeting and sent a delegation to the captain. We never were able to learn what his response was. We could only guess what tightened lips and infuriated glances might mean. But there was no more quarter decking from the YMCA. On the sixteenth day, we plowed up through the Bay of Biscay to the mouth of the Garonne, with the white walls and red roofs of villas and farmhouses on either side. It was suddenly very familiar. I realized that a literature was coming to life for me.

The books came much more to life as we sidled clumsily up to the Bordeaux docks and saw the acres of wine casks against a background of pastel warehouses, soiled up to human height from lorry-thrown mud, and heard the shouts of dockers and longshoremen. There was only a glimpse of Bordeaux, of course; we were piled into a Paris express, and soon we were furiously running out into the sunny land of southern France, green, neat, and bountiful. There really were pollarded willows along the streams and Lombardy poplars defining the roads just as I had seen them in the paintings of the Barbizon school and read about them in Hugo, Balzac, Zola, de Maupassant—no! I have my geography wrong. This is the country of Montaigne. I thought of his tower, not fifty miles from where we were, perhaps much less, and wondered whether it would still be there.

It was in the cool dusk that we drew, coughing and steaming, into the Gare d'Orleans. Not even farmers and mechanics are more characteristic of various peoples than are their station porters and taxicab drivers. Constant contact with strangers seems only to harden their determination to be themselves and to shame others for foreign oddity. The combination of a porter and a taximan that evening reduced me to a very small size, a process continued through succeeding days. Europeans, settled into their grooves, surrounded by monuments, and sustained by an invincible provincialism, had a peculiarly overwhelming effect on me. The intellectual arrogance and cultural certainty of the French might rest on decayed foundations and might be sustained by diminished resources, but it was sustained nonetheless. And in France the visitor's inferiority is intensified by a complete inability to master colloquial French. I was never able to ask even the most elementary direction of a gendarme without having him ask again and then repeat after me, with a different accent, what I had been trying to say.

My first essays that week in the streets and the houses of Paris were tentative. I gathered courage—or acquired a certain indifference —as I went, however, and, in spite of time-consuming duties, soon became an indefatigable explorer. My predecessor at the union, who was leaving for a Red Cross job, was in no great hurry, and we overlapped by several weeks. He was an expatriate of many years who knew Paris as few foreigners ever do, from one end to the other, in every aspect. What was best of all, he knew her in depth, that strange dimension so puzzling to the careless tourist, and he imparted all this knowledge with enthusiasm. I had studied French history in a casual way, but there were so many centuries of it, surviving in some buildings and in the remains of others, that only after I had made myself a timetable and gone over it repeatedly could I place even the main monuments within half a mile of our center at 8, rue de Richelieu. For directly in back of us was the Palais Royal, just next door was the Comédie-Française, around the corner was the Tour St.-Jacques, and within a short distance were the Tuileries. The Tour St.-Jacques belonged to the sixteenth century, the Palais Royal to the seventeenth, and the Comédie to the nineteenth. And when I went through the Place du Carrousel, as I soon did twice every day since I found a room in the rue de Verneuil on the left bank, and crossed the Pont du Carrousel, I looked involuntarily up river past the Pont des Arts and the Pont Neuf at the Ile de la Cité. And to look at the Ile de la Cité was to look deep indeed into the centuries. The Ile had been the heart of France when the wolves had howled in the woods of Montparnasse and kings had hunted where the Champ de Mars was laid out in the eighteenth century.

Since there were two of us to carry on the management, there was some time for orientation. What I found was a middle-sized hotel of some one hundred fifty rooms converted into a club. About a dozen universities were contributing and maintaining resident secretaries, each of whom had a suite for accommodating visiting alumni. It was some comfort for a soldier just in from the front lines, just returned from an ambulance trip, or even just out of some muddy provincial headquarters, to find in Paris a place where he could at least clean up and eat a passable meal. Not many, of course, could find beds, but our clubrooms were always crowded and our dining facilities used to capacity. The French character of the hotel had not changed too much; we had not only the old housekeeper, but the maître d'hôtel who had presided over the restaurant for years. I soon learned the routine. There was not much possibility of improvement: food was a difficulty, but French magic made the best of what we could get; the rooms and baths were as modern as could be found anywhere; and altogether there was not much scope for ambition.

Paris seemed to me at once to resemble more closely the functioning social organism a city ought to be than any other I had ever seen. There was, first of all, its beauty. All vistas seemed contrived so as to give pleasure in gross and in detail. At the end of a street was often a monument; along the street, the conforming style of each building contributed to a composed whole. There were gardens; even the small ones had a sophistication new to me, used as I was to the English park translated by American landscapists. Many of the city fountains were flowing even in wartime; indeed, there was one just below the windows of the corner suite we used for offices.

This was not, as the next one was to be, a war involving civilians intimately and continuously, unless they happened to be caught in invaded territory. The Germans, nonetheless, were quite aware of the effect on national morale of bringing civilians under pressure. In the first few days I was in Paris, we not only had air raids, but also were bombarded by the Paris Gun, built especially to shell Paris. Of these two morale twisters, the Paris Gun was immensely more effective. There was about its belching a terrifying regularity. When in operation it fired from dawn to dusk at regular intervals. This was such a nerve-shattering experience that in a restaurant, for instance, the diners would watch the time furtively and at about four minutes before the explosion was due, lay down their forks and gather up their courage. For at least two minutes before the explosion there would be complete silence. Then, as the tension came to a climax, the dull boom of the exploding shell would release a sigh of relief. To go through day after day of this was just too much for civilians who were not tied to Paris; when an occasional day or night air raid was added, it was easy to account for the comparative emptiness of the city that spring. As a matter of fact, it was possible just then to walk the whole length of the Avenue de l'Opéra and see only a scattering of civilians, perhaps not more than a half-dozen. At least a million Parisians—I heard much higher estimates than that—had found it convenient to visit relatives in the provinces, a procedure made easy by the close ties French families maintain and by the tenacity of their country connections. Many more, of course, were in the army.

If the wholesale desertion was noticeable in daylight even to a newcomer, at night it was positively eerie. There was, of course, no street illumination except for the dim blue lights at infrequent intervals. If there was no moon and the neighborhood was unfamiliar, it was very easy to become confused. Even the patrons of the Folies-Bergère and the cafés of Montmartre and Montparnasse seemed to dissolve in an instant when they emerged into the streets. The encircling shadows simply absorbed them.

The city seemed to function smoothly, which was difficult to credit. Lack of refrigerating facilities, such as we were used to in America, made housekeeping a pressing daily problem; transport, except for the métro, was pretty well broken down; the ubiquitous monuments seemed calculated to inhibit circulation; and communications by our standards were halting. Yet everything flowed smoothly and with far less obvious effort than it would have taken in Buffalo, Philadelphia, or Seattle. After a while I came to see that it was because the city was well planned for the kind of life the Parisian liked. Meat could not be kept, but French cooks liked an empty larder after the day's last meal. The métro seemed unspectacular, but it was possible to get anywhere in Paris on its concentric lines. The streets, which lacked our gridiron uniformity, needed only a little study to reveal their patterns, and they were supplemented by Baron Haussmann's magnificent boulevards. It was a fair and comfortable city, one to regard, as many Americans obviously did, as a second home.

So in a few weeks, I had fallen into a routine. I lived mostly on the surface, not being acquainted with many French people but being more and more attentive to the problems of readjustment for the French as the war progressed and survival began to seem assured. Naturally, with my interests, I gradually grew into at least some appreciation of these issues. My knowledge of the language—I had a daily lesson from a schoolteacher for several months—gave me, finally, a reading facility. Then I could follow the newspapers. Presently I was reading French books and finally felt that I was getting a preliminary understanding of the Gallic approach to living. I did not get to the point of being able to absorb professorial lectures at the Sorbonne or at the Ecole des Sciences Politique as I had hoped to do; I tried on several occasions, but the rapid technical French defeated me. The others with whom I associated at the union were mostly interested in the more precious aspects of the French contribution to civilization, and about these, consequently, I heard a good deal—

literature, art, philosophy, esthetics. What I, myself, was most curious about was the empire idea, rooted in the firm belief of every Frenchman that France was the chosen home of all that was excellent in civilization. This attitude was seldom made explicit: to a Frenchman the exposition of such a theme would seem quite unnecessary. It was also unnecessary, he would feel, to explain why the lesser peoples of the world ought to be willing to come under French domination. It would be so manifestly to their own advantage that argument would be superfluous. And it would not occur to him that questions might be raised about the French genius for colonial management.

My knowledge of French history was, I found, sketchy. I repaired that deficiency somewhat as I went along, but never during this stay did it become for me a completely reliable aid to orientation. I did, however, gradually trace the emergence of the modern nation out of the medieval system. I saw how Languedoc, Provence, Burgundy, Normandy, Brittany, Champagne, and other regions had coalesced around the Ile de France—how the nation had evolved—and how, finally, the Republic had established itself. The eventual union had advantages. It was, for instance, economically self-sufficient, or nearly so, and I came to understand that France's national narcissism might be largely due to this. Even in 1918, with the weight of war and with the overseas colonies beginning to pull away, the air of complacency was unmistakable and almost unimpaired. Peasants kept to themselves on their holdings; towns lived close to their countrysides; regional capitals were unique and flavorful because they were soil bound; and even Paris, self-proclaimed cultural center of the world, dispensed French ideas but drew amazingly little on the cultures of other nations. Peasants and intellectuals alike were indifferent to outsiders.

This astonishing self-centeredness and self-assurance renewed itself by continual reversion to the past. There was Joan of Arc, for instance, who rode her bronze charger so regally in her niche by the rue de Rivoli. There was the Louis of whom Versailles was the surviving monument. Then, of course, there was Napoleon, whose remains rested now in perpetual funereal splendor in the Hôtel des Invalides, a national shrine commemorating the French conquest of Europe. Napoleon represented to the French not the failure of overreaching dictatorship but the conquering power of a unified and expanding people at the moment of their irresistibility. It was hard for any Frenchman to understand that this moment was beyond recall. The refusal to become resigned was symbolized by the crepe draping the statues of Metz and Strasbourg in the Place de la Concorde. It had been there ever since the disastrous defeat of the third Napoleon in 1870. That these symbols of mourning for the lost cities would someday be removed was regarded as one of the certainties no Frenchman allowed himself to question.

But the justification for the larger arrogance was lacking. France was no longer a great Imperium; she was not even a first-rate power, even if her Marshal Foch was the supreme commander and her chief city did function as the allied military capital. Her empire no longer sent waves of revivifying strength centerward. She had not kept up technically; she did not colonize (except in nearby Africa, regarded as home territory). Frenchmen were too educated, too civilized, too self-sufficient and content. They preferred, except in imagination, a narrow existence and the cultivation of intimate and individual talents to the large glories, the risks and the sacrifice necessary to maintain an empire. They kept, in France, the paraphernalia of colonialism: they trained overseas administrators; their army officers were given a high polish; they maneuvered in international affairs as though they had every confidence that theirs was the premier power in Africa, in the East, and in the isles of the Pacific; but it was an empty show.

My duties required no extensive planning. We had crises, of course, when the war came so close as to blanket all other phenomena and to make the observations of life about me seem trivial. Sometimes, when we were bombed by night and day, even in the mild fashion of that war, we felt somewhat ill used. I finally got so that I could sleep through an occasional raid, but this did not happen often. My room in the rue de Verneuil was not far from the Seine, and along the quays there were antiaircraft guns. If we were not awakened by the sirens when raiders crossed the front lines some forty or fifty miles away, we were almost sure to be shaken out of bed by the big guns when the raiders came within range. I found that I might as well throw on some clothes and get out at the first warning. After a while I had an inspiration shared by a few others: if I hurried I could arrive at the Arc de Triomphe du Carrousel before the guns went to work and shrapnel began to fall in dangerous showers. Under the arch itself there was protection from anything but a direct hit, and the danger-ous game played by the planes, the searchlights, and the artillery could be watched.[11] The trick was to trap a raider in the angle of two lights, thus get the range, and shoot him down. More pilots were scared off than shot down, but there were some few hits, as the exhibition of wrecked enemy planes in the Place de la Concorde testified. And it was a spectacle of almost unexampled grandeur.

One day a bomb obliterated the fountain just in front of the Comédie-Française and just below my office window; on another day I missed by a few minutes a direct hit in a small hotel we were thinking of leasing for an annex. These incidents were my closest approach to the shooting war, and I could hardly regard them as important.

From late May to nearly the end of July, of course, we felt that we were practically at the front. Then the excitement of war really set in, and I forgot my ambitions to absorb French culture or to take any advantage of my luck in being a temporary Parisian. By then, a colleague of mine in Carl Parker's group at the University of Washing-ton, whose name was Lilly, had become assistant comptroller of the Red Cross and was stationed in Paris. His office was on the Champs-Elysées, near the army's general headquarters, but he roomed near me, and we frequently spent evenings together. Paris was incredibly lovely in the warm twilight. Quite often we undertook the climb up to the top of Montmartre where there was a favorite restaurant of Lilly's in the Place du Tertre. As dusk thickened, we could see flashes of gunfire off to the northeast and hear the Paris Gun's shells as they screamed over our heads on the way to the center of the city. We sometimes stood by the parapet before the Sacré-Coeur and saw the shells explode. There would be a small cloud of dust, but that was all. It was obvious that the beautiful body of Paris was vulnerable to mutilation, and there were

---

11. My classmate and fellow *Pennsylvanian* editor Jim Austin came to Paris from the front early in the summer for a few days leave. I arranged for lodgings in the rue de Verneuil. There were air raids on two successive nights, and we got up and went together over to the Carrousel. I was amazed to have him say that he was as scared as he had ever been in action. I hoped it was so, because it seemed to make me more part of my generation's experience than I could ever be, not having worn a uniform.

I was proud of Jim Austin. He was promoted in action a number of times. He came to Paris, as I remember, on promotion leaves three times, and each time we went out to find him new insignia.

weeks when the probability of a battle with the city as its center seemed considerable. The Germans had overrun the Chemin des Dames and come down to the Aisne. Their power seemed irresistible. By the end of May, they had captured the Vigny Plateau and Soissons and were thrusting southward from the Vesle. On the last day of the month they were on the Marne from Château-Thierry to Dormans and claimed to have captured fifty thousand prisoners and four hundred guns in the past week.

Lilly and I walked in the twilight, our day's work done, like two French bourgeois, with no responsibility for the immense decisions being hammered out almost within sight to the northeast. We knew a little more than two bourgeois might, for there were no communiqués all during that crucial summer struggle. We at least had headquarters gossip to chew on. We dined. Lilly never ate; he dined. We savored a small wine. We sat over cognac and *café filtre.* We usually had with us a few officers on leave or some of the paperwork military from the Elysée Palace, and we exchanged views of the way things were going and discussed the generals and their tactics. On special days, when a friend had a baby or a birthday or when a journey impended, we went to Laperouse or Foyot's and once or twice to the Tour d'Argent or Marguery's. There was no restaurant of reputation we did not try; but usually, for special occasions, we came back to Foyot's.

It was not so much the food and wine; they were, of course, inspired,[12] but then so were the food and wine in a dozen other places. It was mostly that when we went to Foyot's, General Bliss's four-star Locomobile usually stood outside; often General Pershing's four-star Cadillac stood there, too. Lilly found it impossible to believe that General Bliss did not know the very best of all places to dine. If he thought Foyot's so good that he need look no further, Lilly, too, was disinclined to look further. There was, of course, the minor fact of cost. Eating at Foyot's was not cheap. It might be worth it, but it was really too dear for daily indulgence. Lilly patted his growing paunch and regretted audibly that, evenings at least, he was not a four-star general.

---

12. This reminds me of the criticism of our own restaurant at 8, rue de Richelieu. A visitor said of it one day that it was "good but uninspired." But perhaps we could have done no more.

The crisis in the battle did not come until July 18.

All during June, the tension grew. At the union we had evacuation orders to be executed on notification. We were to be taken to Bordeaux by truck transport; we were ordered to have our records ready. This naturally caused excitement. Our office employees were mostly French and reflected the profound tiredness of the nation after four years of war and the loss of friends and relatives. And now there was the final, almost unbearable, pressure of crucial battles. Hysteria and collapse from exhaustion were frequent. Facing the trial of evacuation seemed to require an almost impossible effort, even though actually it was no very great task. We were ready, finally, and in daily expectation of orders. For the gunfire was unmistakably louder, and the excitement at all the allied military centers was more intense. They were obviously preparing to move.

In spite of the still undecided struggle just beyond the outskirts of Paris, there was a characteristic celebration on Bastille Day, July fourteenth. By then even we in Paris knew that stabilization probably would be reached; but after all the disappointments, it was hard to believe that it would be more than temporary, and that we should not soon again hear of new defense lines overrun, of vast booty lost, and many prisoners taken. We had, of course, heard the talk in allied circles about the French letdown during the last winter and spring. Mutiny is a terrible word in connection with military operations. The French had absorbed so much punishment, the *poilu* was by now so characteristic a symbol of endurance, that such a suggestion at first seemed incredible. Yet we knew that it had happened during the last year and on a serious scale. Had the fatal weakness been cured?

The trouble ran deep. It had its origins in French politics and the betrayal of the armies by politicians. By now Clemenceau was taken to be the embodiment of patriotism. But there had been others who, even when France was far into the war, had been defeatists and had even carried on communications with the enemy. The Painleve government had been superseded by that of Clemenceau in November of 1917; from then on the armies had not had that fatal conviction that they were being betrayed. But Clemenceau had enemies. There was still a peace sentiment and subterranean talk, and exhaustion bred defeatism. The coming of the Americans had been slow, and there had been high-level quarrels, not yet settled, about their use in French cadres. Foch obviously wanted them as relief; Pershing was determined that they should be used only in autonomous units. He had compromised in the crisis of that spring but was still officially determined to have a distinct American army.

Against this background, the celebration of Bastille Day had its significance. For the first time, the Parisians saw American soldiers in impressive masses. The histories say that the turning point of the war came on July 18. It came, as far as Parisians were concerned, on the fourteenth. After they saw those billowing waves of khaki, filling the Champs-Elysées from curb to curb, and felt their freshness and strength, there was no further doubt. They knew their own tiredness, and they recognized its opposite when they saw it. It was the very next day that the Second Battle of the Marne began. As everyone knows, it went badly at first. The attack came on a fifty-mile front, east and west of Reims. West of Reims, the most vulnerable sector, the Germans penetrated the French defenses to a depth of several miles, and on the east they crossed the Marne at Fossy and elsewhere. But that was all. Foch began to let loose a series of hammer strokes that would crush the German armies in the battles of the next two months. Then came Belleau Wood, heroic ground forever for all Americans, and Château-Thierry, and Soissons. The French took heart. It was they who beat back the best the enemy had: in the valley of the Crise they fought eight miles into German territory; and, east of Reims, led by that strange, fierce, bearded and one-armed General Henri Eugène Gouraud, they recaptured Frunay and had their enemy off balance from then on.

Much of the tragic human debris of those July battles was evacuated through Paris. For the first time I saw our American wounded, just out of battle, with no more than emergency dressings. There was one station where the belly-wound cases were sorted and reloaded for hospitals farther south, and some of us civilians went to help during the nights of the rush. These men were to die. Belly cases in that war did not live, and dying was slow and agonizing. True, they were drugged. But they had lain in the woods and fields, been carried in stretchers, loaded and unloaded from ambulances and trains. Here now they lay in long rows under the dim yellow lights of the freight station, and the end was not yet. There must be more loading and unloading, more jouncing before at last they could be washed and tended and allowed to die in narcotic peace. That was the soldiers' ordeal. It had always been the soldiers' ordeal.

Then for a few weeks, while the battles followed one another just north of Paris and the Americans were more and more engaged, we really had a flood of visitors at the union. Men came to us, often a few hours out of the line, filthy, unshaven, and exhausted; we stretched our facilities to the utmost. The battles then moved farther away, and Paris was no longer their center. It began again to be a place to take leave, to enjoy life a little. Presently there was an amazing decadent development: restaurants turned into places of solicitation; obscene night clubs sprang up; Montmartre's *Bals* and amusement places took on a more intense, feverish life. Suddenly Paris seemed to be a kind of civic bordello. So we passed through summer into fall.

If I associated the summer months with my friend Lilly, who would be wholly lost to me when we parted in Paris, I associated those of fall with a few others, such as Leroy Baldridge, the artist-author, who was then on special duty with the *Stars and Stripes.* We somehow fell into the habit of lunching together at the Trois Portes, a tiny but very cheap and very French restaurant with an unmistakably Latin Quarter atmosphere within five minutes walk of the Pont Neuf. Mürger himself might have had a table there. It was near the Sorbonne, near the Academie, near the Beaux Arts, near Lip's, and the Deux Magots. It was one of those old-style places where everything to be eaten came as a separate course—the *viand,* the *pommes frites,* the *chaufleur aux fromage,* the *tarte.* That style forces, for one thing, an attention to *legumes,* which they never get when they are subordinate on a big plate to the overpowering attractions of meat. The madame was the chef at the Trois Portes; she did not welcome strangers, and she did not favor departures from the classic cuisine. We lunched there well and cheaply day after day, once we had been introduced, to hold our franchises. And in the course of this patronage we became well acquainted. Then Roy found a girl, as he was sure to do in such romantic circumstances with his war coming to an end, and I lost him, too.

September is a special month in Paris. The first leaves sprinkle the boulevards and quais; the plane trees have not yet been touched by frost, but rainless weeks have dried their stems and turned them brown. A blue haze, noticeable since late August, thickens and softens the outlines of buildings and monuments at the end of every vista. The fountains are surrounded by bathing birds; the Tuileries and the Luxembourg Gardens have a new and even more formal flowering array for the fall. Children go about their complicated games as though they had to get through them quickly before the chill set in.

The fall of 1918 was no different from any other, except that people were still scarce in the streets. They were trickling back into the city now that the Paris Gun had belched its last and the air raids had stopped. There was an unmistakable air of renewal everywhere. The battles still went on in one sector after another. The British, immediately after the battle of Bapaume, struck toward Cambrai, then the French attacked toward St.-Quentin and reached the Aisne from Condé to Vieil-Arcy. So it went, first in one place, then in another. And on September 12, the Americans, with an army of their own, attacked both flanks of the St.-Mihiel salient and captured 15,000 prisoners and 200 guns. While the lines collapsed in Macedonia and Bulgaria asked for an armistice (on September 5), the Hindenburg line was pierced by the British, and the Battle of the Argonne was opened by the French and the Americans. As October began, the German chancellor was replaced, King Ferdinand of Bulgaria abdicated, and the whole German front crumbled under allied pressure.

We could no longer hear or see the battles from Paris, and we had long since unpacked the files supposed to have gone south with us. We still had floods of soldiers and were trying to find auxiliary accommodations for them, but in this we had no luck. The French hotelkeepers had already begun a campaign of remodeling and refitting for the postwar tourist trade and were making such progress that they no longer cared to consider such a lease as would interest us. They evidently had access to a black market for materials and seemed to have no difficulty finding workers. Everywhere, in the two-mile circumference around the Opéra, while the armies fought their last savage battles and the soldiers with their girls swarmed through the streets and crowded the hotels and restaurants, the business of refitting went on. The result for us was that we were confined to our one establishment. It began to have a shabby look after the tramplings of the last few months, but no one seemed to mind. The food was undoubtedly better now. It was easier to get eggs and butter, and the chefs no longer had to improvise so much. Besides, there was the prospect, now really opening up, of an end to the war. What that meant to us, as well as to the soldiers, was that we might think of going home.

We had a little more freedom as the battle lines moved away. Groups of us went on Sundays to walk in the suburbs or in the forests. We explored Versailles until we had straightened out its romantic relationships with the monarchy (Napoleonic painters had given us the impression that it must be a Bonapartist relic), and we made excursions to Malmaison, Chantilly, Fontainebleau (where the Napoleonic atmosphere was authentic), St.-Germaine-en-Laye, Vincennes, and St.-Denis. But our favorite walks were in the forest around Barbizon, whose associations with the artist-writer school of the late nineteenth century were so recent that the studios of the impressionists could still be seen. The dim, thin, linen-clad figure of Robert Louis Stevenson could be imagined, watching his painter friends at work in the forest aisles or at the edge of the adjoining meadows, and going home to his pension to explain in leisurely stylized sentences how they dignified and softened the landscapes of those rich fields.

One Sunday we went out as far as Meaux by railway and walked all day over the fields where the battle of the Marne had been fought. We pictured that battle as saving Paris in that first savage outpouring of militarism; and we credited Foch with its strategy, though undoubtedly German mistakes gave him his chance. In that battle the taxicabs and buses of Paris had carried new armies out of their city garrisons to strike the enemy flank, and so had special associations for those of us who, by adoption, had become Parisian.

On a Sunday morning in September, Meaux teemed with business. Masses succeeded one another in the cathedral, but it was a market day, too. At the stalls we bought loaves of crusty bread, chunks of cheese, cartons of dried olives, and a bottle apiece of the local wine. With these in our *musettes,* we tramped all morning, studying the battle. At noon we sat with our backs to a tree looking out over yellow stubble, still specked thinly with scarlet poppies (like the fields of Flanders), and talked, as we often did in those last weeks of war, about the meaning it had assumed. We did not doubt, just at that moment of exhilaration, that the conflict had turned revolutionary under Wilson's leadership. We thought he had a practical view of peace. We thought the vested interests in nationalism and colonialism had met their master. Had it not been for the American effort, all of them would have been obliterated by the Germans. That had given Wilson his appeal. The imperial politicians—Lloyd George, Clemenceau, Orlando—would not be able to match it. We looked for a Europe united, in fact, with the rest of the civilized world. Japan was far out in the east; the dependent peoples would hardly be able to resist even if they had some reason for wanting to; and although Russia was for the moment enigmatic, the Bolshevists could not be other than hostile to imperialism. We thought collectivism everywhere had advanced startlingly during the war, since everything had had to be done on so enormous a scale, possible only by government or with government subsidy and direction.

We pictured for ourselves, rising from the wheat stubble of that battlefield beside the Marne, a renewed civilization serviced by the technology developed during the war. Only such a result could justify the ordeal of the French and the British, the millions of Russian dead and the maimed and killed Americans, who might be few but were fine soldiers. This was what man wanted everywhere. Now that they had the leader, they might be able to achieve it.

These castles in the rural haze faded in the noon sun; we got to our feet and went on. But interest in the battlefield had dimmed, and after a while we stopped at a small roadside *estaminet*. It was a quiet time of day, and it was a lonely road. The proprietor turned out to be a discharged *poilu* who had come back to the battlefield where he had lost his leg. He was glad to tell us about the weeks of that four-year-ago struggle. Presently some peasants came in, and although their patois was thick, one of us had French enough to supply the words the rest of us missed. We got along very well. In fact we established peace and a just order of affairs for all the farmers of the world. We could, because we were countrymen of Wilson, and because my friends were in uniform. When the peasants went home to their suppers, the patron and his madame pressed us to share their evening meal. And, as the stars began to show through the casements, we did justice to their casserole. The patron went down into his cellar hole and came up with several bottles of a wine of precisely the color of the stubble we had wandered through all day. He had been saving it for an occasion, he said, and there would not be another—even *La Victoire*—that would be any more fitting. We drank; presently we hurried down the road and the two miles or so to Meaux and just barely caught our train. Next day we sent the madame a little gift of dried herbs in crystal containers from a *magazin* on the Boulevard St.-Germaine.

Ten years later I tried to find the *estaminet* again, to see whether I could recapture some of the afflatus of that September, but like the dreams and wishes of these days when the peace had not yet quite shown itself and we could believe that it would be just and enduring, the patron and madame had gone, no one knew where, and the *estaminet* had taken down its bush.

The end neared. On October 15 Wilson's reply to Germany's peace overtures was published. The British were forcing withdrawal from the Belgian coast in the west, and Brand Whitlock, the American ambassador, who had been so unhappy in his exile, began to anticipate a return to Brussels. The British were, in fact, rolling the German armies back to their home defenses. Erich Ludendorff resigned on October 26; on the next day Austria asked for an armistice. Soon a Czechoslovak state was proclaimed in Prague. The Turks surrendered, thoroughly beaten on the Tigris, and T. E. Lawrence's adventure, except for its tragic finale at the peace conference, drew to its end. We knew on November 5 that the Austrian armistice had been granted. And now the retreat into Germany was faster. There was no rout. The sailors at Kiel had mutinied, and there were tales of disorganization in the German high command. But the armies fought a skillful, costly rearguard action, contesting every yard the allies gained. It was obviously hopeless and the question was: when would force be recognized as a failure and politics once more take over? Or rather: when would the means for the enforcement of politics change?

There were errors in the calculations of those liberals who thought the victory now within reach in Belgium, northern France, and along the mountainous ridges down to the Swiss border would be generously and therefore successfully administered. One error was that even the men of good will, who saw so clearly that only in a world order could national security be expected to develop, did not understand that the time had come when nations had to have their sovereignty limited, just as, in an earlier age, individuals reached a time when they had to subject themselves to common rule. There were too many nations; the means for destruction had become too effective (the tank, the machine gun, and the plane, limited as was their use in World War I, should have furnished a foresight of this) and, in fact, technological advances had created a world community before the fact of national-individualism had given way to international-collectivism.

The other error was that of believing good will to be more pervasive than it was. Many civilians, even in Britain and especially in the United States, would feel that the armistice had come too soon. The enemy had not been made to suffer nearly enough. Inappropriate as these sentiments were to the technological stage now attained by the Western world, they would soon appear, expressed as isolationism mostly, but this withdrawal would furnish freedom for French *revanche*. This would characterize not only the formal peace, but all postwar diplomacy, and would, eventually furnish precisely the atmosphere needed by Hitlerism. We would only have had to look into our own hearts to have seen the probable result of the policies of Clemenceau, Poincaré, and Lloyd George.

We did not know, and if we had known it might not have made any difference, that when the heavy guns boomed from the outer fortifications of Paris on the morning of November 11, and we realized that the Armistice was a fact, it would never be more than an armistice. We thought permanent peace had come. When I walked out of my office, past the theater, and looked down the Avenue de l'Opéra, my expectations were more optimistic than they would ever be again. A weight had been taken away. This is something not easily described. Another armistice in another decade, after an interval of some twenty-seven years, would bring no such lightening. According to their own testimony, war's end always comes to soldiers as a kind of parole from death and so is unforgettable whether or not much is expected from the peace. In this instance, however, there was general belief that the way lay open at last to permanent security from aggression. Wilson had been an effective teacher.

The profound thankfulness of Frenchmen made that day a solemn one. There was rejoicing and celebrating not on Armistice Day but on the next day, as the realization of release sank in. I met an old woman in the rusty black of widowhood coming down the all-but-deserted Avenue de l'Opéra. She was pushing a two-wheeled barrow filled with turnips—obviously on her way to Les Halles. In the topmost turnip of her heaped-up load was stuck a tiny bright tricolor, and as she pushed heavily along, the tears streamed down her leathery face. I thought perhaps her husband had been one of those tough and patient *poilus* who had made up the army of France—those so lovingly written about by Henri Barbusse and so often betrayed by their politicians. Later on, in a hairdressing establishment patronized by permanent members of the Opéra, singing broke out, and, led by the proprietor, the company went through a whole repertory of patriotic songs.

Those regulars must have sung their way through most of the next few days, for several times on street corners, I stopped by gatherings that had hoisted a singer to a fountain brim or the pedestal of a monument and followed his (or her) lead in passionate chorus. That night and the next night the Place de l'Opéra, so often deserted in the months just past, was filled from curb to curb with a mob come to hear the singing. A hundred times I heard the *Marsellaise,* and I heard it again sung from a balcony above a crowd of thousands, but it was no more impressive than when it shook the perfume bottles and rattled the mirrors of that hairdressing place.

There was an impressive *Te Deum* in Notre-Dame; black-clothed civilians streamed in and out. It was the same at St.-Sulpice, at St.-Germain-des-Prés, and at the Sacré-Coeur. It was not then, and not even the next day, that the French let themselves go. The streets were riotous on the twelfth; but it was Americans, British, Canadians, and Australians who were celebrating. The French, for the most part, looked on. Most people, it might be said, merely wanted their opponent crushed, largely because it signified an end to discipline and danger. There might be nothing more constructive at hand than that, Wilson or no Wilson.

Anyway, I wanted now, like everyone else, to go home. Fall had come with the Armistice, and cold, damp days had brought with them a bone-reaching chill. Fuel was scarce. Once in a while I had a fagot fire in my room. But it was inevitable that I would come down with the prevalent influenza. When I did, I did not recover quickly. There were, as there always are in that magic city, compensations. The braziers were lighted on the terraces beneath the awnings of all the cafés—somehow they could get fuel when no one else could—and, bundled up, it was possible to sit with friends over successive apéritifs and appraise current events.

Then the Comédie and the Odéon were again in operation, and I had what of Racine and Molière I could take; at the Opéra Comique I heard the *Barber of Seville, Madame Butterfly, La Traviata,* and *Manon* in as good a setting as they would ever find. There were artists and poets again in the Quartier, and I met a few of them. Life in Parisian attics might be romantic, but it was not surprising, I decided, that a good many others besides Camille had succumbed to tuberculosis under those conditions. One thing did surprise me: how comfortable middle-class folk could be in the apartments of the rue de Bac or near the Etoile even when they had no central heat. While there were a good many of these, I had already learned during the war how many of the others there were in the vast shambles of St.-Antoine and the other slums away from the boulevards. The poverty was no worse than that on the lower East Side of New York or on the east side of Buffalo. In New York, I had heard, there were still two hundred thousand families living in "cold-water flats"; in Paris there were about as many. Wandering in those neighborhoods, I understood how much the rule rather than the exception misery is.

Before the decisive battle of July, I had been taken to a number of leftist meetings of the C.G.T. or of the Communists. Having heard the denunciations of international capitalism and imperialist war quite in the same line of logic as those I had heard in the lumber camps of the Northwest almost halfway around the world, I reflected that similar conditions create similar reactions. Thousands, many thousands, of these workers in French factories had a profound skepticism about the war. They were asking, then, for union with their German "brothers" just as though international socialism had not broken down into outright nationalism at the beginning of the war. How far it went, I had no way of knowing, but I went to several such meetings without assuming any very elaborate disguise; at all of them the crowd listened to earnest exhorters with apparently unanimous sentiment.

It must be remembered that Communists then could not be linked with Russia. It was not yet—though it soon would be—the philosophy of an enemy state, so they could hardly be called traitors. They could be, and were, called disloyal for not extolling in French nationalism, but they were not at the disposal of a foreign power. This did not prevent radicals from being denounced, but the enthusiastic denouncing made them more radical than ever. France was the home of synicalism of a kind hardly distinguishable from Lenin's bolshevism; it had existed in France as long as it had in Russia. There was also a stranger anarchism with no phase beyond the terror it would impose. I had read Proudhon, Sorel, Fourier, and the rest, of course. Not the least of the educational results from my Parisian sojourn was that the political activity I witnessed made these philosophers come alive. The war's ending on a note of victory enabled Clemenceau to use many of his toughest troops for suppression, and there were pitched battles with the leftists in Paris before Christmas.

I thought a good deal about communism. It interested me, as it would continue to do throughout the decades to come, as one of the philosophies with pretension to worldwide hegemony. In this it was certainly a competitor of capitalism and Catholicism. I supposed that nationalism was nearly through with its six or seven hundred years of evolution, but it was to be the organizing principle for the peace of Versailles. I had not only overlooked Wilson's phrases about self-determination, I had also failed to realize that the spoils of victory were not to be foregone and that some justifying principle would have to be set up. It could not be communism or Catholicism; it had to be nationalism. It did not apply, of course, to "dependent" peoples. For them there was to be the elaborate hypocrisy of the "mandate."

The meaning of the victory was partly that nationalism should be given a new run into the future. This I already knew by December, and I guessed what Clemenceau and Lloyd George would do to Wilson if he came to the peace conference. At least I knew what they would try to do, in spite of the masses of their own people who believed Wilson to be a sort of Messiah. Those who were radicals would still be able to go on being radicals; their beliefs would not be those of the responsible postwar statesmen— not anywhere, that is, except in Russia. But the radicalism I found in Paris, like that I had found in the American Northwest, was quite unlike that tradition of Progressive dissent I had grown up in and which had so many heroes in the rest of America, especially in the Midwest. La Follette would not have known what these Europeans were talking about. And Theodore Roosevelt would not have allowed them (if he could have prevented it) to join him in 1912. La Follette, in fact, in a later incarnation, would be denounced as the worst of all reactionaries by the Wobblies of America. And they would be right. He was essentially a conservative.

Was I, also, a conservative? I wondered. I found communism basically even less attractive than capitalism as a philosophy. Capitalism had the seeds in it of self-destruction, but communism had a kind of iron logic I instinctively distrusted. It was of a piece with Newtonian physics, Smithean economics, and other mechanistic doctrines. I was, I could see, an incorrigible experimentalist. What kind of social and political organization we would need for the postwar society would not be exactly capitalistic in the economists' sense and would certainly be collectivistic. It would be unified and of one piece. About that the Communists were right. I could not believe, however, that anyone in 1840 or before had foreseen the details of a scheme or even the general principles acceptable for a yet preliminary industrial civilization.

During the second week in December, I was able to leave a soggy, dark gray Paris for Bordeaux with only a little hope, however, of getting home for Christmas with my small collection of gifts. The chances were that I should have another two-week passage on the old *Chicago*, sister ship of the *Niagara*. Any hope of that was quickly extinguished in Bordeaux. There would, we were told, be a ten-day delay. Several of us who were homegoers spent it together in the Grand Hotel. Apart from the impatience to get home, this stay in France's fourth city, capital of the wine country, was in itself interesting. French provincial life, especially in a port city, is a fat, bourgeois existence, with its tone set by *negotiants* and with the emphasis on comfort. There will not be many amusements, it is true, but there will be a countryside steeped in some productive tradition.

The great Bordeaux merchants feared the wine trade was in a long slow decline. The yield of the famous chateaux vineyards had, for a thousand years—perhaps longer—gone out to all the world. They were fine wines, appurtenant to lives of cultivation, if not luxury, and were drunk with ceremony when there was time for their enjoyment. But there were fewer people all the time who had the necessary leisure for long luncheons or who had the means to support table-laden meals. The chateaus were still scattered about the countryside up and down the Garonne, their vineyards spread about them. It seemed incredible that these great houses could have been built out of the product of so few acres, sometimes not more than ten or twelve. There they were, great stone houses, warm in the winter sunshine, and still inhabited. I had no premonition that I should come back sixteen years later as undersecretary of agriculture for the United States and be given the freedom of many of these cellars and houses I now saw from the highway.

We tasted no wines in the cellars where they aged during our ten days in Bordeaux, but we discovered the *Chapon Fin*, whose cellars were stocked with the aged products of the local vineyards. There were other good restaurants with provincial traditions, where the clientele went to stay for all the hours from apéritif to liqueur. There the papers could be read; there dominoes or cards could be played; there the strictly local news was passed around. It was just past the harvest time; *choux de Bruxelles* were still in season; there were *perdrix aux choucroute en casserole* and pheasant in various guises; the *fine à l'eau maison* was poured from cobwebbed magnums. Since nearly every day we had spent hours in the open, all this bounty in warm surroundings at close of day was richly used, if not deserved. So we passed the two weeks of our delay.

The *Chicago* was so like the *Niagara* that, as I told my fellow travelers, I was sure that I recognized some of the more individual cockroaches. It must be the *Niagara* renamed. We were crowded again; but we made Christmas at sea as much of a holiday as was possible, and, since we were nearing home, the tragedy was not too deep a one. We celebrated American style, with the amused permission of the French. The ship's officers had known Americans all their seagoing lives, but they had hardly passed the toleration stage for our customs. The French have others, and, being French, they are, of course, ordained.

Manhattan's towers shone on a bright January morning as we came up the bay. As I left the pier, I mentally checked off another of life's adventures. I was not sorry to put it in the past.

Late in November, when the prospect of leaving Paris seemed imminent, I had written my father a letter. I so soon recognized it to have been a mistake that I handed it over to an inner forgetting mechanism. Having thus disposed of it, I would have no idea that it affected him so seriously if, years later, it had not turned up as I leafed over for him, a nearly blind old man, some of his more treasured papers. It came, undoubtedly, out of the nostalgia and sense of futility of those last weeks in Paris. What I wrote him was that I had experimented long enough; that I felt now the need to settle down where I had roots; that, in a word, if he wanted me to, I would come home permanently, assume my share of responsibility for the business and take up life on the farm. I reminded him that I had always wanted a chance at a good farm, and whatever would become of the business if I did not assume responsibility for it? I had had no answer from him when I left Paris, but I knew that he could not refuse. It was with a sense of genuine homecoming that I got off the train in Buffalo at the old Exchange Street Station and found all the family waiting for me. My wife and small daughter were there, too. The Seattle house had been sold. The one thing I had known since leaving there was that I would never go back. All the family together had taken a house in Buffalo for the winter, a custom my parents varied in those years by spending some winters, or parts of them, on Florida's west coast.

The next six months were difficult. For one thing I was tormented by successive illnesses, mostly centering in my sinuses and bronchial tubes, but also involving my eyes and lungs. I was more discouraged about my physical condition than ever before because I realized finally that my physical troubles would be with me throughout life. At times I was genuinely glad that I had given up the fierce competition of academic life and could look forward to existence as half-farmer and half-businessman, but most times, of course, I regarded it as a sacrifice in the interest of a sentiment, and perhaps I expected appreciation too openly. My father was good for many years yet, and I would be no more than a helper, except for the farm; I would have no very pressing responsibilities. I could do as much or as little as I liked without much affecting our economic situation. The farm was a smallish but very valuable one just at the edge of the village and about a mile from the canning factory. There was an old house on the property, and I made it over into the kind of spread-out and generous farmhouse I had always wanted. My father had also bought a large tract of land surrounding the harbor, which included about half the big island where most of our summer residents lived and some hundreds of acres of woodland. This land had always been used for picnics, ball-games and Fourth-of-July celebrations. There was also a smaller island, just offshore (connected by a bridge), and under my mother's pressure, he was developing it into a small estate. It had on it a large house and a smaller one. The large house was already being rebuilt, the smaller one would be remade into a summer cottage. For the next two decades, this would be my summer anchorage.

My daughters would know this small island, with its big, galleried house, its gardens, its oaks and willows, and its cottage, as more their home than any other place. They returned to it from wherever they were taken. There, for at least four, and often five, months of the year they could be free with their pets, their toys, and later, their young men. One of the great sorrows of their lives would be the final letting go of Wintergreen Island and its big house. On one side it looked out toward the harbor onto Lake Ontario, so like a sea as not to be recognizably different. Canada was over there, thirty miles away, but it had to be a clear day for any sign of it to be seen from shore, even at the height of a tree. On the other side was a marsh with all the fascinations marshes possess when they are really lived with. Both girls grew to love it.

But first we lived in the farmhouse. All spring and summer I planned and planted. By fall the new orchards were all in place, a fine range of gardens laid out, and an efficient barn built for our small dairy herd of twenty Holstein milkers. I could have the satisfaction of having really created something at last. It was a nice, tidy farm; its orchards were divided among apples, peaches, and plums. There was a fine field of alfalfa and another for corn, wheat, or oats. We had a sizable herd of swine, a few hundred chickens, and cats and dogs enough, for once, to suit everyone. All this had been costly, but my father kept no books in such matters. If we needed a few thousand dollars for improvements, if I wanted a new car or a few new cows, he simply paid the bills without asking too much about what the returns would be. I think he was worried about me, without saying too much about it. I am sure he liked to see my enthusiasm about the farm, but I have often wondered since just how he felt about installing a desk for me in the factory office—not that I ever sat at it much! But what he really felt I should never know. He never put such matters into words.

He had another partner in the factory, but the arrangement was that I should have a full third in the enterprise. I tried loyally enough to do my part, though there was not much I could contribute. The problems of administration were not many, and anyway, all the foremen knew more about the processing than I, after having been away for some years. I got along with them well. They seemed glad to have me back, and really felt, I think, that I was something of a protection from the business risks taken in the front office. Anyway, they came to me with many of the problems of those days when the cost of living was going up so much faster than wages. My father and his partner had no feeling whatever for the difficulties of men living on wages or small salaries. They made so much themselves, and so easily, that genuine poverty had no reality for them. They regarded me, I am sure, as an easy mark, and also, I suspect, as a doubtful business asset, although I thought I was averting trouble.

The fall of the year is a satisfying season in upstate New York, especially for those who are somehow involved in the harvest. There is, if the crops have been successful, a sense of risk undertaken and survived. The work lets up, and farmers think of what they may do in the months until spring. Actually, they may be free enough to go off to Florida and abandon the farm to the Ontario winds and the pelting snows they carry; or they may take it easy at home, carrying out improvements, tinkering with machinery, or taking a short course at Cornell. It is not a bad way to spend the winter. After the factory closed that year, I, myself, might have expected to look forward to something of the sort. The cellar was full of apples, eggs put down in water glass, potatoes in bins, and kale set in sand. Hams and bacon of our own curing hung from the rafters; there were crocks full of sausage, and a store of loins and spareribs. Deep shelves were filled with preserves and jellies, and stacked in the corners were the choicest of the cannery's vegetables and fruits.

Wilson in 1919–20 was a very different place from what it had been a decade earlier. It was no longer an isolated village, cut off from neighboring cities in the months of mud and slush. There were concrete roads running everywhere. They would be open all winter. We had had an influx of new inhabitants, too, people who had come because it seemed to be a good community.

I could not say that I lacked any necessity for enjoyment. I was even free to read and to write all winter long if I wanted to. I could always escape to Buffalo. I loved the countryside. Yet I had a growing conviction that I must not sink into the life so pleasantly available.

When fall came and the canning season was over, I took stock. It had been more and more apparent that I had made a mistake. The reality of being the only son and carrying on in the family tradition was far from the sentiment I had felt about it overseas. There was a good, even generous, living in such a life while I waited to succeed. I might make money and in time, inherit a good deal more. I might, if I wanted, live mostly in and out of Buffalo, where I had already joined the University Club and had renewed my old association with Frank Forster and the other Wharton School men of my time of whom I was so fond. I should be able to keep my family in security and affluence. But there was something seriously wrong. I was, in fact, unhappy again, and devastated by doubt. I had gotten off the track. By Thanksgiving I knew what I was going to do.

Thanksgiving of 1919 was such a feast and family celebration as Americans of English ancestry like best. All the relations, even the remotest cousins who could gather in, sat down together. There were a good many of us. My mother, in spite of a growing prejudice against the kitchen, had been tormented into stuffing the turkeys herself; and she had never, even in her most extreme aversion, permitted anyone else to prepare and lay away the row of plum puddings mellowing in her cellar since September. My father carved, as was the tradition, with the old Sheffield carving set whose bone handles were now so worn; he told the new children, as he always did when he began, that it was a set brought over from England by his father. There were halved Hubbard squashes baked in the shell; heaps of potatoes mashed and whipped; green vegetables laid away before the first frosts; an array of jellies, jams, and pickles; and, to follow, the pies. Afterward we had games and singing. After an interlude outdoors or resting, we ate again, and only then did the cousins and visitors depart. It might all of it have come straight out of Dickens. As a matter of fact, Dickens probably came straight out of it. For this was, indeed, the kind of holiday feast (though they had had no Thanksgiving) that Tugwells had brought with them, along with the carving set, on the sailing ship from the Surrey-Sussex border. It was the kind I could remember back into my earliest boyhood.

It was on that very day that I told my father, somewhat shamefacedly, that I had made a mistake and meant now to correct it as best I could. If I expected opposition, I was disappointed. He said at once that I must do as I thought best.

I had an intimation, a very strong one, added to by every experience I had so far had, that new forces were finding their expression in these years. They were not matters of common sense to be understood by the simple operations of conscience and ordinary intelligence. They were the product of a pure learning now finding its way into use by way of engineering and management. That I would not be a scientist had long ago been settled. This was undoubtedly the basic cause of my dissatisfaction. I might, back in high school days, have approached this learning through biology. My impulse toward it had been strong enough then under Miss Gemmel's tutelage, and my turning away from it had seemed to follow an accidental decision. I could see now that my interest in social studies had been as much an impulse of conscience as of intelligence. But it might be also that I had distrusted my ability to be creative in biology. I had no facility in mathematics, physics, or chemistry, whether because of a bad start and poor teaching or because of a more basic lack of ability. To have forced my way into those fields after high school would have required, at any rate, a resolution I did not have.

Having started on that road, I had very slowly learned that economics, politics, sociology, and the rest, were far from being sciences or even from being approached as sciences by their most reputable practitioners. That had been the dramatic lesson I had grasped from Patten's excitement over the Einsteinian formula for the transmutation of mass into energy. Ever since that time I had had an unfocused expectation of something new. This, up until now, had manifested itself mostly as a critical attitude toward the orthodox economics I had absorbed so thoroughly, toward the social statics of the sociologists, and toward the negative attitude in politics so well represented by our government of checks and balances.

Back from close contact, at least with the experiences of 1914–18, I could see that modern war represented human failure on so vast a scale as to approach race suicide if it should happen a few more times with the increased efficiency of the weapons in use at the end of the war. If war was merely the application of force to diplomacy, diplomacy was merely the formal representation of those economic and political ideas held by the people who were represented by the diplomats. It had not been the Triple Alliance versus the Allied and Associated Powers; it had been Adam Smith versus Patten; it had been Agassiz versus Darwin; it had been Spencer versus Dewey. There had to be an effort to substitute the new sciences for the old orthodoxies, which now ended in collisions of opposed ignorances and prejudices.

I had come to have a genuine fear of the easy life. Unless I took all the risks involved, I would not have the resolution to see my way through. I had some handicaps in the contest to come. The academic competition was not going to be easy. I had been away and had lost most of my old connections. Also, the chilly atmosphere at Pennsylvania would make it difficult to go back. I knew I could not expect to teach there again, but then I could not teach anywhere until I had completed the unfinished work for my doctorate: it might be that I should fail in the formidable tests guarding that fortress.

It was necessary to begin what I must do without the possibility of going back. I put it that way and my father agreed. So in a few days, off I went, entirely too late, I thought, to begin the academic year, now more than two months old, but so anxious to seal my new resolution that I thought nothing at all of such red tape. I wanted to plunge in, now, at once.

My first talk with Patterson, who would be in charge of my work, was not encouraging. He did not refer to the long drawn-out Nearing episode, but he did say that I was too interested in causes to be a real scholar. I had had, with some exceptions, mediocre marks as an undergraduate, and even as a graduate there was not much to show that I possessed any exceptional ability. I could not claim much on such grounds. I merely said that I was going on unless the department formally refused to accept me as a candidate and asked him if he would not make his own judgment as I progressed. I guessed that what bothered him most was a fear that he might be harboring another Nearing.

I was discouraged enough by his coldness, however, to go over to New York on the following weekend and explore in talks with representatives of the economics and sociology departments at Columbia whether I might work better there. I saw at once that, in transferring, I would encounter several difficulties. The emphasis was different, and I would have more difficulty meeting the Columbia residence requirements than I would at Pennsylvania, where I had just about completed such formalities. Also my work in English literature I was offering for a "minor" would be lost; such a crossing-over seemed absurd to the Columbia people. So I resolved to go back to Pennsylvania in spite of Patterson's disfavor.

Talks with former teachers—Kelsey and Lichtenberger in sociology, King and Young in political science, Smith in geography, McClelland and Weygant in English—contrasted encouragingly with Patterson's assessment. They said I was making the right choice. All of them seemed to think that what I had done in the past gave every reason to believe I should succeed. Moreover, all of them admitted me to such courses as I thought would help me to prepare, even though I was two months late. They simply ignored the regulations.

What lay ahead, then, as I settled down to work, was some six to eight months of intensive study, the first I had had, wholly as a student, since the beginning of my graduate work. All the time since 1914 I had been doing full service as an instructor, and getting on toward the doctorate had been an added chore. In those days instructors carried hard schedules of teaching, too, so that I had always come to my studies tired, and sometimes, when my health was especially bad, really exhausted and unfit. But this was the ordinary thing for young university teachers; scholarships, now so plentiful, were then very scarce. Anyway, the fact that my father always made up my deficits would have prevented me from applying for one.

That year was a trying yet pleasant one. I had to prepare for three exacting examinations in the late spring: a major in economics and minors in sociology and English literature. I did not see how I could actually fail in economic theory; sociology I thought I should pass without great difficulty, although I needed a review of theory; English literature might turn out to be most difficult of all because of the problem of memorizing so many facts, not because of an inadequate grasp of the subject matter. The drudgery of sheer preparation would be considerable in the two minor subjects, and I knew that I had to demonstrate in courses, in discussions, and in written papers that I had possibilities as an economist. It was on this judgment, really, that success depended, more than on any formalities.

That winter with no distractions I turned out an enormous quantity of work. Output of this kind is never exactly measurable, but I never went to a class without full preparation, I wrote far more than was required on assigned papers, and I took care to excel in course examinations. After a few months, I felt that I was winning. I had had too much experience and was too realistic to deceive myself. I thought some of Patterson's chilliness had softened. And I was accepted again by the Wharton School group as one of them.

The faculty engaged that winter in another struggle involving academic freedom. A new dean had been appointed, an engineer-businessman from the public utility field: William McClelland.[13] It was amusing to see such old hands as E. S. Mead, Carl Kelsey, the

---

13. He had begun as an instructor in physics at Pennsylvania in 1900 but had progressed rapidly by way of the Philadelphia Rapid Transit Company and his own consulting firm to the vice-presidency of Stone and Webster. He would not stay long in the deanship; he would presently go on to Cleveland and Washington as a private power executive.

Huebners, J. R. Smith, and the rest teach the businessman (who had been appointed by the trustees to eradicate the last taint of radicalism from the Wharton School and to put an obstreperous faculty in its place) how professors can function in politics. They led him into every embarrassing ambuscade possible and then enfiladed his forces with an absolutely demoralizing fire of publicity. He never had a chance. McClelland doubtless never knew it, but he was the victim of all the smothered annoyance the faculty members felt because of their futility in the Patten and Nearing incidents. They did not intend to be worsted again, and they devoted themselves singlemindedly to the enemy until he withdrew.

I had demonstrated to myself that I had not lost the capacity to absorb and to learn. Before summer, however, the real crisis for me had passed. I had visualized that crisis as occurring at the time of my major examination in economics; actually, it arrived in April, precipitated by the invitation to teach at Columbia. I took my letter in and showed it to Patterson, who gave me his judgment. He had seen that I was encouraged, he said, but he was convinced that I did not have the dedication to see an academic career through to success. He would, for instance, not think of adding me to the staff at Pennsylvania even if I had had no disability as a member of the old Nearing group. I had much better not accept the Columbia offer. I should only disappoint both them and myself. He said again that I would be diverted by causes, which in the end would be fatal.

I did not tell Patten of my troubles. He still lived in West Philadelphia and breakfasted daily at the University Club downtown where I was always welcome. Many times during the year I had gone to see him. I knew that he was responsible for the Columbia interest in me, so I simply told him of the offer and of my acceptance. He was pleased. After a lifetime of academic service, he was gradually retreating into the shadows of age. His frame, always gaunt, had bowed and shrunk; it seemed an effort now for him to lift the clodhopper shoes he always wore as he plodded along Philadelphia streets. He still pursued the routine he seemed not to know how to break, but there was a tragic exception: he could no longer go daily to Logan Hall. The war, as I have said, had been a grief to him. He had thought it would result in victory by the wrong people for the wrong ends. And now that it was over, he thought the settlement justified all his fears.

The war settlement, succeeding his forced separation from the university, had given him an exaggeratedly futile and aged feeling.

Yet in the few years of his retirement, he had gone on participating in his fashion in what was taking place. He had, for one thing, engaged in a lively controversy with E. R. A. Seligman about war finance.[14] He felt that the war ought to be paid for currently; this, for once, put him on the sound side and his opponents in the weak position of defending inflation. His was essentially the simple argument that since food was eaten, munitions used up, and so on, only after they were made, the income produced in the process of making them must be sufficient to pay for them. The only excuse for saddling future generations with debt for production already consumed must be so that bond holders could go on collecting far into the future. In this way those who had fought the war would have to pay for most of its cost after they got home to those who did not fight it, when actually the costs had already been met.

Seligman, then head of the Department of Economics at Columbia, was supposedly the foremost American authority on public finance. I thought he had allowed his financial affiliations to influence his economics; but he had given Patten the opportunity to work out a classic statement concerning the relationship of national extravagance to the means of paying for it. This was a lesson I should remember in the future. It would cause me then to take a "sound" position as against those who believed in deficit finance. I should think then, as Patten thought now, that goods produced are income; that when they are used, the income is transformed into energies capable of complete payment for the processes of production. Advances to start the productive processes ought to be returned, and could be returned out of the income produced. Only in this way could deficits be avoided. And deficits are better understood as debts of one group to another (later) group. The end of deficits, long continued, is likely to be repudiation. Hard economic facts thus have their way in any case.

Because of many discussions with Patten, I had come to realize

---

14. "Taxation After the War," *Annals* 64(1916):210–14; "The Day of Financial Reckoning," *Moody's*, January 1916; "The Financial Menace to America of the European War," *Annals* 60(1915):123–29; "Problems of War Finance," *Yale Review* 7(1917):73–89. "The Tomorrow of Finance," *Annals* 76(1918):257–71; "Liquidation Taxes," *Annals* 75(1918):165–81; "Mandeville in the Twentieth Century," *American Economic Review* 8(1918):88–98. To this last, J. H. Hollander and E. R. A. Seligman replied in the *American Economic Review* 8(1918):338–49; "Making National Debts National Blessings," *Annals* 82(1919):39–51.

that these financial arguments were hardly more than diversions to him at that time. His mind was running in far more profound channels. He was, in these last years, trying to penetrate a more remote and esoteric realm. My occasional and informal contacts with him furnished the enlightenment in that year of grinding study. When I was with him a certain afflatus seized me. No one had ever made so prolonged an attempt to follow his thought, to understand his premises and his methods; but the leaping boldness, disregarding many of the steps between beginning and end, always left me breathless. I had to ask for help. Sometimes he went back and retraced the argument until I could pick it up where I had gotten lost. It was often our next meeting before I could even ask apposite questions. But this was creative intelligence functioning on its very highest level, and I knew the privilege it was to have contact with it. Patten took such pains with me that his efforts could only be interpreted as a hope, at least, that his influence would continue. His unspoken but clearly shown faith in me carried me through all the difficulties of decision and saw me finally dedicated to university life.

I can commit only a few pages of this chapter to some account of what it was that Patten was trying to achieve in his last years and was discussing with me in 1919–20 and in the year or two afterward when I visited him again in Philadelphia. The material was not gathered together in one book; it appeared in scattered form in several different journals between 1913 and 1920.[15] This period was given to

---

15. The first of this series of articles appeared as "The Genesis of Human Traits" in 1913 in *Popular Science Monthly* 83:149–57. Evidently preoccupation with the coming war prevented further pursuit of his subject until 1917, when "The Track of Evolution" appeared in the *Science Monthly*, October 5, 350–58; and "The Mechanism of Mind" appeared in the *Annals* 71:202–15. Then, again, the war intervened. The bibliography (*Annals* 105 [1923]:358ff.) contains references to numerous articles on subjects having to do with the conflict, but nothing more on this other subject until 1919, when "The Genesis of Consciousness" and "The Divided Self" appeared in the *Monist* (29:223ff. and 432ff.). Then, also in the *Monist* for 1920, there appeared "An Analysis of Mental Defects" and "Cosmic Processes" (30:107ff. and 406ff.).

"Cosmic Processes" is the last title but one in Patten's long list of published contributions to American scholarship. I need not comment on the fitness of these

thinking out what appeared in these seven short articles. Death intervened, I must presume, before they could become a book,[16] if indeed he could have found a publisher. The new generation had found him unpleasantly challenging.

In this work, Patten began in the same realm of knowledge that had so attracted Carl Parker and had so mightily modified the rational assumptions of economics and politics. There were others who saw the need. Thorstein Veblen, for instance, had a psychological theory at the root of all his work;[17] C. H. Cooley, in *Human Nature and the Social Order,* and F. H. Taussig, in *Inventors and Money Makers,* the one a sociologist and the other an economist, were others who had seen the need to revise their assumptions. And there was, by now, a whole school of behaviorism coming into vigorous life.

Patten, then, in turning to the flow of life and energy through men and their aggregations, was not breaking into so novel a field, except that the more orthodox body of economics was, as it had always been, dependent on preevolutionary biology. College students were being taught out of such texts, and more young men than would seem possible were developing into neoclassicists of a more limited kind than even their predecessors. There were, by now, even at Pennsylvania, a half-dozen of that sort.[18] But Patten now had got

---

themes developing at the end of such a career. I might just add, and sadly, that the last article of all appeared in the *Freeman* and was called "The Failure of Liberal Idealism."

16. As is shown by fugitive notes in the collection of papers I have caused to be deposited in the library of Columbia University, though I could never bring them into any further recognizable form. Most of Patten's papers were destroyed by a careless janitor after his lonely death in West Philadelphia.

17. As long ago as 1898, he had published in the *Journal of Sociology* (September:187–201) an article called "The Instinct of Workmanship and the Irksomeness of Labor." That was a long while before Carl Parker discovered that primitive war was important in man's work life. It was not until 1914 that Veblen's book *The Instinct of Workmanship and the State of the Industrial Arts* (New York: Macmillan) was published. From the beginning he had brought biological and sociological data to bear on economic theory, as, for instance, in "Why Is Economics Not an Evolutionary Science?" in the *Quarterly Journal of Economics* 12(1898):373–97; and in "The Preconceptions of Economic Science" in the *Quarterly Journal of Economics* running through three successive issues in 1899 and 1900.
It is of interest here that in 1899 Veblen published a review of Patten's *Development of English Thought* in the *Annals* 14:125–31.

18. The most prominent of whom in later years would be Raymond T. Bye, from 1926 professor of Economics in the Wharton School and author of *Principles of Economics.*

beyond revising economic theory. He had devoted much attention to it in the past, but now he was trying to understand and to interpret the forces of the universe being brought to the use of man.

His point of departure was the solid knowledge available by that time in biology, ecology, and related sciences. His aim was to show the position of man in his environment: his relation to its materials and forces and the full possibilities of changes in himself. By drawing on newly available data and rearranging them so that their significance was apparent, he believed he could establish a new foundation for a social science. He had been troubled, as others had been, by the dead end reached in evolutionary theory. The dogma that acquired characters are not transmitted had left the biologists without any explanation of the origin of species or even a satisfactory theory of changes within species. They had not been able to establish mutation and favorable selection in the laboratory. Yet there must be observed phenomena to support a new departure. The psychologists, in an important area, were similarly at a loss. The postulation of an unconscious, functioning below the threshold of consciousness, was merely an evasion of the real issue. Cause had to be linked concretely with effect; action and its antecedent had to be connected. This was the real problem.

Patten believed that known phenomena had been interpreted in ways that confused rather than illuminated. Shallow fitting of facts had extended beyond all possible utility explanations such as the noninheritance of acquired characters and the existence of a subconscious. The truth was that living beings had changed in the direction of their wish; and actually, unless reason was to be abandoned altogether, it was "axiomatic that the content of consciousness is a reflection of the physical forces which underlie it." To escape from such dilemmas as these, Patten had gone back to the nature of man and matter and had presented new hypotheses to rationalize the known data.[19]

In "The Divided Self," for instance, he began with the contrast between the inorganic and the organic. The inorganic, he said, is at a stable equilibrium. This provision is made for survival. There must

---

19. Students of a later generation will recognize suggestions of the behaviorists B. F. Skinner, George A. Miller, and their school. It was this that Lightner Witmer glimpsed when he remarked that some day Patten would be rediscovered.

always be mechanisms for meeting conditions that are the opposites of each other. These extremes he called poles. For instance, a tree must have one set of mechanisms for meeting the conditions of winter and another for those of summer. The one requires damping down, suppression, withdrawing life elements—all in the interest of mere survival. The other requires pulsing life, expansion, and growth. Mechanisms of this sort exist in every living thing. They promote adjustment to, and progress in, their environments. More light or less, more food or less, higher or lower temperatures—to these conditions the organism must adapt itself.

These are the conditions (and here Patten became the economist) of a surplus economy. And evolution in living species may be measured by the growth of double mechanisms. The higher the organism, the greater its power to make dormant or active its various mechanisms for promoting survival or growth under particular conditions. Translate this into psychology, and the individual is seen as having two selves, one seeking to withdraw and conserve, and another seeking to expand, generate new wishes, and take hopeful risks.

On this basis Patten formed a theory of evolution quite in contrast to the Darwinian explanation. He assumed that germ cells varied and that this variation was the starting point of evolution. The belief in acquired characters had broken down because of the inability of Lamarckians to show how changes in somatic structure modified germ structure. The same reasoning, however, also showed that germ structures could not vary; why would they? A sound theory must rest not on accidental variation but on the influence wish has on structure. If wishes could modify structure, a satisfactory theory would emerge. So mutation, said Patten, is the result of internal antagonism, of the divided self. This self, as the result of conflict, casts off its static parts and is regenerated in the direction of better accommodations to its environment.

> A new species thus arises through a sudden splitting of the antecedent organism and not through a gradual variation in its germ cell. The causes are internal, recessive, and hence not observed until the split occurs and the accompanying regeneration reveals a new type of being. The sudden change is not sudden at all if we watch the right spot for its manifestation. We must start with surplus energy and trace its gradual transformation into wish pulses and wish structure to get the key which unlocks the mysteries of organic evolution.

Dealing with the nature of the human mechanism in "The Genesis of Consciousness," he insisted that the functions of assimilation, circulation, and muscular activity were its most important elements. These form the kinetic system of autonomous organs where energy is generated. It is through this system that the materials of the environment are acquired, digested, circulated, and discharged. There is another separate set of mechanisms for adjustment and for direction; these form the nervous system. The former is for growth and activity; the latter is for preservation, continuity, and consistency. Digestion, circulation, and muscular activity are far older and more fundamental than the activity of the nerves. They respond to heat, light, and gravitation by simple impulses to advance or to retreat; so they respond also to surplus or deficit in the environment. The one causes expansion, the other contraction. The imposition of nervous controls upon the kinetic system is somewhat like an electric current forced over resisting metal and causing light. A similar kind of action explains the genesis of consciousness. This is the basis for understanding how thought can rise to the level of progress. The from-within elements of consciousness are older than the from-without elements. "Life was blind before the rise of the nervous system, but though subordinated, its ultimates still persist. The path of progress consists in freeing the elemental life pulses from distortions which ages of adjustment have imposed."

These were new suggestions. They emerged, as Patten said, only when he had given up such concepts as "ultimate, permanence, reality and primary," and had understood that "we should not think of things as being supported, caused, or ultimate, but as parts of series through which they manifest themselves."[20] Thought is confused by not holding on to the idea that all change resolves itself into changes of form but never of substance. The substance must be followed through its embodiments in structure, not regarded as having come to rest in any particular one of them. Certain impulses flow on and on in an endless, improving circuit. We produce food; it generates energy; energy creates thought directed into consistency by the nervous system; it emerges as action. The circuit is thus completed.

What Patten was getting to, I understood, was the rejection of

---

20. "Wish and Will: A Reply to a Letter by Mr. Salter," *The Monist* 30 (1920): 130ff.

contemporary cosmic theory resting on older finite concepts. The acceptance of these had led to the conclusions, then so often restated, that the universe was running down, cooling off, and that man drew on toward the end of his career as the physical conditions appeared to which he could no longer make adjustment.

Patten's reorientation also required the restatement of physical theory.[21]

It is impossible here to elaborate the hypothesis that energy, momentum, and speed are conserved and not dissipated. I did not understand then, as he talked; and I do not yet wholly understand as I read, though I am, I think, beginning to comprehend. He talked, as he wrote, in vast leaping jumps, assuming that his hearer and reader had a knowledge of all the sciences and the power to remarshal all this knowledge for the purposes of restatement. Yet I gathered some inspirations, and I have spent much time in my life working them out. I found at once that I had a changed view of the cosmos, and that the old certainties had completely disappeared. I also had a sense of universal force working through temporary embodiments in structure and improving through the continual renewal of applied energy directed by human thought. Also I escaped from the dead end of noninheritance, that biological nihilism subscribed to by a whole generation.

Even at the distance of more than half a century I recall vividly the colloquies at this level during that year. Or rather, I recall what questions came to my mind. Most of them occurred across the breakfast table in the old University Club. The ham and eggs disposed of (that was Patten's invariable morning meal) and the plates pushed aside, I would raise objections, try to bridge gaps.

I cannot now reproduce his answers to my many flooding questions. Usually a question would evoke a half-hour of answer, and I would be able to follow only in part because it assumed a knowledge of science and philosophy I did not have. Only when it touched the scientists and the philosophers to whom the social sciences owed their origin would I be able to follow with any confidence. I resolved, frequently, to improve my education as soon as I could escape from my present pressures.

But what did result was that I became permanently biased. If I

---

21. This restatement was published in *The Monist* 30(1920):406ff.

had to describe that bias—and I must admit that it has influenced me throughout my entire life—it would be in terms such as these:

The universal forces are becoming known in a shadowy fashion: whether they are to be described as finite we cannot say, being aware only of those we have partially uncovered. But their nature is to be roughly thought of as circular, endless, accelerating—as a pulse running in an ascending spiral. Man is a kind of factory for improvement, sending out stronger pulses as forces move through him. The soil and water of earth, light, motion, gravitation—these are the nurture he changes into renewed forces, meanwhile also improving his own nature. This is not an inevitable spiral: the betterment wish has carried him up to such civilization as has been achieved. At the accelerated pace to be anticipated as man approaches the reaches of spiraling change just ahead, he may make gross and fatal errors; and these may permit the forces he has unlocked to overwhelm him; but there is no rule that this must happen. It is a question whether structure can contain the immensely more rapidly surging pulses of power now running through it to be transformed into new structure and modified forces. There is no reason to believe that inability to withstand the flooding energy is inherent and inevitable. There is no reason either to think that the resources and natural forces are being exhausted; rather, new and more powerful ones are being opened to use. These are more difficult to discover and use, but the intelligence and energy required for this effort are supplied by the forces themselves. It is, as Patten said, an upward-pulsing spiral, self-renewing and constantly improving.

Man's hope and possibility in this is that he may successfully collectivize; that the strength and intelligence of many men may be brought into one renewal effort; that he may perfect a collective mind superior to any individual mind, perhaps by many times, and thus capable of coping with forces of vast volume and energy. Patten had labored to bring about such an improvement in social devices as would reach toward the mastery of a nature become too much for the lagging structure of individual man. Nature was taking man over into a new realm. She had given up the effort to make supermen; she was trying to create a supersociety, not supermen, by putting men together and thus multiplying their capacities.

Sometimes, as I left these sessions with the old man, the universe came thundering into my ears, and vague, bold visions of new societies shaped themselves in my mind. Examinations seemed only annoyances on the way to the work I had at least to attempt.

III

NEW YORK

1920–1932

When in 1925 I looked back on the past five years, the impasse Patterson had forecast for me had proven to be mistaken. My work at Columbia had been successful, and my academic future seemed assured. Everything before this appeared to have been a kind of apprenticeship. As yet I had not actually achieved much, but I could feel that I had made a place for myself. I had passed some landmarks: I was now a Ph.D.; I had become an assistant professor and so was started on the normal progression; also I was beginning to have some confidence that I could write and be accepted as a scholar.

I had even more to be thankful for. I had made friends; I had found congenial colleagues, and they had become understanding companions. In this and in other ways I had been fortunate from the first at Columbia. I had not yet begun, or perhaps was just then beginning, to feel that I must do more to meet the responsibility I felt for the injustices and unnecessary hardships imposed on so many of the people I saw every day on the New York streets. This impulse would grow stronger and would presently interrupt my academic life. But these were years of prosperity, and although the conflicts between workers and employers were frequent and sometimes violent, and although the country's farmers were having hard times all their own, these were not troubles that we knew much about. The hyperactivity of Wall Street might be approaching an exposure of its hidden dangers, but no one would have known it from the outward signs.

My successes at Columbia, such as they were, did not come easily. I still had some making up to do. For instance, I had never gone further in mathematics than my high school courses. My physics and chemistry were of the same elementary level; I knew almost nothing of prehistory or of astrophysics and not much even of biology, although I had once thought of specializing in it. When I needed such material and collected the necessary books and manuals, as I did from time to time, I found my way blocked. I have said before that I did not regret my Wharton School education. My reservation was that its graduates were prepared best for a career in managing affairs or, incidentally, if they had taken pains to acquire it, a knowledge of the social studies sufficient to start them as teachers, analysts, or researchers. But I realize that those who had had the liberal arts kind of schooling were quite as deficient in the social studies. This was not so obvious somehow, I suppose, because opinions or conclusions about economic, political, and social affairs are not usually held to so high a standard. Even with my graduate years added to the Wharton School experience, I still did not feel the same ease in the liberal arts or the natural sciences that some of my friends from those fields seemed to feel in my disciplines.

The work I had been given to do up to that time had not been beyond my powers if I held myself to a rigorous schedule. That I did, recuperating in the long summers at Wilson. There came a time after a few years when I did not seem to freshen. My sinus troubles got worse and were terribly intensified by long allergic sieges every fall. It got so, finally, that I was in physical discomfort almost continuously and slept very little, a matter certain to become more serious. But this would be after 1925, well on into the time when I could fairly consider my career to have been established.

It really seemed almost providential that I should have come to Columbia College (it was mostly in the college that I was to teach during my years at the university) just as the course in Contemporary Civilization was being organized. For that was the first of those comprehensive undertakings with the social science and cultural subjects so prevalent a few years later.[1] It was, in fact, the beginning of

---

1. I recall how surprised I was, twenty years later, to hear of a great to-do at Harvard over comprehensive studies of this sort. It was done there with characteristic soul-searching and after the production of a ponderous report, giving the impression that a new idea was just being discovered. We had broken the ground at Columbia, and by then some 200 other colleges had followed; but the winds of doctrine had reached Cambridge late. They reached Chicago somewhat earlier and with the improvements to be expected from the attentions of Chancellor Robert M. Hutchins.

the end for the elective system—"department store education"—that had spread from Harvard throughout American colleges during the last decades of the old century and the first decades of the new. We were no longer to offer incoming students their choice of a dozen or more courses in economics, politics, sociology, history, geography, psychology, and philosophy, and to allow them to select those few they thought desirable—perhaps because they were reputed to be easy. The cultural studies were being amalgamated into a blend that would seem relevant to life in the contemporary world. It was, we felt, the teachers' job to provide the materials for an education, not the student's to overcome difficulties and digressions in finding them.

This was a complicated matter, for all of us were specialized in the fashion of American graduate schools, and none of us had had an undergraduate education such as we hoped to provide for our students. I was very conscious of my glaring deficiencies in science, philosophy, and the history of peoples outside the European tradition. The natural sciences were the foundation for the social sciences. In undertaking to pose contemporary social dilemmas and to explore suggested solutions, we went back more certainly to Descartes, Newton, Cuvier, Lyell, Darwin, Kelvin, Tyndall, Tait, Gibbs—a long list of mathematicians, physicists, chemists, biologists, and geologists—than to Smith, Mill, Malthus, Marx, Ricardo, Marshall, Jevons, and other economists; to Compte and Spencer, social philosophers; to Locke, Hume, Bentham, and Montesquieu, political theorists; or to the great historians of the past.

It was the scientists, really, who had laid the foundations of the knowledge we now had to deal with; the social philosophers of various sorts had erected superstructures, often on imagined foundations. But there were the philosophers. In our generation there was only one Dewey, and in the preceding one there had been only one James. They had, however, been giants and gifted teachers as well, but the ability to give new impulse to men's thinking was scarcer for an obvious reason: the volume of knowledge was expanding beyond any one person's comprehension. This had not been true for very long. Going back fifty or a hundred years, most of those who were claimed as progenitors by economists, political scientists, and so on in our specialized age had not thought of themselves as such. Adam Smith had held the chair of moral philosophy at Edinburgh; Mill had written on liberty and logic as well as on political economy, and there had been no chiding for trespass on others' territory.

It was perhaps presumptuous of us to essay a return to the philosophers' generalizing function. Yet the atomization of knowledge was a serious matter for education, and education was our responsibility. Students in American colleges had, until then, spent too many years in dilettante activities. We proposed not to approach economic questions as though all undergraduates were embryonic economists, or political ones as though they were future government experts, but rather to assume that they were responsible members of society who would be expected to act as citizens should in a democracy. There were some who would be economists or political scientists, but very few. Many more were intending to find careers in industry, commerce, law, medicine, or engineering. They, too, were entitled to appropriate initiation.

We did not always select our teachers well; some of them proved to be unsuitable, but that might have been expected. When we failed, we merely looked for new recruits. Anyway, it was the most congenial undertaking I had ever shared. I was not in at its very beginning. I cannot claim even to have had a really formative part in shaping the first year, yet I joined in the work with such enthusiasm that I can legitimately share the credit of the founders as the enterprise expanded.

I was developing other interests as well. I had to. For even though these teachers were trying to experiment in amalgamation, the university as a whole was still departmentalized. It was only as an economist that I could hope for preferment. But economics was being merged with history, politics, sociology, psychology, and philosophy in Contemporary Civilization. In later years there would be further specialized offerings. Those of us who were believers in the new approach may have had designs on these advanced courses, too; in fact, we did soon begin a substantial transformation. In the early days, however, all of us who joined the Contemporary Civilization group took on its work in addition to our departmental duties. The elders in our respective disciplines were in the faculty of political science (the Graduate School) in Fayerweather Hall, and they held our respective fates at their disposal. They were not likely to be impressed by any contributions we might make to a synthesis. To them we were aspiring economists, sociologists, or historians, and they held us to their own strict criteria. Not even Herbert Hawkes or John Coss could gain us much credit for our efforts in Hamilton Hall.

Hawkes and Coss were, respectively, protector and manager of the Contemporary Civilization course. Hawkes was dean of the College and Coss was professor of Philosophy; Contemporary Civilization was their creation.[2] Service in it could therefore be expected to have certain rewards, at least, if not departmental ones. The best of these for me was that it took me into the university's inner circle, so to speak, as nothing else could have done. As I soon discovered, the conception of this college enterprise, so fruitful for American education, was to Hawkes and Coss no more than another among many ways to serve an institution they had given a deep and indissoluble loyalty.

It was a privilege to work with them, a privilege I shared with the whole group of instructors. As members of it came, served with us, and later went on to other institutions, the number of those who had had this experience must have grown toward the hundreds. This was one of the ways Contemporary Civilization spread to other places.[3]

---

2. Herbert E. Hawkes was a mathematician who succeeded Frederick P. Keppel as dean of the College and became at once one of the two most powerful members of the current administrative group. John J. Coss was the other power in administration. He was director of the Summer School and known to be leaned on heavily by President Nicholas Murray Butler for difficult jobs. He was at one time supposed to be Butler's favorite candidate to succeed as president. Coss never took this very seriously. There had been numerous others (and there would be more), and Butler outlasted all of them. He would, in fact, outstay both Hawkes and Coss.

3. In the introduction to the fourth edition of the syllabus in August 1924, there is a list of those who cooperated in its preparation. The names include only four of those who had been listed in the 1920 edition: J. J. Coss, H. J. Carman, H. L. Friess, and H. W. Schneider. Of these, three—Coss, Friess, and Schneider—were members of the philosophy department, serving in the college. Carman was a member of the history department, also serving in the college. He would eventually succeed to Hawkes's deanship and hold it until 1950, but this would be after the death of Coss.

Those who had served in earlier years and then gone on included two who became college presidents and eight who became professors, either at Columbia or elsewhere: W. E. Caldwell, Irwin Edman, A. P. Evans, E. D. Graper, A. L. Jones, B. B. Kendrick, S. P. Lamprecht, R. D. Leigh, F. C. Mills, P. T. Moon, and W. E. Weld.

Those who were then teaching and who helped to make the syllabus, were: R. C. Atkinson, H. J. Carman, J. J. Coss, A. G. Dewey, D. L. Dodd, D. M. Fiske, H. L. Friess, C. A. Gulick, James Gutmann, E. B. Hewes, H. B. Howe, J. E. McGee, J. G. McGoldrick, Thomas Munro, R. F. Nichols, J. H. Randall, I. W. Raymond, H. W. Schneider, John Storck, D. D. Wood, and myself.

I had luck in another direction as well. Professor E. E. Agger was in charge of economics teaching in the college; he was not only one of the kindest men who ever lived, and ready to take any pains for a younger colleague, but he was also a liberal-minded sort who liked to see originality developing. This last was of considerable importance to me at that time. I was gradually taking a deviant line in economics, and a hard-shell theoretician of the old school would have seen to it that I either conformed or departed. That was the way economic orthodoxy protected itself then; I have observed that it still does.

My deviation, after five years at Columbia, was becoming serious, but I was too unknown to make any stir outside my own circle. Agger was quite well aware of what was happening; in spite of it, he supported my first promotion. I thought the receiving of that distinctive blue envelope in April, telling me that I had become one of the academic elect, was a moment unlikely to have many counterparts in my career. It far surpassed the satisfaction of becoming a Ph.D. That, in my case, as in most others, was progressed toward so messily and granted, step by step, so gradually, that most of its gratifications were lost in the process. Promotion was different. I had earned that. I had had no backers; no one's interest was involved. I alone could claim the achievement.

Patterson back at Pennsylvania was still unconvinced. I had gotten little help from him on my doctoral dissertation. I had made a tactical error, too, in my choice of subject, though it had been a natural one for me to make. My interest in the direction and control of economic enterprise had led me to question how much could be done, short of public ownership, to contain and coordinate the rapidly expanding industrial system. It was obvious that the antitrust laws were quite unable to protect the public interest. In spite of all the prosecutions, corporate enterprises grew more powerful and more reckless year by year. Only one group of these had been held within the bounds of decency, and then not always, but more frequently than others. These were the public utilities. The difference was that when an antitrust suit was over and the court order for its breaking up (if the suit had been successful) had been complied with, the private corporations' lawyers, who were the best to be had, immediately began the exploration of new ways to accomplish the same outlawed results. Unless a new suit was brought in the course of years and new dissolutions were ordered, as seldom happened, monopolizing went happily on. The dissolved trusts were still capable of restraining trade, fixing prices, and mulcting consumers; and it was obvious that they would continue to be. The ingenuity used to evade charges of conspiracy was too much for the clumsy pursuit of government prosecutors; but the public utilities were "common callings," so for them there was permanent regulation.

It seemed to me that the long struggle of the reformers with the traction, water, power, warehouse, and other similar interests was turning out to be a good deal more successful than the efforts of the federal government to break up the oil, steel, sugar, and other monopolies. Especially in states where the public utilities had had less success in corrupting legislatures (notably in Wisconsin), and where, consequently, there had been established public service commissions with adequate powers and capable personnel, there had been a decided change for the better. Rates had been kept low and standards of service high, and, significantly, the utilities themselves had prospered.

I had thought there might be something here worth careful investigation. It might be that industries themselves, to be successful in a permanently rooted way, needed to be held to the course we always said was characteristically American, but all too often was not. High productivity and low prices were principles more often honored in the breach than in the observance. Also, I was certain, some way had to be found to stop the drift toward business dominance of all society. This was a terrifying feature of the twenties, coming then to a kind of climax, as a matter of fact, after decades of progress toward concentration and the almost final failure of all kinds of control. My thesis, called "The Economic Basis of Public Interest," undertook to investigate only part of this problem. It was a study of leading Supreme Court opinions to see whether the economic tests for bringing businesses into the category of "common callings," and so under the police powers of the states, could be determined.

It was obvious, I suppose, to those under whose supervision I worked where I hoped to come out. If I could show that businesses other than those usually admitted by the courts to be "affected with a public interest" had precisely the same economic characteristics as those traditionally called public utilities or those more recently brought within the definition, I might have made a contribution to public policy. Of course, it would not have been a happy solution from the point of view of the academic defenders of laissez-faire, to say nothing of those enterprises now operating almost as freely and recklessly as they liked. Making my point would not make me popular with either businessmen or academics.

I had begun the work with the encouragement of Leo S. Rowe and Clyde King, but they were now gone from the university, and I had to deal with the constitutional lawyers in the law school at Pennsylvania. They gave me a bad time, not because my thesis was disturbing, but because they thought it nonsense to try to establish it by economic analogy. It was not legal research or a legal conclusion. Finally Patterson had had to have pity on me and give reluctant approval, although I always suspected that he had grave doubts. He may possibly have been influenced by the acceptance of a compressed version by the *American Economic Review* for publication while he still had a final decision to make. At any rate, in June of 1922, I journeyed to Philadelphia and sat in Houston Hall among numerous other aspirants to receive the formal graduate degree. I recall about that occasion mostly how hot it was. Under our black gowns, most of us had stripped to undershirts. Josiah Pennington, now the provost, and Dean Ames of the graduate school—both portly men—who wore heavy morning coats under their robes and had an active part in the proceedings besides, were objects for pity. After the ceremony we scattered. We should never assemble again.

Eight months of each of those Columbia years were spent on Morningside Heights, but the other four were spent in Wilson. The farm had been sold, and the family was now concentrated on Wintergreen Island. In earlier years, as I have said, the nearby park had been a gathering place where school picnics and Fourth-of-July celebrations had been held; it had even been a favorite resort for picnic parties from Toronto and other lake ports coming for day excursions. Back in my teens, I once saw the ancient sidewheel steamer Argyle tied up to one of our piers, having come in with what must have been the last of these loads of trippers. These days were long past. Nowadays the railway and the interurban electric lines were taking people elsewhere. Although there were occasional picnics, the resort equipment of the park—merry-go-round, restaurant, ice cream stands, and the like—stood in neglected desuetude, and what had been an amusement ground was well on its way back to forest.

Wintergreen Island lay within the bay and was reached by a thirty-foot bridge. It was an oval of an acre or two, lying end-to off the shore, its marshy meadow on the landward side, alive in summer with red-winged blackbirds; it ended in a bordering bank of bushes and trees, so that the marsh was a green enclosure. On the other side was the deeper clean water of the bay. We looked straight out to the lake between thousand-foot wooden planked piers, one running outward from the island and the other from a headland on the main shore.

The park was several hundred acres of enormous old oaks, beeches, and hemlocks, covering islands and headlands, some inaccessible except by small boat, and in between were stretches thickly grown with cattail reeds. There were channels, miles of them, where canoes could slip silently under the overhanging branches of willow and hemlock growing along the banks. My father had made a kind of ill-starred attempt to sell all this as a real estate venture, but in the end it simply remained a forest. The promotional activities had, however, resulted in paths and roads. Beyond the forest was a golf course whose greens lay surprisingly among the fruit trees on what had once been apple orchards.

On the island itself, a large summer boardinghouse had been transformed, with the use of what seemed in those days to be inexhaustible resources, into a double-balconied country house. It stood toward the shoreward end of the island, and its broad front porches looked one way up the estuary with its weedy marshes and lily-covered shallows. That was west; to the north was the fresh-water blue of the lake. The house, within its surrounding balconies, had huge raftered rooms. There were a dozen fireplaces for burning a constantly replenished pile of logs. The kitchen was a long sunny room looking east; and the diningroom, where the family gathered on Sundays and holidays, was a large octagonal room standing out from the house over the marsh. It was on the southeast corner, and early in spring or late in fall, the sunlight there and the fireplace between them tempered the damp and chilly air off the surrounding water.

My father surprised me one spring, when I came home from New York City, with a study cabin completely fitted for the kind of work I was doing, and calculated, in spite of my small daughters, to give me solitude. We owned several cars, of course; and what with the golf course so near by, the many close friends about the country, and the work I was now doing, the Wilson months, with no teaching for distraction, were pleasant and productive. I prolonged them when I could, going at the first possible moment in June and coming back to Manhattan on the last possible day before the fall term.

It was there in Wilson that I wrote my early articles and books. In an attempt to turn economics toward a more realistic assessment of modern problems, and because it was needed for Contemporary Civilization, I conceived a new sort of text for introducing students to economics. I induced Thomas Munro, a friend from the philosophy department, to work with me. He did not help much. He went on, indeed, to become a philosopher of art. Before long he was lecturing at the Sorbonne on aesthetics—recognition indeed for an American—and was permanently director of the Cleveland Museum of Art. But before he went, we produced *American Economic Life and the Means of Its Improvement.* Another colleague, Roy E. Stryker, illustrated our book with charts, diagrams, and pictures. When it came out in 1925, all of us had some reason to be proud. It was, we thought, quite satisfyingly in the Dewey tradition. Hawkes and Coss praised us for it; if the economists treated it with no more than toleration, as a beginning effort, we were satisfied that we had at least done our students a good turn, and perhaps the social studies, as well as the art of teaching.

Somewhat earlier than this (in 1922), Wesley C. Mitchell had come back to Columbia. Some years earlier, he had gone to the New School for Social Research, along with a number of others, when President Nicholas Murray Butler and the Columbia trustees had suddenly at the war's beginning weakened in their professed devotion to academic freedom. Charles A. Beard had left specifically because of this issue, to return only briefly in his late years. Many of those who had stayed on as members of the faculty and had not protested were left with scarred consciences. There were some who had approved the trustees' action; others, like John Dewey, who had spoken their minds, resigned from committees and expected dismissal. In the end, however, discipline had not materialized.

A young man coming from another environment could often hear outbreaks of old differences. I had had some experience of my own with intrusions into academic life and was prepared to understand the quarrel. The Columbia professors sometimes seemed to regard it as a local and isolated matter. I knew very well that it was part of a larger issue and that it was not likely to be settled soon. Dissenters would always have to contend with those who were upset by unorthodoxy and who possessed (or thought they possessed) the power of suppression.

I had no occasion to take sides. During my years at Columbia the shadow of the Beard resignation, especially, would deter those who might otherwise have undertaken to force conformity. Beard was one of the eminent historians of his generation, and leaving Columbia had not interrupted his work in history. He was always referred to in professional meetings as *"formerly* professor of History at Columbia University." The same thing happened whenever his numerous articles or books were referred to by others, and no one was more often discussed. It could be said that he was a living reproach to his more timid colleagues. For a whole generation he helped to protect all the rest of us. I along with others who might well have had difficulties owed him a debt we were glad to acknowledge.

That his resignation had more effect than the Nearing dismissal at Pennsylvania was largely owed to his standing as a scholar. His courage had not been greater than that of Lightner Witmer at Pennsylvania, whose *Nearing Case* was a better documented record than anything resulting from the incidents at Columbia. The two faculty members who were dismissed—Professors Cattell and Dana—had not offended in the same way, of course; they were opposed to an incipient war, not to domestic injustices, and so could be called unpatriotic.[4]

---

4. The Cattell and Dana cases were not the first at Columbia, but they were the most notorious. Butler, until just before the war, had been an active proponent of conciliation, especially as president of the Carnegie Endowment for International Peace. But, like many others, the justification for the war overcame his commitment to peace; so, in fact, had mine. Both Cattell and Dana were pacifists who did not change; both, as so often happens in these cases, were difficult. If Beard had not resigned, there would probably have been no more serious repercussions than had occurred as a result of Nearing's dismissal.

Beard's resignation was sent to the trustees about a week after the Cattell-Dana incident and was associated in everyone's mind with it. In reality it had a wider causation. The trustees, he said, had been showing more and more tendency to behave as though faculty members were employees. It was as a result of long consideration and not "in a fit of petulance," as he explained in a letter to the *New Republic* (December 29, 1917), that he resigned. In this same letter he went back over a good

Wesley C. Mitchell was a different kind of person. On occasion he would take unpopular positions and hold them doggedly. He was not adverse to protest when it would be of use, but he was modest. He was the sort of scholar who had to explore the last corner of his subject before admitting to any competence in it. He worked at the description of economic behavior in a system with so few uniformities that bare enumeration was almost impossible, say nothing of generalization. He was really just beginning his treatise on the business cycle, and it would require more than the rest of his life to complete, even though he had the National Bureau of Economic Research to widen his own efforts and with it a succession of able helpers. He also lectured on the history of economic theory and seemed to divide his interests about equally. It was only seeming, however, for the interpretative book so many of us hoped he would complete never appeared. It was not much of a change for him, really,

---

deal of academic history, especially the appointment of W. D. Guthrie (a corporation lawyer, brother of one of the trustees) to succeed J. W. Burgess as professor of Law without consulting the faculty, and the conduct of the trustees in subjecting him, the year before, to an inquisition on his views and then ordering him to warn all members of the department against teachings "likely to bring disrespect for American institutions." Both Dean Woodbridge of the graduate school and President Butler had assured him that such an ordeal would not occur again. But in March 1917, the trustees had published a resolution indicating that another committee was to conduct still another inquisition. The faculty of political science had voiced objections; and there the matter had stood when the Cattell-Dana dismissal had taken place.

Beard's letter of resignation became a much-quoted document. Its sentences of condemnation had a life of their own. They were so effective that even years later Beard could return to the faculty of political science. What Beard said was this:

> Having observed closely the inner life at Columbia for many years, I have been driven to the conclusion that the University is really under the control of a small and active group of trustees who have no standing in the world of education, who are reactionary and visionless in politics, narrow and medieval in religion. Their conduct betrays a profound misconception of the true function of a University in the advancement of learning. . . . I am convinced that while I remain in the pay of the trustees . . . I cannot do effectively my honorable part in sustaining public opinion in the support of a just war on the German Empire or take a position of independence in the days of reconstruction that are to follow. . . . As I think of their [the faculty's] scholarship and their world wide reputation and compare them with the few obscure and wilful trustees who dominate the university and terrorize the young instructors, I cannot repress my astonishment that America, of all countries, has made the status of the professor lower than that of the manual laborer, who, through his union, has at least some voice in the terms and conditions of his employment. . . .

Things had changed, however, and that Beard had returned was evidence that wartime excitement had passed.

to move to the New School for Social Research and then, a little later, to come back to Columbia.[5] And it was done quietly as always.

Although he eschewed academic politics, Mitchell had considerable influence among the older men in my own department because he was so widely recognized. I consulted him more often than anyone else because I so greatly admired his integrity and abilities. Among the others, I could not find so much to admire. E. R. A. Seligman, for instance, was the head of the department and the author of several books on public finance. As such he had an international reputation. He had a magnificent library, the result of a lifetime of collecting, kept in the kind of private institution I had never seen until, as an instructor, I was asked with a group of graduate students to spend an evening at his home. I have since seen such collections in English country houses, survivals from another century, and a few in America, gotten together by wealthy friends, but it was new to me then. Seligman was a member of the international banking family of that name; there were plenty of resources to support the library and to go on adding to it. He was not yet an old man, but with his white beard and ponderously bright manner he assiduously cultivated the appearance of venerability. His contributions to public finance were perhaps considerable, yet I have never been able to dissociate my memories of him from a certain incident.

A little later—just before the depression—he was engaged by the General Motors Corporation to carry out a most elaborate investigation of installment selling, a recent practice being criticized by some economists as having a suspicious relation to the inflation of those years. This vast research proved, in two richly produced volumes, that installment selling could not be blamed. Several skeptical colleagues were heard to wonder what the General Motors executives would have said if the results had been different; throughout the uproar over his study there was never any question about what the result would be. The vast load of installment debt made a substantial contribution to the depression beginning a few years later. Frozen

---

5. During the war he was director of research for the War Industries Board and so author of the price section in the *Report* of its activities so useful to later scholars. In 1937 a group of his essays would be collected and published under the title *The Backward Art of Spending Money*. This would furnish the occasion for repaying my debt to him. My "Evaluation" may be found in the *New Republic,* October 6, 1937.

assets were the most intractable obstacle to recovery and reactivation of the economy after the debacle of 1929.

H. R. Seager was still another kind of person. Next to Seligman, he was the departmental senior; and, as a matter of fact, it was he who nominally supervised our undergraduate teaching. Although Eugene Agger was the executive of the college, he had not been promoted to a professorship and would presently leave for Rutgers University, where he would stay, firmly fixed in everyone's affections, until his retirement in 1948. This left William E. Weld and then me—for Weld left the next year—in charge. I had, therefore, very close relations with Seager at first, until he made sure that I had the confidence of my dean. From then on I had no supervision to speak of from "across the street" and only such advice as I often sought, especially from Mitchell.

Those first years were important to me, and Mitchell's friendship and trust have always sweetened my Columbia recollections. Seager was the author of a widely used text with some cautious departures from strict orthodoxy, mostly ones he had been encouraged in by Patten. Seager was one of the many scholars of that generation who had been students at Pennsylvania in Patten's great days.[6] Our mutual interest in Patten was deepened just after our old teacher's death when I undertook at his urging a biographical study and, a little later, the editing of a volume of Patten's essays in economic theory, never before brought together in a book. Seager thought well of this and wrote its introduction.

One of the presidents of learned societies who had studied with Patten might have been expected to have written his memorial. After consulting with them and with other of his more devoted students, it seemed unlikely that it would be done if I did not do it. What I had in mind at first was a somewhat fuller study than I was ever able to complete; still I was able to find out a good deal about his youth and education, his years in Germany, the interlude of discouraged elementary teaching before he was brought to Pennsylvania, and his

---

6. Shortly after Patten's death in 1922, a memorial service had been held in Witherspoon Hall, the scene of so many Academy of Political and Social Science gatherings. Six learned societies were represented by their presidents, and all six had been students of Patten. This was evidence of a greater influence than was ever exerted by any other teacher, with the possible exception of John Dewey, I believe, or perhaps William James, in American academic history. And, of course, it has not been repeated since. The great growth and diffusion of learning has made such a personal influence unlikely to happen again.

first years at the Wharton School. This was all new to me. I had known him only as an elderly savant.

I now began to catch glimpses of him as a farm boy, dreaming along the furrows of Illinois fields; as a pupil at one of the early academies, so characteristic of mid-nineteenth-century America but so unlike the educational institutions of my time; as a student at Halle, struggling with a language he never really mastered. I began to understand how the abundance of midwest America had shaped his thought and made him so optimistic and how experience of the changing American scene had led him to believe that free enterprise would evolve into an adequate system of economic activity. In the course of it, I often had occasion to see how events, not precisely like those he had experienced, but, after all, comparable with them in having fortunate conclusions, had formed my own attitudes. I was as much an optimist as Patten and as much an evolutionist. I had less patience because I was less learned, and I may have been less tolerant because by now the contrast between poverty and riches had become so much more offensive. But these were matters of degree, not of kind.

I think now, as I look at it, that my biographical essay was overeloquent and that, in spite of my efforts, it did not convey my conviction of Patten's genius. If it is admitted that it was not meant to be exhaustive and that it was occasional (written at the request of the American Economic Association), it is all that could have been expected. I wish now that in the following years I had taken the time to write a really adequate and lower-keyed commentary on his life and work.[7]

Besides my Patten studies, I was still following up, in various ways, the psychological leads Carleton Parker and Will Ogburn had introduced me to in Seattle. There was plenty of encouragement for it at Columbia—much more than I had ever found at Pennsylvania. Wesley Mitchell was interested in it, too. As a student of Veblen at Chicago, he had come to consider the perennial wars of competition absurd. His "Making Goods and Making Money" was only small

---

7. The Patten articles were "Some Formative Influences in the Life of Simon Nelson Patten," *American Economic Review* 13(1923); "Notes on the Life and Work of Simon Nelson Patten," *Journal of Political Economy* 31(1923):153–208; and "Bibliography of the Works of Simon Nelson Patten," *Annals of the American Academy of Political and Social Science*. The edited book was *Simon N. Patten, Essays in Economic Theory* (New York: Knopf, 1924).

evidence, really, of a very deep interest.[8] In his lectures on theory, this appeared as a critique of the English economists bearing on the concept of value. His sardonic exposition of the "felicific calculus," descended from Bentham and hardened into law to suit his successors' purposes, was one I should never forget. I went to his lectures and must have heard each of them at least twice. I was later glad of this, for they were never published.

Veblen's had been a far more iconoclastic interpretation of social behavior than Mitchell's own; it had been savagely critical of the alien culture in which he had had to make his way as a scholar. There was a good deal of the sourish and disillusioned northerner in his attitude, and although his serious students defend his cynicism as pure detached assessment, I never found myself convinced.[9] Mitchell did not have this feeling of alienation. He was at home in America. His work on the business cycle was one of the earliest approaches to pure science in economics.

My own psychological explorations were restimulated by contact with Woodward, Thorndike, and others at Columbia whose books I had read. There also was the influence of the biologists, especially T. H. Morgan and Donald Lancefield, his younger associate. Old interests were revived, and I began feeling for the integrating impulses from all these specialized fields. These, I was convinced, were badly needed. Then, of course, there was John Dewey. His presence was at once a liberating and a unifying influence throughout our company of scholars. I went to hear him, but this was not always very rewarding. He thought tortuously, slowly, and intricately, as he talked. It was a major enterprise to understand him from such contacts, but most of his books were hardly better. He was as difficult to read as he was to hear. Only very occasionally would a gem of a sentence emerge from his turgid prose to repay the labor of following him to the end.

---

8. Later published in *The Backward Art of Spending Money and Other Essays* (New York and London: McGraw-Hill, 1937).

9. Cf. my "Veblen and Business Enterprise," the *New Republic*, March 29, 1939, afterward republished in *Books That Changed Our Minds*, edited by Malcolm Cowley and Bernard Smith (New York: Doubleday, Doran and Co., 1939). The comprehensive *Life* of Veblen was written at Columbia by a then graduate student, later a professor, Joseph Dorfman: *Thorstein Veblen and His America* (New York: Viking, 1934).

So I followed him mostly at second hand, although when I went to him with specific questions, they led into expanded conversations. After five years, I felt I had some grasp of his philosophy, and I considered myself one of his disciples. I was, in fact, to call the sort of economics I was trying to develop "experimental" (or, sometimes, "instrumental") in his mode. The chief novelty in *American Economic Life* was the section on consumption and choice. In it I felt I had married Patten's *Theory of Consumption* and Dewey's *How We Think*. But most of all, my generation owed to Dewey liberation from old concepts, if it was wanted. He encouraged my turn away from classicism in economics and politics and my admission of the future as the chief influence on the present. This was a complete reversal, of course; pragmatism meant something more than judging things or institutions by working tests. It meant that the future could be brought into focus, judged in advance as a working hypothesis, and altered before it was reached. This was and is the essence of planning. I found a comprehensive justification for much of my own work in Dewey. I felt myself deeply in his debt.[10]

Another enterprise undertaken during those early years at Columbia was an extensive exploration of contemporary developments in technology, especially scientific management and its relation to economic theory. I have said that after years devoted to the study and

---

10. It can be imagined what satisfaction I had in Dewey's review of my *Industrial Discipline and the Governmental Arts,* beginning as it did with understanding paragraphs:

> The presentation is in my judgment by far the most intelligent analysis of our present economic situation and its impact upon the social order. It is neither a condemnation, a laudation nor an exposition of a dubious philosophy of history. It is an intelligent analysis of forces at work with a statement of how they work and a comprehensive grasp of the unutilized possibilities latent in these forces. . . . I cannot close without saying that I know of no work from which hot headed radicals and supposedly hard headed businessmen can learn as much, if they would, as from this book.

This review of a book to be discussed later was published in *Occupations,* November 1933.

the teaching of orthodox theory, I was dissatisfied.[11]

Classical theory had become a hardened logical system in circumstances quite different from those of the twentieth century. It could not, therefore, be taken either as a generalization from contemporary economic experience or as an hypothesis for the solution of future problems. It was dangerously close to being merely a speciously attractive, highly elaborated abstraction, relevent to nothing in the real world. It could not be concluded that because its central subject matter was the valuation of goods and services, there was any special relevance to what went on in the market place. It was more precisely an exercise with artificial conditions: a series of theorems, all of whose elements were assumed, and if any attempt was made to substitute actual observed elements, the whole edifice crumbled. In other words, it did not explain. Although I understood well enough the value of hypotheses in science, I was learning that they are not considered to be valid unless they accept reality, reduce its apparent disparateness to simpler relationships, and provide a provable (that is, experimentally provable) explanation of the events they pretend to comprehend. Classical economics was an exhibit of nonscientific reasoning. I questioned the usefulness of saying that it was what it was not.

My disquiet came from my own particular kind of receptiveness to the new attitudes in science and philosophy so prevalent on Morningside Heights in the twenties. It was not only Dewey's instrumentalism, it was the consciousness that classical physics was breaking up and that something new was replacing it; that anthropologists were discovering new uniformities of behavior and new depths in history; that the astrophysicists had new ideas about the origin of celestial

---

11. We provided, in Columbia College, an advanced course in economics similar to elementary courses elsewhere, except that we expected rather more of our students. The orientation was the same, but the intensity was greater. We used several texts: that of Taussig, which I already knew practically by heart, and those of Seligman and Seager were the most frequent; but we often went to Marshall, Clark, or Jevons for readings. Our students were put through the rigorous course of classical logic. The difference at Columbia was merely that not all of them were required to undergo this discipline, only those who were intending to go on with further work in the social studies. An intending engineer, physician, or natural scientist, need go no further than Contemporary Civilization, where the emphasis was instrumental—on problems, not on theory. After my first two years, I always taught either this intermediate course or a still more advanced one for graduate students in theory.

bodies; that the biologists were deepening their knowledge of genetics and growth; and that the behaviorists were showing the relations among men and their societies. Then, too, because of my preoccupation with scientific management, I was acutely aware that economic institutions were escaping the old categories.

The muscles of postwar America had developed enormously, and limited productivity was no longer a restriction on national growth. Patten's "surplus economy" had arrived with explosive effect, and we were entering his "creative economy"—or could if we would. There was enough and to spare of everything, and more of it was being demanded by all those who had hitherto been admitted parsimoniously to sharing. This was the result, mostly, of those activities I had so long been aware of among the engineers and their various co-workers in industry. Few economists paid any attention to these developments; most of them were as innocent as children of all this range of knowledge and seemed to be indifferent to any suggestion that a reworking of theory was necessary. For this conviction I owed much to the emphasis in the Wharton School on actual industrial experience. We knew all about Frederick W. Taylor and scientific management; we had watched his progression from simple time-and-motion studies to the rationalizing of management as well as work.

I thought the method of most importance for reassessment was Dewey's instrumentalism. What this might imply was a series of newly taken generalizations concerning business behavior, not different in method, perhaps, from those made so long ago by Smith, Mill, Malthus, Ricardo, and the rest of the early masters, but resting on the realities of the changed contemporary world. These generalizations could then be tested for validity, one after another, by using the developing techniques of statistical analysis, themselves so improved that they constituted a new scientific tool. I can see now that I was feeling toward the conception of a development plan or model whose construction and use would later on become the central instrument of social articulation. At that time I was only certain that our theory neither explained adequately what went on in the economic world nor offered a starting place for the solution of its problems.

Others were troubled, too, however reluctant to admit it. Seager's text, for instance, written years before, was being rewritten. He was giving less and less space to theory and more and more to those chapters, begun as appendixes, but gradually assuming more importance, having to do with "problems." Seager himself had made a long study of trade union organization, of employer-employee relations, and of methods of fixing wages. He had discovered that payments to workers were not merely the price of labor, fixed in an impersonal market and impervious to the influence of imponderables. In fact, he knew well enough how "uneconomic" most wage bargains were. And he was not one of those who believed and said that departure from the classically fixed wage rate would be ruinous to the economy and (as the iron law of wages had it) bound to harm workers themselves, because the better employers would succumb to the competition of others whose wages were "economic." He knew that the system was a managed one, and that its relationships might be of varied sorts, some fair and some not.

This was not only true of the labor problem but of other problems as well: tariffs, taxation, agriculture, railways, public utilities, and the like. Not only Seager, but Taussig and other textbook writers of the generation ahead of mine, had given more and more space to "practical" discussions. No one knew more about tariffs than Taussig (who had once been a member of the Tariff Commission); about public finance than Seligman (who had had innumerable official commissions); or about labor than Seager (who was a noted conciliator). And their discussions were first-hand and authoritative. But what these chapters had to do with the theory in the front of the book it was impossible to say. Our modest *American Economic Life* had at least the virtue of a coherent approach without the pretense of universality. We added the subtitle *And the Means of Its Improvement.* Its first part was a description of poverty, comfort, and riches in America, and it went on to suggest ways those who now lived in poverty might move—or be moved—upward: by increased productivity, by more equitable sharing, and by more reflective uses of goods and services.

If we hoped that this different approach of ours would be copied in other texts, we were disappointed. Of the crop of texts in our generation, ours would be the single exception to still another rewriting of classical theory with problem chapters added. Most of them, I might say, would be inferior to the older ones. I had thought then, in the early twenties, that a renaissance was due. There had been, after all, a later industrial revolution of even greater consequence than that which had furnished the materials for the theories of Smith and his successors. The expansion of productivity had made new levels of living possible for everyone; it had, moreover, brought about such changes in the organization of industry as to make the old assumptions obsolete. How many manufacturers were now also proprietors? How many owners were their own managers, making face-to-face bargains with their workers and directing their efforts? How many were confined to one area, had a local market and never intended to move? The truth was that classical economics had come out of the age of handwork industries, water-wheel mills, corner stores, horse transport, and sailing ships. Now there were great impersonal organizations and sophisticated management. Not scarcity but surplus was the ever imminent threat to equilibrium, but economists still reiterated the same old theory.

I thought if a new beginning were made with its foundation in contemporary facts, something of genuine use might emerge. It was the responsibility of the economist to understand industry and to rationalize its functions, but he was being left behind. There was now a generation of industrial engineers and financial specialists who were essentially uneducated to begin with (because they had been taught an irrelevant theory) and who saw no difficulty about confining themselves to furthering the interests of the businessmen who were their employers or clients.

These specialists were not by any means all in private employment. Many of them, in fact, were teachers in the many schools of finance and commerce on the Wharton model. The Wharton School itself, after recent purges, was much more allied with business than its original faculty would have approved, and newer schools (including the one at Columbia) had never been intended as anything else. It was no accident that the era of commercial expansion had also been the era of expansion for these faculties in the universities. Even Chicago, least vocational of all universities and most devoted to the ideal of liberal education, had its school of business; and that at Harvard was almost a caricature, so high a gloss was put on its pretensions. Meanwhile economists in departments of economics were either being left high in the classical air with their theoretical unrealities or were attempting feebly to compete with their colleagues in the schools of business, who were genuine specialists in advertising (incredibly, but actually, every school of commerce had its professor of advertising, sometimes several of them), public and private finance, transportation, real estate management, insurance, and the like.

To this there was no objection. What did seem objectionable was the capture by business of professorships. The teachers of all of these subjects quite characteristically spent part of their time at the university and the other part working as experts for private firms. This was, indeed, counted an academic virtue: it showed that they knew what they were talking about, and that students intending to become advertising experts, bankers, or stockbrokers could safely allow their training to be directed by authorities so competent that they could command pay for their services. It seemed to me a questionable virtue. The distortions it caused made any kind of appraisal impossible because it precluded weighing by an acceptable ethic. Surely service for self-interested, profit-making concerns, seeking to make them more efficient—whether in production or in the exploitation of their workers or their consumers—was not the proper function of a university or of a university's professors.

For this kind of thing there might be technical schools, appendages of the businesses themselves or, at least, forthright in their intentions and scope. But the intrusions of such subject matter into the university's curriculum could only result in the perverting and undermining of its mission. That institution had an ancient and previously unassailably honorable relationship to society. It was the custodian of learning, the definer of aspirations, the critic of morals. If an economist had a right to a place in such an institution, it was not as a sycophant of business or of any other interest, not even as a defender of contemporary culture. He ought to have the knowledge of all that went on, perhaps even knowledge only to be gotten from inside, but use of it ought to be for a higher purpose than the furthering of exploitation. It was no use to pretend that much could be done about this now that business was so powerful and had brought into its service so much intelligence. Radicalism of any sort—that is, departure from harmless orthodoxy—was quite easily detected at an early stage and could be smothered.

I think Coss and Hawkes understood this even though they found it difficult to question any decision of the moneyed men they trusted. They had, at any rate, a fierce jealousy for Columbia's honor. I argued with them that the university's purposes were being perverted and even that its good name was being jeopardized, but so strong were their beliefs in the status quo, in the goodness of the powerful, that I could never bring them around to my point of view. They still resented Beard's action and blamed him for questioning the trustees' good faith. They could not regard Beard, as many of us did, as a defender of university tradition. It was not so much that the university was being invaded by Philistines: I was, in fact, all for most of the Philistines. Philosophers could not afford to neglect the newer subject matter; if they did they would some day discover that their students had left them while they dealt so meticulously with irrelevancies. No, it was rather that it seemed impossible to use the activities of industrialism as the subject matter for intensive study, a field of learning, without becoming adjuncts of the business system. It would have been relatively easy to have found many allies for objection to the intrusion of such studies into the curriculum, but that would have meant making alliances with faculty reactionaries, which included most of those in both the humanities and the sciences. If these colleagues had any economic notions, they proceeded out of an easily explained feeling that the patrons of their society had earned respect. They saw no reason for risking trouble by allowing status to subjects with no cultural importance.

Nevertheless, I had a potentially powerful argument. I could contend that the impulse to create the Contemporary Civilization enterprise had come out of the same culture I was describing. Coss, Hawkes, and the other originators certainly had had in mind precisely the difficulties I was making too explicit for comfort. Theirs had been a more direct, less informed (as to actual economic functioning), but no less reformist, approach. They had called it an educational enterprise, but it had all the implications I now pointed out. They were, I must say, quite willing, even eager, that as far as economics was concerned, our course should have the orientation I suggested. It was to be a detached approach to industrialism and the contemporary problems it had brought with it that we were to work out. And they were quite willing, moreover, to trust me with it.

I find myself at a loss to put my differences and my agreements with Coss and Hawkes as precisely as I should like. I respected them so deeply that I could not question their honesty. We worked together for a common end. We were dedicated teachers and administrators and it seemed to me then that we had more like beliefs and intentions than differences. Only at this distance do I see that they lent themselves, because of their very virtues, to an undermining of our educational enterprise. What was wrong with them was what was wrong with our culture. I was not so old as they and not so experienced. Also I was not by nature dogmatic. I argued with them, but I did not know then how right I was and how wrong they were.

There was no reason why I should feel any responsibility except that I had a natural desire for allies among so many hostile forces. As for economics, the National Bureau of Economic Research, with Mitchell directing it, might develop much of what I was hoping for. Of course, if it did, I should be excluded. I had no aptitude for statistical economics and no desire to devote myself to it. But I thought there might still be a place for theorists whose fresh appraisal of economic forces and facility in generalization would lead to new orientations, just as the new hypotheses in the natural and physical sciences were doing. I had noticed that the quantitative economists were productive in proportion to their imaginative conceptions—that, in fact, statistics were useful mostly for proving and disproving hypotheses. Such work was fashionable, and its uses were apt to be magnified; but I thought it would settle down to its proper position.

Still, economics, as apart from the specialism developing in the schools of business and in the institutes, had to go a good deal further than it had toward making sense of economic phenomena. It had to relate itself, I thought, to the expanding industrial system emerging from the past and proceeding rapidly, now amended, enlarged, and enriched, into the future. It not only had to rationalize that stream, it had to help in directing it toward the objective of all our aspirations —the increase of well-being.

After discussing the problem with friends, I wrote letters to a few of the younger men in other places whose work had seemed to show a similar interest. I suggested a symposium volume to be called *The Trend of Economics.* I did not, I said, propose to direct the contributions they might make to any common subject matter. I merely wanted them to write something of appropriate length dealing with or illustrating the present state of our discipline and perhaps suggesting ways for its more fruitful development in the future.

Most symposia are frightful tasks for their editors. Mine was easier. There are usually refusals; I had none. There are often those who are unable to do what has been promised so that postponement is necessary; that did not happen to me. It was, in fact, a happy experience; one or two of the others even helped me to read the proofs. After the younger men agreed, I even went so far as to ask three others, our elders by a little, but genuine creators, as I thought, to contribute, too. These were Wesley Mitchell, J. Maurice Clark, and Albert B. Wolfe. Their contributions were important statements.[12] I wrote one of the essays myself and called it "Experimental Economics." Into it I put all that I had on my mind after my first few years at Columbia: my experience in teaching Contemporary Civilization; my fraternization with scholars in other fields; my inheritance from Patten and the Wharton faculty; the behaviorism I had learned from Watson and Thorndike; and the philosophy I had gotten from Dewey. The general feeling about my essay was, I sensed, that it was not economics. I still thought, however, that the attempt to provide unifying generalizations must be done over and over until some agreement about the formulae for the shaping forces of our time had been reached. Only then could we begin to bring them within the ability of men to manage.

This impulse to find wider and wider generalizations containing and giving meaning to the contemporary world and the complex forces working in it was the strongest intellectual, and perhaps moral, urge I had. The need I felt for *meaning* was almost physical, and I had the strongest of convictions that tying together and finding direction was not only possible but also a condition of progress. Even in these first years at Columbia when what I had to do every day demanded concentration, the outside world was insistently present as a kind of muttering undertone, since the campus was part of the city. Our Contemporary Civilization course gradually organized itself as a kind of intellectual history. All of us, I think, felt more and more

---

12. The list of authors and their contributions was as follows: "The Prospects of Economics," by Wesley C. Mitchell; "On Measurement in Economics," by Frederick C. Mills; "The Socializing of Theoretical Economics," by J. Maurice Clark; "Communities of Economic Interest and the Price System," by Morris A. Copeland; "The Reality of Non-Commercial Incentives in Economic Life," by Paul H. Douglas; "Economic Theory and the Statesman," by Robert L. Hale; "The Limitations of Scientific Method in Economics," by Frank H. Knight; "Some Recent Developments of Economic Theory," by Raymond T. Bye; "The Organization and Control of Economic Activity," by Sumner Slichter; "Economics—Science and Art," by George Soule; "Regional Comparison and Economic Progress," by William E. Weld; and "Functional Economics," by Albert B. Wolfe. This volume was published by Knopf in 1924.

the need to discover for ourselves why a developing technology possessing such promise for men—of relief from drudgery, of emancipation from poverty—had not also brought assurance that the serious troubles we feared might be averted.

In the twenties, we did not yet expect another way, but we did expect before very long to be involved in an economic break up. There were international troubles, most of them the result of unwise settlements after the last conflict. After about 1925, it no longer seemed possible that a United States of Europe might result from the efforts of Aristide Briand, Gustav Stresemann, E. A. R. Cecil, and the other statesmen then in power. Americans were very little concerned about the East, and the Harding-Coolidge freeze of relations with Soviet Russia under the guidance of Secretary of State Charles Evans Hughes seemed likely to persist indefinitely. It was, nevertheless, a time of spreading disquiet. And it was not only about foreign affairs that questions hung in the the air unsolved.

How could so prosperous a people believe so little in the faith they professed? The disbelief did not appear on the surface. It was not to be seen in the press, and it was not heard about from politicians. That submergence was part of the trouble. The press was beginning to be recognized as untrustworthy. The moderately independent papers were disappearing into the vast empires of Hearst, Munsey, Block, Scripps, Gannett, and half-a-dozen others, businessmen who intended to run them as profit-making enterprises primarily, but secondarily as propaganda organs for the business system. And there was by now an equally deep suspicion about legislative representation, a fear that it had been permanently impaired by the prevailing corruption—not just passing scandals attributable to an individual or two who were taking advantage of democratic tolerance, but an extensive and persistent perversion. It was often remarked that the Teapot Dome scandal had caused unaccountably little furor, but this was only seemingly true. The lesson had sunk deep enough into people's minds and stayed there, a festering cynicism. By the mid-twenties it had spread very widely. Everyone seemed to be on the make, as on other occasions in American history, and nothing seemed so interesting as sharing in gamblers' gains.

The days of the muckrakers were long past, but those who had been young during the revelations of that time were now adults. They had followed Lincoln Steffens, whose remarkably revealing autobiography was now being read, into confusion. He had ended on a note of complete pessimism: that what was best in men led to the worst behavior. Political bosses and their business allies had transformed the American commonwealth into a kind of immense bucket shop, all from the best impulses in the world: love of family and friends, working to get ahead, loyalty to colleagues. School children were taught an adulterated account of American political and social life, and it was called "civics." It could not possibly seem to them to have any relation to the sharp practices of the business world or the political manipulations going on around them. They were expected to grow up believing in one kind of thing and practicing quite another. And when they left school, they were thought pretty stupid by those out in the world if they allowed the morality they had been taught to influence their behavior.

This contradiction infused much of American life by now. What people professed and the way they behaved were sharply different. There was an agreement to preserve this separation. To erect an ethical system from current behavior would have been to produce an intolerable confrontation for institutions buried under so many layers of hypocrisy. And, as a matter of fact, from about this time on, the conspiracy became next to universal. Press, pulpit, and educators joined in.

The perception that a specific disaster was almost upon us was not manifest to any of us. We were not seers. Some of us were deeply troubled about the current ethical confusion, about the separation of action from direction, and about the laying out of logical cells where intelligence operated without overlaps. We did believe that some calamity must result, and some of us said so. There were few who listened.

The course in Contemporary Civilization was a small contribution toward a preventive, or possibly—for we believed in education —a remedy. We hoped to draw together for consideration both fact and fancy, to show people as they thought they were and as they really were, to make a rationale of social action and to extrapolate its trends until they appeared as consequences. We meant to be thorough, that is, we felt the obligation to show how what was going on had come about, and then to discuss with our students where the ongoing tendencies might take us all, especially them, in their generation. There were also possibilities of a managed future. These we dwelt on as alternatives to the prospect if no management should be undertaken.

Sometimes Coss and Hawkes used to chide me gently about being "radical." I replied—and meant it—that *they* were the radicals. Nothing could be so explosive in the 1920s as showing young men the prospects they faced and guiding them to decisions concerning choices they must make. I gradually came to understand that, incredible as it seemed, Coss and Hawkes were not allowing themselves to realize that this was an inevitable consequence. I had run across similar blindness in other places. It had been a familiar trait of my father's business associates; it had been true of many of the soldiers in the recent war; it was true of the economists about whom I complained. But these colleagues at Columbia were not ignorant of such evasions; indeed, we still sometimes called Coss "Colonel," a reminder that he had served in the wartime psychological service directed by Walter Dill Scott. If anyone could, he ought to be able to suggest the integration our society so badly needed. I recall how I was finally convinced of the extent of their blindness when I discovered that both these friends of mine had voted for Harding in 1920 and —in spite of everything—for Coolidge in 1924.

Contemporary Civilization was recognized by earnest educators as a useful conception. That it was necessary was shown by the spread of the idea to other institutions. The specific Columbia technique was not always copied; but electives were always abandoned for an integrated and comprehensive curriculum. It was not only good in conception, it was being worthily implemented. The first of the texts to result was Irwin Edman's *Human Traits and Their Social Significance.* [13] It was an attempt to give a general view of psychological realities, from man's simple inborn impulses and needs to the hopeful fulfillment of these in religious observances and in the activities of artists, scientists, and philosophers. Later on in his forword Edman said of the origin: "The book follows more or less closely that part of the syllabus for the course in Contemporary Civilization, which section of the outline was chiefly the joint product of collaboration by Professor John J. Coss and the author."

If I had read *Human Traits* with more understanding, I might have found an explanation of what in Coss puzzled and tantalized me, the more because of my fondness for him and my feeling for the

---

13. Published by Houghton Mifflin Co., 1920.

university where he set such an admirable example of service. I should have noted that when man's fulfillment was spoken of as lying in the "deliberate activities of religion, art, science and morals," economics and politics were not mentioned. Indeed, I think it was Coss's wish to exclude these or at least to exclude whatever developed that might be challenged. He wished it so much that he could only be gotten by sharp reminders to acknowledge that the most serious of our impending problems were economic.

Yet he and others like him in that age were themselves builders and changers. He was trained and specialized in university environments, and an administrative revolution was going on, not only in the universities but elsewhere. The pattern was new, the energy being poured into it enormous, and what would result would be such a revolution as the world had never known. But that it would have fatal defects was almost inevitable. How should it not when it was done blindly? I realize that I dwell here on an almost incredible weakness in the twenties. That it existed has been amply demonstrated by what has happened since. Yet if I were challenged to prove it and to specify its incidents, I should be at a loss. If my challenger wanted to show that my colleagues had a philosophy as inclusive as I could ask, he would be able to prove it from my own citations. True, in his introduction Edman did not mention as ends of man his schooling in economics, sociology, or politics; but the "problems" later arrived at in Contemporary Civilization were mostly economic or political. And, indeed, the exposition in *Human Traits* of the social nature of man is one of the most comprehensive and lucid in the whole book.[14]

Coss knew what education was for and what it could do. His advocacy of the comprehensive courses was proof of that. Edman, too, as an expositor of Dewey was persuasive concerning education as an agency of social change. In one place,[15] after quoting a passage from Dewey's *Democracy and Education,* which begins: "Society exists through a process of transmission quite as much as biological life . . .", carrying the implication that society has organic characteristics and is dependent on constant recreation under the guidance of education, Edman himself went on to say:

---

14. Ibid., chapter 5.

15. Ibid., pp. 107–8.

Education, however, may not only transmit existing standards, but can be used to inculcate newer and better expectations and ideals. In the adult, habits are already set physiologically, and kept rigid by the demands of economic life. In the young there is a "fairer and freer" field. Through education the immature may be taught to approve ways of action more desirable than those which have become habitual with their adult contemporaries. The children of today may acquire habits of action, feeling and thought that will be their enlightened practice as the adults of tomorrow. All great social reformers, from Plato to our own contemporaries like Bertrand Russell, have seen in education, therefore, the chief instrument, as it is the chief problem, of social betterment. We may train the maturing generation to approve modes of behavior which the best minds of our time have found reasons to think desirable, but which could not be substituted immediately for the fixed habits of the adult generation.

The "modes of behavior which the best minds of our time have found reasons to think desirable" would be political and economic, as well as artistic or scientific. There was no considerable difficulty about science or art—not that there were no artistic or scientific controversies, but that they could be settled without resort to violence. Economic and political questions were continually causing civil disturbances, sometimes indistinguishable from war.

These were my teaching years. I did my best. Five days a week for a whole academic year I met the same students in the same classrooms. I should have thought they would have been sick of me long before the end of the second term. I had always demanded more than all but a few in each group could give. Yet even at the end we remained friends. Many from those first Columbia years were still friends after many years. We met infrequently; time dimmed my recollection of their names, their characters, and their habits of thought; but recollection bound us together. Some of them became professional men, some businessmen, some teachers, like me. I never afterward had a dissent from the opinion that the course in Contemporary Civilization was a strong influence in their lives.

What gave teaching its opportunity was the five-day week throughout the year. During it we, with our students, ventured into uncertain territories. They knew that our only advantage was that we were a little older and had done more reading and thinking about the future. As a teacher, I was more interested that they should make progress than in anything else. Day after day we met in a group no larger than two dozen. After a week or two we knew a good deal about each others' attitudes, after a month or two we were intimates. They were an extraordinarily mixed crowd. Some stand out in my memory: one lad from Jamaica who was, as he studied, an elevator operator; a South African from somewhere up on the veldt; a son of a rich Chicago father who had been a famous Bull Mooser; one who was then, and remained for some time, an active Communist publicist; several who were sons of more or less prosperous businessmen; several who were terribly handicapped by having had parochial school preparation and were by then resenting their deficiencies. I remember many sorts from many places, even some veterans who were older than average.

They had reading to do every day—twenty to fifty or so pages of it. It was usually not too difficult, mainly informative, and it was held together by the syllabus. We more or less discussed the reading, but we were free about it. If those with business backgrounds and the veteran who had turned Communist differed about a point of human nature or logic or a social problem, we stopped to have it out even if it took a week. My agreement with them was that they were responsible for the reading; they would be rigorously examined on it—not by me—and would be judged accordingly. No examination, I told them, would show whether they had grown wiser, more tolerant, or more useful. That was my responsibility, and as far as I could, I would beat their prejudices out of them, sharpen their awareness, heighten their sense of responsibility. I must say that my students did as well as any others on examinations;[16] as to the rest, who can measure educational results? I still think the enterprise worth all I put into it.

Those were times when the cost of living was rising, and it seemed especially high on Manhattan Island. So without really needing to, I took on small jobs to supplement my salary. New York offered many temptations to do that, and most of us succumbed, often unwisely. There was never a year, I think, in all my service at Co-

---

16. After about 1923 we had a special examiner, Ben D. Wood, an expert in educational statistics. We pioneered in what we called "objective tests," and much of the technique now common educational property was worked out there under his direction. I must remark that one of the most surprising results was our discovery that teachers made little or no difference in examination results, a matter of some chagrin to those of us who fancied we were superior practitioners of the art.

lumbia—except the first—when I did not double my income by extra teaching, by speaking here and there, and by writing. I soon had two fairly regular connections of this sort: one was teaching two or three nights a week at the American Institute of Banking; and the other was regular book reviewing for the *Saturday Review of Literature.* The bank clerks were usually as tired as I was, and the time for them and for me was mostly wasted. Pursuing these courses made promotion easier for them, and teaching gave me a steady income. Presently I was so adjusted to it that it seemed necessary.

Book reviewing was hack work, too, I suppose; at least it is often spoken of that way. Yet for me it never seemed so. There was a kind of fascination in this tenuous touch with literary New York. I kept to political and economic subjects, but I went to the editors' weekly luncheons. Henry Seidel Canby, formerly a Yale professor, had gathered a group of critics who gave the *Saturday Review* an unrivaled importance among writers. At his gatherings, Canby entertained those who had recently caused some stir. Frequently they were visitors from elsewhere. It was on such an occasion that I first met William Allen White and at once asked him to explain his Republican regularity. He replied that even a newspaper editor could not get too far from his readers. I must admit that he loosened their rigidities. He was at least a progressive Republican. Years later, when I had become a notorious New Dealer, he would preside at a critical dinner and pit me as "the young champ" against Eugene Meyer, publisher of the *Washington Post,* as "the old champ."

On another of these occasions, Canby had as guests (at the Hotel Webster on Forty-fifth Street) two young men from Yale who were thinking of a new publishing venture—a weekly news magazine to be called *Time.* They were looking for opinions and ideas but especially for guesses as to whether they could hope to succeed. I would give something to be able to recall what I said when it came my turn to speak, but I cannot. My recollection fades, too, about conversations with Elinor Wylie, Stephen Benet, and, more often, because he was on the staff, his brother, William Rose Benet. But I never really made my way into their circle. I was an economist, and economics was to them a dull mystery. Gradually, as book reviewing became impossible, my contacts loosened and fell away.

I had many opportunities to lecture to groups of all kinds—innumerable in New York—and I did quite a bit of it. I found the immigrant Jews who dominated the clothing trades especially eager to understand more about American life and willing to explore all its mysteries with open minds. They were eternally curious. I liked that. The discussions were sometimes exhausting but invariably interesting. After those first few years, however, this, too, was something I gradually had to abandon. Finally, as my opportunities widened, I spoke only occasionally and wrote more and more. What I wrote was not always publishable, but much of it was; and since it was fairly successful, it became a regular and cultivated occupation.

We were going on, from 1925, into several bursting years, optimistic in spite of growing reservations. Columbia was very much part of it all. Nicholas Murray Butler (it still seems unnatural to speak of him without using the three names) had from the first insisted on the locution "Columbia University in the City of New York," and the identification was genuine. The intellectual tides of the city swept into and out of the gates on Morningside Heights and so through the university. The effect on that overrunning metropolis was no doubt minimal, but certainly New York gave Columbia character.

There was not much of a distinctive and separate social life for either students or faculty—less than in Philadelphia, for instance—but since we instructors were held together, even if loosely, by the need for meeting our frequent classes, and because our college library was a much frequented center, we did form a kind of community. This was much more true of those of us who were comparatively young. We had more classes to meet and had to be more attentive to our students than the professors in the graduate school. They might live in a suburb and grace our environs only a day or two a week; many of them did just that. There were members of my own department who, years after, I had seen no more than once or twice, and with whom I had never exchanged more than a casual word. They had lives of their own somewhere, we supposed, but it was not on Morningside Heights.

There were differences among us in this respect. Those who were gregarious and whose work often brought them together had a circle with shared interests and cooperative effort. A university community is a temporary one, but not strikingly so. There are always members leaving for one reason or another and others joining; but friendships can be formed and relatively long-term projects carried out. Sometimes these attachments are as strong as those among the undergraduates; often, indeed, they mature through a decade or two, building up shared experience resting on mutual help. They can come to be needed, so that forced separation for any cause may be tragic. Members of such a group especially bound together by their feeling for the university will cling to it almost as they would to a happy marriage and dread its ending.[17]

But we were not thinking of retirement then. We were thinking more about what we had to do to become accepted and permanent members of our chosen community. Very few instructors in Columbia College ever became university professors. Professors were much more often chosen from among already proven scholars in other institutions. An instructor could usually look forward to no more than a few years of service. He would then have to find himself a post elsewhere. If after some time he proved to have outstanding talent, he might be called back, but that, too, was unlikely; he was in competition with the whole scholarly world, and the professorships were few.

I speak of this because it explains something of the ordeal young teachers sustain, and because those of us who undertook to reconstruct the teaching of social studies were worse off than most others. We had departmental criteria to meet as well as those imposed by the unification we had undertaken. Not many of us were promoted at Columbia, and those of us who were had survived a grueling competition. It is no wonder that the incidence of ills attributable to tension and worry was very high. I did not escape. For some time I had an excess of respiratory and digestive troubles, only gradually overcome by a regimen I detested.

I have not said much about what the university was like in the twenties. The casual visitor could have walked up Broadway from 110th to 125th Street and not realize that the university had been passed. Barnard College and the Theological Seminary would have

---

17. This is why the retirement policies of many institutions are so cruel. The casting off of those approaching old age, insisted on by the administrators, is often absolute and deprives teachers at the very time they most need it of the support of old associations. There must be a better way.

been on the left just after leaving 116th Street, but a dormitory and the journalism building would have risen on the other side between 114th and 116th Streets. On the same side were business, mines, engineering, and the teachers' college. At 116th Street pylons backing a formidable female figure on either side might have been noticed, and with a little imagination, the visitor might guess that they were intended to give the impression of a portal. Going through and crossing on 116th Street at Amsterdam Avenue were another matching pair. Back from the street and above it on the north, the library dominated its plaza—a classic pillared building, one of Stanford White's parthenons. It sat above a wide stone stairway on whose lower terrace *Alma Mater* reached out welcoming arms.

About this center the red brick renaissance buildings of the various schools were disposed as blocks enclosing small rectangles. It was amazing into how small a space this plan had permitted the positioning of law, architecture, philosophy, political science, and natural science on one side, as well as the chapel, and on the other business, mines, engineering, and the union. There were even a half-dozen vacant blocks gradually being filled in as the funds could be found, but very gradually, because somehow, in spite of flowing prosperity in the nation, funds seemed harder and harder to find. Either that, or, as was said by the sour oldsters in our neighborhood, the new medical center out at 168th Street was getting everything. They hoped, they often said, "that Nicholas Miraculous was building himself a good place to die in."

That Butler's presidency would run on into the forties and that he would die, blind, deaf, and helpless, not at the magnificent medical center he had put together, but at neighboring St. Nicholas's Hospital, were dispositions of fate. By then, however, I had been long since separated from the university. I could not have been convinced that such a prospect was likely, however, because I was so intimately concerned with its affairs. I thought of myself as a permanent tenant of Hamilton Hall where I spent my working days; and Hamilton Hall had been built to endure indefinitely. However, like all the other buildings, it was not designed for inevitable expansion. We—teachers, students, and working staff—had to accept crowding as best we could, and, in fact, we became accommodated to its inconveniences and, if pressed, might well have admitted an unwillingness to see it changed.

As young academics, our college group was properly critical of the more bizarre manifestations of our environment, and, as is now generally appreciated, the twenties was a decade rich with vagary, not the least among its statesmen.[18] There can hardly ever have been three successive chiefs of state who furnished such rich material for caricature as Harding, Coolidge, and Hoover. It is as incredible now to read accounts of their activities as it was for us then to read about what had gone on in the administration of Grant just after the Civil War, the low point up to that time for our government and its presidency. Later students were inclined to think their teachers made a better story of it then the facts warranted, but actually no exaggeration was necessary. Like most young Americans, I had regarded presidents not so much as politicians who, largely through accidental availability, had achieved the White House, but as embodiments of the staid virtues. The school histories, by slurring over a good deal and playing up a good deal else, had given us that kind of picture.

This was not far from the same kind of stereotype parliamentary politicians had created for British royalty. When the British discovered that the vagaries of inherited sovereignty had shifted the focus of their stereotype, they would take the extraordinary measure of forcing Edward VIII to abdicate. The amazing blandness with which they would substitute a complaisant nonentity for a vivid character and go on assuming that nothing had happened to the Crown would be most revealing indication of what a determined elite could make a whole people swallow. Americans were worse off. They had to go on pretending that Harding and Coolidge were much like Cleveland or Taft had been, not to take the best examples but ones it was possible to respect.

I had almost arrived at the end of my stay at Columbia before I saw the way out of the educational difficulty such examples revealed, and then I arrived at it as a by-product, so to speak, of other ideas. I was becoming something I should later learn to call a planner but had not yet accepted the label. At this time—until after the

---

18. Frederick Lewis Allen in *Only Yesterday* had a good deal of fun with all this. What he said was true, but he did not uncover all the various forces shaping the future. For that he need not be blamed, since it was not what he set out to do. Readers who have followed me so far might trouble to read or reread Allen's account of what we Americans were like then. He might remember also that we were reading Thomas Beer's *Mauve Decade* and regarding that earlier time as later readers would regard the decade centering at 1925.

depression and its financial crash furnished an opportunity for reassessment—there were few doubts about our free enterprise economy. At least there were none in the minds of American leaders of any sort. How could there be in the midst of such fabulous prosperity? But as I have said, I had been fascinated by scientific management since my Wharton School days. Lately I had been studying our changing agriculture—the one depressed segment of the prosperous American whole. These two interests led me to considering the future. Eventually I realized that orienting education to the future was the educational device we needed. It might replace our Contemporary Civilization. It could be another conglomerate with the same purpose and method.

I had better now speak of this preoccupation with scientific management; its influence on my agricultural, ecological, and consumer interests can follow. It was not new for me to see industry more realistically then did the writers of the classical texts. I had had some experience of my own as I was growing up, but also Taylor's principles had first been used for educational purposes at the Wharton School. As a consequence, I had a firm belief in the wholesomeness of allowing actual and going technique to furnish the factual material for theory. This was the way to make of social science what it pretended to be. Taylor by now had completed his work, but a school of followers was going on with it. They were, in fact, at the point of extrapolating the principles of shop management into a novel approach to industrial organization. Production, instead of proceeding by rule of thumb out of the accumulated experience of foremen and superintendents, was now, in most large shops and factories, being taken over by precision-minded engineers who worked with exact observation to determine the best materials and the best processes for producing goods and services. It was during this decade just following the war that mass-produced goods were proving more durable than hand- or semihandmade ones for the first time, a victory owed wholly to the final acceptance of analysis and precision. In principle, production was no longer managed; it was planned. If the planning was as exact as theoretically it could be, industrial operations would be revolutionized.

This, of course, was taking a lot of fun out of business. Old-fashioned factory foremen could no longer swell around with their chests out, giving peremptory orders out of their experience and concealing their mistakes. Now there would be records and measurements. Everything in the new dispensation was neat and tidy. Ideas and creative contributions were only wanted when the preliminary paperwork was being done; after that they were unwelcome, and, in fact, could not be entertained at all, because the established rhythm depended on repetitiveness only to be modified when the blueprints were being remade for the jigs and dies, the endless conveyors and the fitting and cutting machines. The metallurgical industries were having a vast expansion; makers of machine tools were prospering; and the time had come when Henry Ford could install a many-thousand-dollar rig to stamp out the tiniest parts of his new Model A.

These, however, were contributions from the past, really—no more than Taylor had forecast several decades ago. They were, it was true, just becoming prevalent. Most of the old generation of foremen and managers had resisted until they had had to retire, defeated but unconvinced. Observation of these delays—amounting, as I have said, to several decades—would have made me doubtful, if I had not been before, whether enlightened self-interest was really a controlling rule in the economic world. Businessmen in that generation were possibly the worst-educated group ever to come into substantial control of a culture. The economists ought to have expected them to be actuated by naive, unrealistic, and—as Carleton Parker had said—purely theoretical considerations, rather than being governed by logical projections of expected results. Such sustained and disciplined thought was not to be expected from speculators, living from deal to deal. Being practical men, they were susceptible to curious and even outlandish interpretations of society as a whole, of human motives, and of men's professions.

During these years the "business" type was retreating to selling and advertising or to gyrating in and about the exchanges where stocks and commodities were gambled. It was, in fact, a golden age of speculation. The engineers were enlarging production capabilities enormously, but wages were not being increased as rapidly as productivity, and prices were not (as, according to the textbooks, they should have been) coming down along with costs. In other words competition—among employers to get workers, among manufacturers to sell products—was decidedly not regulating economic processes as economists said it was. They argued that conditions of free competition had never been established. But what the nation needed was not deduction from perfection but a hypothesis explaining actual economic processes. The result, as it was reached in the late twenties, was the production of more goods and the offering of more services than could be sold. For the time being, profits were high, and speculators could win. Because businessmen were unrealistic, they were tempted to believe that the most obvious signs of danger were evidences of success. It was, they said, "a new era."

Economists were at this time being drained off into fringe activities. The young men who were now going into business from the universities were becoming bond and stock salesmen, advertising executives, or perhaps insurance agents, adding themselves to that growing number who were doing by high-pressure methods what was supposed, in the books, to be done because of enlightened self-interest. They were enticing people to buy, and when buyers had no more funds, inventing ways of persuading them to borrow on future incomes and then buy. There was installment selling of everything: automobiles, of course, but also the new electric gadgets, especially refrigerators, kitchen helps, vacuum cleaners and the like, the rapidly developing radio, and even stocks and bonds. The selling of securities added further productive capacity to that already producing more than could be paid for out of current incomes.

I thought the simple, rational processes of scientific management, so effective in productive operations, ought to be extended now to all production, services as well as goods. I realized, however, that much better management could not come about until the logic of planning was more completely accepted. It was like the situation in a factory where serialization was as yet incomplete. It did not make much sense to have here and there an efficient process if, between the processes and before the product was finished, there existed delaying gaps. The pace of the whole was, in fact, the pace of the slowest. Engineers were closing breaks in single factories. When they filled the last one and production moved with a new celerity, uninterruptedly month after month, fed by materials delivered on split-second schedules, the product was enormously enlarged and the unit costs were spectacularly reduced. The same principles were obviously applicable to larger and larger operations. A Taylor was needed now for the economy as a whole.

This was not very well shaped in my mind, and I had no very clear notion of the mechanisms for carrying it out. It was not a difficult transition to move in thought from the factory with completed serial operation, being set in motion in accordance with well-articulated plans, to a complete industry so arranged, even one with widespread and complex operations. The difficulties were not engineering ones. They were more general. Or rather they had to do with the serious defects in what was inaccurately called a "system." Some of these had their origin in nature and human nature—"acts of God" and the vagaries of man. But these were responsible actually for only a small percentage of inefficiencies; many more were attributable to deliberately created uncertainties or those arising from the fact that not only venturesomeness but adventuresomeness was encouraged. The aim of business was the making of profit; and where there were no ventures and no risks, there were no spectacular profits.

A stock-and-bond house in New York or Chicago might float a security issue for an ambitious enterpriser who wanted to open a gold mine or drill an oil well, to build a new factory, or to furnish a new service. The mine, well, factory, or store might or might not have any prospect of success: the real question was whether the prospective buyers of securities could be made to think it had. The salesmen of the stock-and-bond houses in those days were furnished with a prospectus containing some information mixed with highly colored fantasy. Using such persuasives, capital was gathered up from various sources. After the stock-and-bond house had deducted a nice percentage, the 60 or 80 percent of the investors' funds remaining went for the purpose set out in the prospectus. It might turn out that the mine was superficial or the oil well dry; or the factory might make a product the public would not buy at a price high enough to be profitable and would presently have to be shut down. Such ventures failed, but the financiers made money.

Any number of variations could be made on this theme. It was, and still is, called free enterprise, and its virtue was supposed to be that it got new ventures started and enhanced their vigor in operation. But note that it was always done to make money rather than to furnish a needed good or service—the paradox Veblen and Mitchell expounded so effectively. To the economist who would say that money could not be made if the good or service were not wanted, the answer was very often that it could. That is to say, the venture might pander to a weakness for "conspicuous consumption"; or it might otherwise, through the arts of salesmanship, ensure the wide distribution of nearly worthless or even undesirable goods. It could be pointed out, however, that the original purpose had often been served when the stock-and-bond house and all its satellites—the financiers and promoters—had made their profit from it. For them that was the desired end. That this was not a very effective way to raise levels of living or even to get the everyday work of society done had been thoroughly enough established by the critics. The proof of all they had said would be made abundantly available in a short time. Errors in judgment (or deliberate misallocations) in setting up enterprises must be cumulative. The chance that many securities so conceived and widely distributed would be the foundation for profitable ventures was not very great. Many of them would turn out to be worthless. This would lead to successive financial disasters, since most of those who were entrusted with investors' funds were involved in the process. And the scale of the operations made it likely that future disasters would be cataclysmic.

I was becoming more and more convinced of the possibility of using the principles known and tested in industrial planning and management to operate the system in an entirely different way. The risks could be very much reduced, the capital available could be made almost certainly productive, and the worst losses from indirection and misallocation could be avoided. What was required, I thought, was to put production rather than financing first, to take the management of the system away from the adventurers who had already been banished from the shops and factories, and entrust direction to those whose purpose would be to make goods and services rather than money. No one who had studied Taylorism and its delayed spread throughout industry needed to be told that any such change would not come quickly. The vested interests of the factory manager and his foremen had been very weak compared to those of the speculators who would be displaced by planned management. Every passing year of financial prosperity enabled the businessmen to build their advertising and selling costs and their interstitial services into institutions whose regulation would grow progressively more difficult.

It was already evident that even in the welfare state of the future, they would be almost impregnable. Their proliferating propaganda for free enterprise and against collectivism was not taxable. It was accepted as a cost of doing business, and its legitimacy could be challenged only with difficulty. The propaganda already permeated the press and the radio, the principal means of mass communication, and already business sycophants were far more welcome than critics in all positions of consequence.

It was a dismal prospect. Obviously only one kind of attack on such institutions could have any effect: one from inside. Every possible danger from outside had been elaborately prepared for. Any critic was, by definition, an enemy of "the American way of life." The extraordinary "red hunt" conducted by Attorney General A. Mitchell Palmer while President Wilson had lain sick in the White House had failed in the immediate purpose of making Palmer the Democratic candidate in 1920, but it had left its slime, poisoning the springs of national politics. The fright it had brought to honest dissenters had toned down criticism even of the base betrayals of government by Harding's Ohio gang. It was a foretaste of what might happen again to critics who failed to sing the praises of business as loudly as the worst charlatan on the payroll thought he ought. It was worse even than that; there were many employees who could stay where they were only by *inventing* disloyalties or acting as provocateurs.

Business was riding high. Production costs, because of factory efficiencies, were rapidly decreasing; taxes were being reduced by compliant Republican regimes (in Coolidge's administration they were reduced four times), and the incidence of reduction was favoring the highest taxpayers. The treasury was headed by Andrew W. Mellon. No extravagant business expenditure was too fantastic to be counted as a cost and so exempt from taxation. It was necessary, even so, to distribute large cash dividends, although they were made to seem far smaller than they were by the fractionalization of shares. Sometimes one share became two, sometimes five, sometimes ten, but the new shares continued to earn a four-dollar dividend. The speculation when one of these divisions was about to occur was intense. The insiders, of course, knew what was coming, but others could only guess, and Wall Street seethed over the fire of easy profits. Another thing: during the whole of this decade there was a suspiciously stable level of prices, showing, if not conspiracy, certainly a cessation of competition. Also the average wage did not rise. This made it impossible to sell all the proliferating goods even on installment plans.

It was not a propitious time to insist on such ideas. They would be unwelcome almost everywhere. Nevertheless, they seemed to me most neglected and most needed, and I continued to write and speak about them.

Industry's Coming of Age and *The Industrial Discipline* were written in Wilson during two summers. The actual writing was shortened by a complete working out of the text beforehand during early morning hours in Hamilton Hall. Also, I owed a good deal of what finish they possessed to trips back and forth to Amherst and to discussions I had with friends there. One year I visited there three days a week. An economics professor was lacking, and I helped to fill in. I usually drove up and back. Images from the drive up the College Highway into New England in the crisp fall weather, with the lavish beauty of the painted hills all around until the leaves fell, and later the sharp, clean brightness of the snow are still mixed in my mind with thinking out the elements of a modified system for the crazy scheme that thumped and muttered, creaked and protested all around me. It was not so pleasant in winter; still the lonely drives gave me time for considering.

In this enterprise I owed very little, I believe, to learning. In order to prepare myself, I had, as a matter of fact, offered courses for several years called "Proposals for Economic Reorganization." With my students, graduate and undergraduate, I had read through the literature of Utopia from Plato to H. G. Wells, had gone again into Marxism, had studied British gradualism in the Fabian literature, and the current craze in Britain, Guild Socialism. So I did not neglect my study, but I was not greatly impressed, except by the Fabians. For most of it was, if not preindustrial, certainly pre-Taylor.

It must be possible, with the multitude of new devices for paperwork and calculation, to reduce uncertainty until it comes within limits restricted enough so that allowances can be made without disrupting the steady progress of the whole. This would begin by isolating each risk and either eliminating it or squeezing it down. Simultaneously it would be necessary to set up social objectives and to discover the best means for attaining them. This was the essence of Fabianism; and this was what a factory, using the Taylor system, did. It was furnished with a job to do, after a good deal of figuring and consultation. Then the layout of the necessary facilities was studied for maximum output with a minimum input of energy, human and other. In the same way, it was conceivable, a whole economy could set target quantities of goods and services. The facilities to produce them could be laid out, and the processes of industry could be expected to operate in an orderly fashion. There was no theoretical difficulty about it. There would be vagaries, but they would not amount to any large percentage of the whole.

The real difficulties were not of this order at all. To state the matter in engineering terms was to be hopelessly unrealistic. The trouble was that so many individuals had the privilege of exploiting and disrupting what regularity and discipline there were. Such an attack was allowable at any stage in the process and at any level of operation. Facilities were being shifted about, not to furnish needed service, but so that money could be made from manipulation. It was more or less the same with most of our services and products. Ruined facilities for making goods, built with disregard for the probability of permanence in the first place, littered the industrial landscape. Others were springing up on the chance of being wanted and because investors' funds could be assembled with a profit to promoters. As far as the nation was concerned, only one large industry had an outlook and compliance device. That, paradoxically enough—because it was the most individualistic of all industries—was agriculture. It was possible to go to agriculture for lessons on the possibility of knowing what could be made to happen and trying to get it to happen in all producing fields.

I did, in fact, turn to agriculture after a study of the change brought about by Taylor, but first came my initial study of the impact of scientific management, called *Industry's Coming of Age.* It was a modest attempt to assess the technical stage now reached without, apparently, any notice from economists who were interested in what went on at the centers of the economic system. By inference I suppose I was accusing them of having their noses in their books while the world around them was being shaken by innovation, but I certainly did not say so, although I had said something like it in the essay for the *Trend of Economics.* It was intimated by my seniors in Fayerweather Hall that *Industry's Coming of Age* was neither theory nor statistics. Either of those was a recognizable category for original contributions, and up to now I had been thought (though I was overcritical) to be on the way to becoming a theorist. They thought that I had merely gathered up and made available the results of engineering practices over the last decades. This was a technological matter, not a theoretical one.

This book, I think, caused my superiors to decide, Mitchell

dissenting, that I might stay on at Columbia, perhaps, because I seemed to be administering the teaching of economics in the college successfully, but that I was not likely to develop into a real economist. They therefore wrote me off. Within the next few years, although I became a professor, other younger men were given the preferred positions at the graduate level. I was passed over. I had despondent moments about this, and, of course, some soul-searching ones. If I was to be of any use at all, it would have to be because I had the insight and understanding to offer *tours de force.* It seemed to me that economic theory waited for a comprehensive rationale, as science had waited for its unifying theories. I thought I had discovered the area where it would be found and that I had hinted at its nature. But no one else thought so or encouraged me to intensify my search.[19]

I more or less decided then that if any of those hints and approaches—there had been several in the past few years—came to anything, I would make another change. I knew that both Coss and Hawkes thought I was the kind of person who ought to make a career of college or university administration and had recommended me for a number of such positions. Nothing had actually come of them, although there had been several I might have developed if I had really been interested, and now I thought I might have been mistaken. If my talents as a theorist were really limited, I could at least be a useful administrator.

---

19. Professor Fred Hoyle, reviewing the fourth edition of Einstein's *Meaning of Relativity* (the *Sunday Times,* April 16, 1950) stated rather clearly the physicists' conception of scientific method: "It consists of two steps. The first is to guess by some sort of inspiration a set of mathematical equations and the second is to associate symbols used in the equations with measurable physical quantities. Then the connections observed to occur between various physical quantities must be obtainable theoretically as the solutions of the mathematical equations. That is to say, the result of every physical experiment must be predictable from the equations."

For social science the method would not be greatly different. There would certainly be in the beginning an inspired generalization stated in wide and inclusive, but precise terms. Observed phenomena thereafter would fall, if the generalization proved to be correct, into the relationships it had predicted. But, of course, social phenomena can be and are managed, and who manages them, and with what purpose, are necessary elements in predicting what they will prove to be; this makes social science more complicated, if not different, than physical science. Also prediction is not regarded as the only test of scientific method.

None of the offers I had or might have had seemed to me sufficiently attractive. The future of the independent college in America, as contrasted with the university made up of many colleges, was not at all clear to me. My experience, except that at Amherst, had been exclusively with universities, and I was inclined to feel that their advantages were such as to jeopardize the future of the small liberal arts institutions. No chance at any large place was offered, finally, and I went on working much as I had before. The weight of disapproval, although largely amorphous and unexpressed, except as Wesley Mitchell conveyed it to me in a friendly fashion (dissociating himself from it but not minimizing its reality), was a burden in my middle years at Columbia. There was much to mitigate it: the friendship of my college colleagues, the rewards of teaching, the satisfactions I occasionally had in a piece of work. Then, too, I was more and more accepted into the governing group of the university and was, as a matter of fact, elected to the University Council as a representative of the college faculty. Services of this kind were privileges, not tasks. For, like Hawkes and Coss, and, as I now understood, many others of my elders, I had come to feel that institutional sense of oneness, of identity, felt, I imagine, by the members of a monastic order. Whatever promoted the university's good seemed more worth doing than anything merely intended to further my own interests. The rejection of my loyalty to Pennsylvania was in these ways more than made good.

Life in the 1920s was often frustrating for those of my political persuasion—political progressives or radicals who were not permitted to believe that we had any rightful shares in our nation's affairs. We were, in fact, all but regarded as social misfits—not that an obscure professor was regarded as anything at all, but only that I identified with those who were political outcasts. Harold Ickes, for instance, must have been feeling very much the same way in these years, and so, perhaps, were Bronson Cutting, Hiram Johnson, Robert La Follette, Robert Wagner, Jerome Frank, William O. Douglas, Henry Wallace, and others of many origins, interests, and sorts who were in a situation like my own. We were all Progressives, and we were in a minority. But this made my concentration on the university more intense. People who serve an institution for a long time, in almost unnoticed ways, are often very happy. Sometimes they know it. I knew it at Columbia, and later I was to know it at Chicago. It went a long way toward compensation for never being quite acceptable to many of my academic colleagues. It was thought that I could put things well but was not likely "to make a contribution."

I had to regard this as failure, even if there were compensations. I had tried to do too much and do it too soon. I had counted on an understanding of long-range intentions from the fragments I had put together. It would have been better to have published nothing, or at least very little, and to have worked out my ideas slowly and quietly, and then, if they had been unacceptable, only I should have known about it. What I had done was to follow my normal tendency to think as I wrote and to work out my ideas from one tentative statement to another. What I was intent on was distant and difficult; I only glimpsed it myself at times of sustained effort, which brought on a kind of exaltation. It was clear to me, though, that I had not really seen the vision whole or held it in view long enough to grasp its shape and design. Not having seen it clearly, what I had written about it could be no more than marginal—hints, intimations, penetrating a little into the chaos, but not really making a synthesis. There was no real reason to expect, either, that I should succeed any better in the future, though as to that, I always had hope, sometimes faint, sometimes strong. It was certainly true that the genuinely creative moments of most discoverers had come earlier in life than the age I had now reached, and if I had not been able to make mine by the age of thirty-five, it was not too likely that I ever should. Still I did have a faith that kept coming up powerfully even in my worst moments.

How is failure lived with? I found out in the years 1925–32. The trick was mostly to do something all the time and to do it intensely. At least that is what I did. Besides, I had extremely interesting tasks. One of these, I was a little amused to see, threatened to gain me the favor I had not been able to win from my more serious efforts. This was my study of agricultural policy. Actually, it had rather long consequences, since it would take me into public life, but it was certainly not entered into as a field of specialization with any very serious intent. My first interest in it was wholly subsidiary to the more comprehensive one of integration, for agriculture, as I have intimated, was the one clearly comprehended field of economic activity in the whole economy. This was paradoxical. Farming was still a small-scale enterprise for the most part. The old pattern of owner-managership still prevailed (in reality there was a growing number of tenant farmers, but most of them worked under close supervision, and their units were small). Farmers competed disastrously with each other in the markets and indeed always had grave disadvantages in dealing with those who bought their products. Nevertheless, the very obviousness of their weakness in a business economy had resulted in attempts to offset their disabilities by indirect means. Farmers had political strength, and that had counted in gaining governmental cooperation. There was by the 1920s an agricultural college and research station in every state,[20] and attached to each institution was a system, reaching into nearly every county, of advisers on agricultural practice, commonly called county agents.

This system, being managed from a state center and being financed with federal aid, could and did offset to a degree the isolation and inexpertness of the individual farmer. If he consulted his county agent diligently, he could be kept informed about productive practices. He also had some help in his even more bothersome problem of marketing, although county agents were never quite sure how far they could go in protecting their clients against middlemen. The agents not only gave advice and dispensed information, they also gathered data, which economists at the state colleges made some use of. There was also a Bureau of Agricultural Economics in the Department of Agriculture in Washington, into which the data from the whole nation had been flowing for years. More was actually known about agriculture, collectively, than about any other widespread activity carried on in America. That some attempt should be made to use it in the farmers' interest was inevitable, in spite of the middlemen's influence in the federal department—especially during Republican regimes.

A devoted civil servant, W. J. Spillman,[21] had seen that the

---

20. These were the so-called land-grant colleges, mostly founded under the Homestead Act of 1862 and having had as their first financial aid the funds from the disposal of government lands; but these original funds had been supplemented by various federal aid measures, such as the Hatch Agricultural Experiment Stations Act of 1887 and the Agricultural Extension Act of 1914.

21. Author of *Balancing the Farm Output* and one of the important figures in the shaping of agricultural policy during these years.

farmer could meet the middleman and the processor with equal strength in bargaining if he could gain as much control over supply as they had over demand. He could never do this as long as his operations were carried out individually, without knowledge of what was needed or how much others were likely to supply of the need. Spillman organized what was called "the intentions to plant" program. This went as far as was possible in a voluntary system to redress farmers' disadvantages. By a system of quick crop reporting, possible because of the widespread county agent network, it would be known before the season began how much of each staple crop would be planted. Multiplication of this number of acres by the average per-acre production would furnish a likely total of the supply for the whole country. If this total threatened surpluses or deficits, word could be sent out and each farmer asked, again by the county agent, to reduce or increase his planting by a certain percentage. Something like a balance could thus be reached.

The catch in this was obvious and, as a matter of fact, limited stringently the effectiveness of the operation. Farmers who thought others were going to reduce acreage would increase theirs to take advantage of the shortage. Voluntarism had this drawback, but there was, nevertheless, a nationwide system capable of being used for achieving balance. When it became clear that it would never work well because of those who did not cooperate, advocates of government intervention began to appear. Only through government could the majority discipline the minority. Soon the farm bloc in Congress would be pressing for action, but it could not agree on any method except passing on to foreigners the farmers' problems by exporting surpluses—at below domestic prices if necessary.

During these years, there was fierce activity in the financial centers; money was being made and lost in manipulation and speculation. The farmers' troubles were peripheral as far as Wall Street was concerned. All the promoters' dreams, it seemed, were coming true. Speculation in big markets, especially in New York and Chicago, was truly fabulous. It was the champagne-and-diamonds, glitter-and-show extravaganza so well caricatured by Art Young, the famous *Masses* cartoonist. The market cities were where the easy money was spent. An observer, if he did not look around carefully, might think the prosperity more extensive and significant than it really was. There may have been clerks, elevator boys, and other little people who made killings on Wall Street. There must have been; there was so much talk about it, and so many others were persuaded to risk their savings in trying to make a killing, too. Actually the prosperity was not widely diffused. Real wages during the boom decade hardly rose at all. And the farmers, however overlooked, had been in desperate trouble since 1921. They, with their workers and families, were more than half the population at that time.

By 1921, after peace had returned even for ravaged Europe, the changeover from armaments to civilian production was not difficult for industrialists. Steel makers could turn from armaments to automobile parts, structural steel, bridge members, and other peacetime goods. So could other manufacturers. In fact, they found a market eager for civilian goods after several years of shortage. But the farmers, who had extended their operations because Hoover's Food Administration and President Wilson himself had begged them to, found that the home folk could not eat any more than they had been eating during the war and that the Europeans could produce their own food—or if they could not, they were unable to buy more in America, since no more loans were being made to finance the purchases. Farmers had been encouraged to mortgage their land, extend their holdings, buy expensive machinery, plow up the western plains and consign an unprecedented volume of wheat, corn, hogs, cattle, and cotton to the central markets. These had suddenly shown huge surpluses. Prices had broken, then tumbled and plunged. Wheat, for instance, had fallen from two dollars to fifty cents; cotton from thirty cents to five. In fact, as farmers always maintained afterward, this had been the result of a deliberate conspiracy. The push, they thought, had come when the Federal Reserve Board had raised its rediscount rate before their fall marketing had been completed. This grievance would be carried for a long time.

Such a disaster to so many producers could not have been ignored by any president except the one who happened to be in office and the two who succeeded him. It was not ignored by Secretary of Agriculture H. C. Wallace, but he had exhausted himself in the effort to interest his superiors and in the end had failed. Harding and Coolidge took no advice from him. Secretary of Commerce Hoover told them that anything remedial done for farmers would be taken amiss by the business community. Representatives in Congress from the agricultural states felt the pressure from home, and however reluctant they might be, voted repeatedly for relief. It was around this nucleus of congressmen that the "farm bloc" was formed. All the weight of business bore against them, and the processors' powerful lobbies alternately worked with and betrayed them. They did make a considerable stir, however, and were heard, if not heeded.

There began a rich offering of suggestions, most of them requiring magic for success. The problem was to relieve the farmers' distresses without offending businessmen. None of the several suggested plans for accomplishing this impossible feat could, of course, meet the conditions, but the air—for the radio had by now become an accepted medium of communication—was alive with discussions. So, as a matter of fact, were the more serious journals. The result was confusion confounded. Legislators, seeking earnestly for some remedy, were more mixed up than anyone else. Farmers were growing more and more desperate. Something would have to be tried.

Interest in a public policy for agriculture was not exactly new for me; but the added incentive for studying it now was the favorable climate for exploration. Every politician hoped for a solution, and some sort of compromise legislation was becoming more likely year by year. One difficulty still was that there were three national farmers' organizations: the Farm Bureau Federation, the National Grange, and the Farmers' Union. Each was disinclined to accept any suggestions agreeable to the others. Their lobbyists in Washington spent a good deal of time jockeying for position. They had not been able to convince the Republican administrations that relief was necessary, but as the surpluses grew greater and prices fell further, more and more farmers went bankrupt or became tenants. In consequence, agitation steadily increased. It was heard in Washington, if not in New York. It frightened members of the Congress even if it did not penetrate Wall Street's new-era blandness or the circle of Harding and Coolidge advisers.

It was in this atmosphere and for these reasons that I began to study the problem more intensively and to write about the situation of the farmers in a business economy. I was naturally critical, but my real interest was in the discovery of a formula likely to redress the balance temporarily while a more lasting solution was looked for. What little agreement existed in Congress on action to be taken centered in what were called the McNary-Haugen bills. These were the first crude approaches to the control of those whose lack of discipline was fatal to attempts at voluntary acreage adjustment. I analyzed these and offered certain criticisms. They were administratively defective, certainly, and they had not, I thought, hit on a central idea of sufficient appeal. As yet I had no comprehensive suggestion of my own, but I was beginning to see a possibility.

There would be an election in 1928. In the summer of 1927, Coolidge, vacationing in the Black Hills of South Dakota, issued his "I do not choose to run" statement. From then until convention time in 1928, other candidates were frantically searching for a politically feasible way to appease the farmers. This was difficult for a Republican, but Governor Frank O. Lowden of Illinois had the kind of connections and background the other candidates lacked.

What Lowden himself lacked was an idea. I was startled to have a note from him in the fall of 1927. He asked if, when he was in New York a little later, he might come to see me. I suppose he pictured —in fact he admitted as much when we met later—the author of certain judicious articles as an elderly professor. Of course I replied and said that I should call on *him;* whereupon he asked me to lunch at the Commodore. I was impressed. This was my first experience with real political activity. His suite was extensive, and there were numerous secretaries and assistants coming and going. The luncheon was interrupted several times. I had asked if I might bring Harry Carman with me, because he, too, was interested in agricultural matters, and the governor finally found himself so deep in discussion with the two of us that he peremptorily shut off interruptions so we could settle down to a long talk. It is of no importance now because Lowden's political ambition was frustrated, but it meant much to me because it gave me a glimpse of a good political mind confronting a dilemma.

The governor may have been interested in agricultural policy because of its possible uses to him personally, but he had a firm grasp of all the problems. As (in my opinion) any citizen should, I told him he was welcome to my services. I admitted that I was an incorrigible Democrat, but that only amused him. I saw him once or twice thereafter and sent him a good deal of material for speeches. But since it soon became apparent that Hoover was to be the candidate, I did not exploit the invitation he repeatedly renewed to visit him at his Sinissippi farms in Illinois.

My acquaintance with the governor, slight and tentative as it must have been for him, meant a good deal more to me at that time than I consciously realized. A medievalist might be valuable to an academic institution; a geologist might also be useful for several reasons; so might a biologist; but I had discovered that one who could be called expert about something heated by the play of interests upon it might be in even greater demand—by politicians if not by academicians.

Before I even saw Governor Lowden, my agricultural studies had been interrupted by an unexpected opportunity to go to Russia in the summer of 1927. The trip was undertaken under sufficiently favorable auspices but turned out to have enough farcical elements to furnish Stuart Chase, Bartlet Brebner, and myself, particularly, with amused recollections for years to come. It was to have been a trade union delegation, but in the end there were fewer genuine trade unionists than "experts" who were asked to accompany them. The unionists were James H. Maurer, the grand old mayor of socialist Reading and president of the Pennsylvania Federation of Labor; John Brophy, president of District 2, United Mine Workers of America; J. W. Fitzpatrick, president of the Actors and Artists of America, usually called the vaudeville union; Robert Dunn of the Civil Liberties Union; and Silas B. Axtell, counsel for the International Maritime Union. Going along besides Stuart Chase and myself were: Paul H. Douglas of Chicago; Bartlet Brebner, my historian friend at Columbia; Jerome Davis of Yale; Arthur Fisher, liberal Chicago lawyer; A. H. Hopkins, national chairman of the Committee of 48; Carleton Washburn, superintendent of schools in Winnetka, Illinois; and Carlos Israels, son of Mrs. Belle Moskowitz, of whom I shall have something to say later.

The impresario of this enterprise was Albert F. Coyle, editor of the *Journal of the Brotherhood of Locomotive Engineers*, who had all the instincts of a showman but less ability to organize than anyone I ever met. Until we arrived in Russia and were taken in hand by Intourist, he seemed to improvise each day's activities, continually causing us to miss trains, lose members, and arrive at rendezvous with hosts who had never heard of our coming. There was always an explanation, a voluble one, and somehow everyone was repeatedly gathered together and started toward the next objective. We were gone from home only ten weeks; yet in spite of the casual arrangements and the uncertainty prevailing after Coyle admitted to having lost all his funds in Warsaw, I think, as I look back, that I have seldom crowded more experience into so short a time.

The bag of trade unionists captured by Coyle was not very impressive. The more conservative union politicians knew very well that they ought not to go to Russia even if they should return to damn everything they saw. This was the prudent attitude, even though the communist phobia was already diminishing toward the time when President Roosevelt in 1934 could recognize the Soviet regime; similarly the Russians were in the midst of what was called the New Economic Policy, initiated by Lenin as a practical means of getting a start toward industrialization. Tourists were being encouraged, outside assistance was accepted, even if sourly, and actually some American capital and a good number of technical personnel were being used. It was only ten years after the revolution, and the country was just struggling out of the dishevelments left from that upheaval. Trotsky still had a ministry, although by now not an important one, and the forced reforms of agriculture had not yet been undertaken, although there were many state and collective farms. But for several years, Gosplan had been an object of enormous interest to students of government, and such information as could be had about its workings was eagerly studied. Compared with later exchanges, it seems to have been a time of quite free intercourse. Soviet literature was available; economists, agronomists, and scientists took part in international meetings; a large purchasing organization had been established in the United States (Amtorg) and took pains to court American opinion. On the whole, although we were not really well informed, we did have a good deal of preliminary instruction, and there was every reason for getting more.

Lincoln Steffens, after his trip to Russia with William Bullitt in 1919 on behalf of President Wilson, had returned to Paris and announced dramatically that he had seen the future and that it worked. At the time, it seemed to most of us Progressives who had had no real contact with Communists, Russian or American, that there were vast possibilities of progress even if they were in spite of than because of communism. To begin with, there were the enormous half-explored areas of the Eurasian continent; also there was Gosplan and state operation to provide the opportunity for planning and direction. As development went on, this might avoid the spectacular wastes of business and draw all the national energies together into one powerful effort.

It was too early to judge success or failure in 1927, but it was not too soon to lay the groundwork for further appraisal. For myself, also, there was an interest in Gosplan as a means for economic integration. Liberals, however, had difficulty distinguishing between Gosplan and dictatorship and between dictatorship and the operations of the secret police. I was a long time in seeing that planning may be—indeed must be—clearly separated from execution. Twenty and thirty years later liberals would still be writing diatribes about "planned economies" when they meant dictatorships. I should not be so long as this in getting straightened out, but I had not arrived at it in 1927. This confusion, arising originally from orthodox prejudice, but being uncritically accepted by others who should have known better, would be responsible for depriving the United States of central planning for several decades. On the way, there would be some notable casualties, such as the National Resources Planning Board, a useful agency whose members went as far toward appeasing congressional reactionaries as any government agency could but which was killed anyway in 1943.

The journey began pleasantly. We crossed on the old *President Roosevelt,* most homelike of all the ships I have ever known (before she was retired, I was able to cross on her twice more), and landed at Plymouth. Instead of going up to London on the boat-train lying at the docks, four of us hired a car. So in the high summer we rolled slowly up across the southern counties, taking three days, stopping to see Exeter and Salisbury Cathedrals and Stonehenge, sampling here and there strawberries and clotted cream and the meat pies and cheeses of tradition. A few days in London were a magical coming-to-life for me of places I had read about from childhood. I saw everything through literary lenses, as any American is apt to do on his first visit. Even the palace of Westminster was the place where Anglo-Saxon liberties had been hammered out in the great exchanges of the past rather than the debating club of twentieth-century politicians hanging on to an empire becoming restless for independence.

We crossed to Belgium and Holland. There—omitting any account of numerous mix-ups—we were taken in hand by trade union representatives. We saw Antwerp, Brussels, and Amsterdam by bus: cooperatives, housing projects, union headquarters, and a few factories. At Dortmund, Chase and I played hooky for the first time and stealthily visited the Heine Museum while the others went to a steel plant. Our success in this was an intriguing discovery, one that we recognized we might abuse. Nevertheless we persisted. The habit had one debatable consequence. Stealing off one day to see modernist paintings in Moscow, we missed an interview the others had with Stalin. It was a poor guess on our part; we had been good the day before and gone to see Trotsky and thought we had done our duty by the high command. Paul Douglas, who was more determined in his earnestness than usual that summer (for a personal reason) reproached us for lack of seriousness.

By then, however, we were about to separate anyhow, I going on a journey down the Volga and up into the Urals, Chase to study Gosplan, Brebner to analyze the operations of the typical provincial town of Poltava in the Ukraine, and the others to make various other excursions. Our small group was gone from Moscow for some two weeks. We were several days on the Volga, where I was much amused to hear the Volga boat song over Moscow radio, while hearing everything but that, it seemed, from the boatmen themselves. It was amusing, too, to discover that what we heard was true: when the steamer stopped, usually for several hours to handle grain or freight, most of the passengers got off to buy melons or cucumbers and bread, then to stroll, men forward, women sternward for a leisurely swim and sunbath. Our interpreter, and the captain, who was also amused about the boat song, undertook to teach us some folk music, and for years after, I would, on the slightest provocation, attempt "Stenka Rasin"—that and "Beulah Land" being the only reliable songs in my repertory, although with help, I would furnish the body for "She Was Poor but She Was Honest," as well as a few strictly Congregational hymns and some old tunes left over from country hayrides. I had some success in teaching the captain "Beulah Land," my pay to him for "Stenka Rasin."

At Kazan, after stopping off at a number of what must once have been rather magnificent country houses but were now children's rest homes, we disembarked and found ourselves assigned to a private railway car for the trip up toward Cossack country, north to Ekaterineslav (where the Czar and his family had been executed), back down to Perm, and then, hitched to the Trans-Siberian, back to Moscow.

We stopped often and long; also we traveled slowly. Our coach was ancient but gaudy, left over, we figured, from the old days when first-class *Wagon Lits* service had been available. We had an attendant, and he had an institution, tended with an assiduity we came to respect in the chill air blowing down from the Asiatic wastes: a huge brass samovar, fired by wood and going most of the time. Wherever there was a factory (they were visited daily, I protesting because I had come to see the state and collective farms), each of us in turn was expected to make a speech. We suggested a little bitterly that we wanted to learn and so would rather listen than talk, but it was no use. So we spoke. But that was no use either. After doing our factual best to tell a crowd something about one kind of activity or another in the United States, *they* always began to make speeches. And always *they* told *us* what our country was like. They were quite certain that we were either ignorant or lying; they quoted supposed facts about hours and factory conditions, wages, productivity—everything having to do with work. They ignored our protests and corrections. This, it should be recalled, was in 1927, before a generation had had time to grow up in the thick atmosphere of official misrepresentation. What it must have been like later, I would be able to imagine. For this alone, I was glad of that experience. I knew from then on how determined dictators come to manage their people.

After a few days, I did succeed in arranging for trips into the deep country. After that, wherever we stopped, I went off with an interpreter and a droschky to see what I had come to see: the old peasant life turning into collectivism. It was not, at that time, turning very rapidly. There were both collectives and state farms where the government had been able to commandeer estates before the peasants could seize and divide them into small holdings, but it was difficult to conclude anything about them because of their recent organization. The agronomists seemed to me remarkably similar to our county agents and well enough prepared to make changes quickly with a powerful government behind them.

There were some country scenes straight out of Chekhov and Tolstoy as the collectivists made us welcome. Sometimes, when the dancing and singing got started, we escaped the speechifying, and all too often there was an earnest Communist present to stop any undue merrymaking. They were the puritans of the regime, holding on to discipline, taking orders literally and seeing them through regardless of custom, resistance, or violence to any liberties the peasants might value. They were enemies in the country then. Many of the peasants hid their produce, sold it in the black market, refused to join collectives, and were generally recalcitrant. They had gotten a firm grip on their land, and they intended to keep it. I understood why later on the Kulaks were liquidated. I am sure they could never, by any amount of oversight, have been made loyal Communists.

On the other hand, the villages had many of the cooperative features of the old *mirs.* Part of the community cohesiveness and self-consciousness might well have been owed to oppression. Village isolation was more easily enforced because transport and communication were lacking. It was quite evident that with less tyranny from bureaucrats and tax gatherers, the peasants would have had what they always wanted. Their lives were primitive relative to some other condition of life, but they knew no other. They were rich in home-grown and homemade necessities and even comforts. The resistance to schemes for modernization, and especially collectivization, would be stubborn. A Russia of log villages scattered haphazardly across the steppes, each living independently, did not lend itself to what the Communists had in mind for the nation.

Rural Russia was the middle ages, preserved with museumlike fidelity. There were none of the appurtenances of Western civilization: no telephones, no internal combustion engines, no electricity, hardly even any paper and printing. On the wide sea of the plains, the pattern of the village—muddy, snowy, or dusty in season, with the wind blowing over it immoderately, and with the violent heats and colds of a northern continental climate assailing it—was repeated endlessly. Yet in the atmosphere there was tension. The stocky, bearded, blue-eyed peasant, deliberately affecting stupidity, must have known that his situation was too good to last. People from the cities, if not his own detested landlord, had always tried to take from him more than he could give up and live. Yet he *had* lived, by artfulness, by sheer toughness, by refusal to die even under the whip. He was obviously nerving himself for another bout with unfriendly fate, and every outsider was looked at with the eyes of those who profoundly believed that nothing good could come from elsewhere.

I thought the peasant might possibly defeat the bureaucrats. Meanwhile the agronomist did what he could. Better seed and better breeding stock were beginning to be disseminated from central stations, machinery was being introduced, and even the tractor, with all its train of consequence, had been heard of in the villages and was already in use on certain big state farms and collectives. The question in Russia, I thought, on long, slow drives over the rutted tracks that passed for roads, was whether the peasants' stubborn resistance to change could be overcome. Everyone would soon know that the party, after years of frustration, would decide that their race with time required stern discipline, and the rural holocaust of the thirties would result. But as I had my short look, that struggle was just beginning.

In Perm, our coach was put on a siding before being hitched to the Trans-Siberian. We visited more factories while we waited. I had another amusing moment, when, coming to the end of an assembly line in a factory where they made a familiar cream separator, I saw workmen attaching the enameled nameplates of the Wisconsin firm whose machines had obviously been copied. It was impossible not to wonder whether they believed the label necessary to the operation. Afterward, on occasions when I was tempted to relate this and similar other incidents to illustrate the Russian situation, I hesitated for fear of strengthening the all too readily believed impression of stupid incompetence.

We had some time in Moscow after our journey. I used it to gather material, to talk to officials, and to sightsee. We were subjected to a good deal of entertainment. For some reason it was thought that a good way to impress visitors was to stage youth gatherings, workers' meetings, and excursions to rest homes and hostels in the surrounding country. I suspected that we were being used as capitalist exhibits. It was obvious that our hosts had been told what to look for when they gazed at us, for although we were taken to inspect, we invariably landed on a platform to be sharply interrogated. I simply stopped going; I often went instead to see what could be seen on my own. There was no objection to this, but there was some puzzlement that the youth organization of the so-and-so plow factory should not be an irresistible attraction. I did get in two more trips to the country, but farming in the Moscow district had less interest than in some others, and I learned nothing new.

Our time was so short, however, that almost before we could really exchange the impressions we had gathered on our separate ventures, we found ourselves again on a train going out toward Warsaw, Berlin, and Paris. I was back in New York in time for the fall term.

We were not through with Russia. A few summer weeks there was not much, but it represented more experience than most Americans possessed. We had gathered enough material to put together a very respectable symposium volume in the course of the next year called *Soviet Russia in the Second Decade*. My contribution was an account of agricultural organization. The writing of this made me curious, in a way I had not felt before, about agricultural policy in other countries, and I made up my mind to have a look at as many of them as I could manage in the next few years. I suspected that some of the problems perplexing our government might have been solved in one or another of the European countries.

The problems of the Russians, of course, were quite different from ours. They were not bothered with surpluses; they provided credit for farmers; and the processes of dispossession at work in the United States were reversed there. The farmers were still getting land away from their landlords instead of giving it up to them. They might not be able to keep it on the terms they preferred, but they were certainly not a depressed sector of the economy, drifting to the city, abandoning the land, and generally to be pitied. To be a peasant was to be ignorant, isolated, and reactionary; but these old conditions were getting better, not worse.

The reaction of my colleagues—especially of my seniors—at Columbia was typical of the public in general. There were a few who were interested in our observations, but only a few. Seager was so intrigued that he took a party on a similar trip the next summer.[22] That we had gone to Russia at all was mostly regarded as vaguely disloyal; that, having gone, we should exhibit a detached and appraising attitude was at least unusual. Even among those who were our everyday familiars and who knew us intimately, we offered so serious a challenge to deeply held prejudice that they too were inclined to question our reports. The times I was told that I had been shown only what the Communists wanted me to see were innumerable. None of us were partisans of Russia or communism; we were, in fact, liberals to whom the dictatorial features of communism seemed intolerable.

I finally wrote a temperate article for the *Political Science Quarterly,* saying that after reviewing Soviet economic intentions, modifications of the Russian system in the direction of freedom and of our own in the direction of collectivization might in time reduce differences to manageable ones. I saw nothing, I said, to be excited about. Russians had not changed; if they had a police state now, the only change from the past was that it had Politburo rather than czarist direction.

I was not especially conscious of it at the time, but I was there-

22. Seager died of a heart attack during the trip.

after to be a little suspect. None of the Nearing case odium had been carried over into my Columbia career as it might have been. There had been no feeling that I was the unreliable sort until I went on this Russian journey and came back friendly to the Russian people, even if convinced that communism was a sinister system. I would have these suspicions to contend with for a long time.

New York in my time, however frequent the old English and Dutch names may have been in the inner circles of the great financial and commercial firms, was conspicuously the home of later immigrants. Some of them had come from overseas—and not from Holland or England—and some from every corner of the United States. Remarkably few of my colleagues seemed to have been natives of the city; Morningside Heights was a kind of island in a restless sea. Even physically it was islandlike, standing as it did considerably above its surroundings. It rose gradually from the south, beginning at Ninety-sixth Street, but much more abruptly on all the other sides. Down a slope to the west was the wide Hudson with its Riverside Park; to the east the tides of black Harlem, swept up to the foot of stony cliffs; and on the north, streets went down to the Harlem valley. We lived and worked thus somewhat apart from, but very close to, the city's busy body. Broadway, Amsterdam Avenue, and Riverside Drive ran through our precincts, carrying heavy loads of traffic. We looked on one side over a dismal stretch of rooftops hiding slums, deteriorating year by year, and on the other over at least the upper reaches of an active harbor. It was impossible for even the most unworldly scholar to detach himself from the currents washing through the campus. The Broadway subway took us to Times Square in ten minutes and to Wall Street in twenty. The *New York Times,* carrying the heaviest freight of information from all the world of any journal ever known, lay fresh and voluminous on our doorsteps every morning. We could not very well escape knowing a good deal of what went on at home or abroad, in New York or in Iowa, Mississippi or California, China or Africa. It not only filtered through our precinct but through our minds as well.

Our efforts, it must be said, did not seem to have practical consequences. The America of the twenties was rolling toward its judgment without benefit of academic advice, and anyway there were those among us who were rather its apologists than its critics. What criticism there was often did not go to the moving causes. There were thoughtful seniors among the faculty who shaped for us verities concerning a careless civilization: Harold Urey, T. H. Morgan, Michael Pupin, Walter Rautenstrauch, E. L. Thorndike, Thomas Reed Powell, Wesley Mitchell, Carlton J. H. Hayes, James T. Shotwell, Selig Hecht, Howard Lee McBain, Franz Boas—and, of course, John Dewey—were among them. They would have been giants in any company. Nevertheless, we could learn a good deal more about the past than about what was likely to come. It was said of history, and history's sister subjects—anthropology, archaeology, paleontology— that guidance for contemporary decision might be found by studying what had happened in other times. I never doubted that, but I discounted it. The cultivation of learning about vanished civilizations was done mostly for its own sake, not for light it might throw on our surging movement into the future.

It was one thing to produce knowledge about man and his environment; it was another to draw the lessons. The duty of social scientists was to explain, not to justify the existing environment. The world was a long way from being perfect, what with wars, depressions, crime waves, and so on. But to listen to a good many of the apologists of that day, it was impossible to conclude that the American environment could have anything to do with generating these problems. So much energy went into defending established customs that this sometimes seemed the purpose of the effort. That this system was rooted in competition; that much of it, as Steffens had said, was indistinguishable from racketeering; and that because it called out the worst in men, it ought to be changed was fiercely rejected. Veblen had been content with this conclusion; another generation of scholars, accepting his view, nevertheless felt the need for working at the constructive tasks of betterment. They wanted to bring their learning to the specific service of the future. This was the reformers' hope in the twenties.

One who had reached such conclusions and who had strong impulses to contribute something toward a better future could, on the whole, work satisfactorily at Columbia and in New York. He would have moments when the decisions he must make would require differing with friends, but these never made great difficulties for me as they did for some others. I can think of one possible reason for this as I look back. I was not overly given to imputing motives or judging others. When colleagues disagreed with me, I was not disposed at once to say that they had been cowardly or unconscientious. This situation was eased also, I suppose, by satisfaction in my college work. There was almost no gathering of cliques, playing of favorites, back-biting, or jealousy. Everyone really seemed to be helping everyone else. There were necessarily times when some of our number had to go, but they always went, I think, with kindness in their hearts for those of us who could stay. Indeed, they usually went as missionaries for our Columbia ideas concerning higher education.

In those predepression years, there was room for tolerance, and just the having of it was a comfort. I presume that the senior professors in economics and perhaps even Hawkes and Coss, who were in a sense my sponsors, were asked some searching questions when I went to look at Russia and came back asking for understanding. Questions must have filtered down from the upper levels. It may well be that a sharper eye than I realized was kept on me from then on. There were arguments, acrimonious within reason, but I was never made to feel unwelcome; indeed, I do not believe that I was.

I was, however, being drawn into outside activities. Evidence of this, disappointing in the end, was my contact with the Smith campaign for the presidency in 1928. This did at least bring me closer to a group I had long admired and felt much in common with: the staff of the *New Republic.* Certainly it was a notable occasion for me when Herbert Croly asked me to become a contributing editor. This was in 1928, and for the next eighteen years, during professorial, then governmental, service, the connection would not be broken. I know now that I served through that journal's good time, not the greatest —that was during Croly's more active period in Wilson's presidency and the immediately succeeding Republican years—but still one with considerable impact on public policy.

Croly's purpose was not to improve men in the biological sense but to educate them, draw them into a continual discussion of public affairs, and thus improve their public behavior. His *Promise of American Life* was one of the books, along with those of Steffens, William Allen White, H. G. Wells, and others, I had read as an undergraduate at the Wharton School. It had had just that mixture of optimism and critical warning calculated to move me. The nation could become transcendentally rich and worthy; the materials were present; but there were disquieting possibilities of another sort.

Croly said that those who were powerful in the land were not concerned about well-being and justice for all; they were, in fact, on the make, without vision, and therefore likely to perish. The Bull Moose discouragement of 1912 had driven many of the young generation to accept the determinism of Marx; others had merely given up in disgust and resolved never to be taken in again by phony leaders. There was plenty to do in making a career; and many simply gave themselves up to it. Croly's offer of new hope was the complete opposite of Steffen's nihilism; it seemed to lead to something on our side of the water such as the Fabians had been developing in Britain: a kind of middle way between the rigid dogmas of communism and the cruelties and wastes of free competition. It infuriated the intellectuals of the *New Masses*—it was milk and water to their raw meat— as well as the reactionaries, who saw it leading to a drastic reformism more disturbing and dangerous, actually, than an open revolutionism they could denounce. Croly was insidious in this way, offering a chance to be of use to those who dissented from the indifference so characteristic of our attitudes and who hoped for the fulfillment of the American promise he defined so persuasively.

The first issue of the *New Republic* had been published in November of 1914, just as the first moves toward international conflict were being made. My mentors at Pennsylvania were attracted to the journal. Subsequently I had read it week by week. As nearly as a preachment could, it gave us a text to live by. It helped to reconcile us to participation in the conflict; later it justifiably denounced the peace of Versailles; and in the postwar years it still held out the possibility of better things to come.

The *Promise of American Life* had other readers than discouraged young university instructors. Among such others there happened to be Willard Straight and his wife, who belonged among the most affluent of American families. They, too, were concerned about degeneracy in public affairs. In subsequent conversations, they discussed the idea of a magazine edited by Croly and subsidized by the Straights. The understanding was summarized in a memorandum that could serve as a statement of progressive aspirations in those years.[23] It was large with belief that a new world could come into

---

23. It can be found in Groff Conklin, ed., *The New Republic Anthology* (New York: Dodge, 1936), pp. xxxiii–xxxv.

being, the product of man's will and the riches he commanded. What the intellectual could do, even if excluded from direct participation in affairs, was suggested:

> Formative criticism which proposes to reinforce the will rather than to betray it is bound to be radically progressive. Consistent conservatism is necessarily dogmatic. It attaches final authority to some particular formulation of political and social principle and demands of the loyal believer that the legal or social dogmas be accepted without question and without modification. But this is precisely the kind of intellectualism which falsifies the relation which ought to exist between thinking and willing. It is the kind of thinking which in the long run will be the enemy rather than the ally of active enterprises—the enemy of the adventurous impulse which had prompted men to abandon their customary paths and to take their chances as social explorers and builders. The enterprise on which the American nation has embarked is that of seeking the realization of a comparatively complete political and social democracy. Whether or not the enterprise shall be attempted is fundamentally a matter of will—that is, of faith.

And what was said about human nature was wholly in agreement with conclusions some of us had arduously reached. Americans, he thought, had a better chance of achieving humanistic ideals than their fellow workers in Europe:

> The operation of economic processes is steadily depriving too many Americans of the opportunity of labor upon which they could formerly count and of the enjoyment of the fruits of their own labor. Year by year the proportions of the American people who work in agriculture and industry, and who do not, and have no reason to, consent to the existing methods of producing and distributing wealth, is increasing. They feel themselves chained to an economic machine which their masters either cannot or will not control. The danger is that they will finally revolt and destroy the machine without much regard to the effect of their destructive work upon their own welfare or that of society. . . .
>
> The ordinary American citizen who works with his hands, and many of them who are supposed to work with their brains, for a living, are not getting a fair chance. The existing economic institutions of society are responsible for the default. It is extremely difficult to remedy the default, and there is every reason for attacking the problem with consideration and caution; but somehow it must be attacked. The people now responsible for the political and business management of

the country are evading it. They are standing pat, or they are making a great parade and noise about insignificant and futile concessions. There is just one way to shock their complacency. The disfranchised majority must take advantage of their numbers and reach in the direction of all the economic and political power that they can.

If discussion is to amount to more than a shock-absorber, it needs to be transfigured by a common conviction of the latest regeneracy and brotherhood of mankind. Only in an atmosphere provided by such a conviction will deep class conflicts be fought out and ventilated until a constructive solution is reached. The contending parties will remain contentious in spirit, peremptory in their claims and coercive in the final methods unless they share with their opponents an affirmation of the latent possibilities of human institutions and traditions.

Early in 1914, Croly foresaw the devastating war about to begin. It seemed just then that the ardors and talents of that generation might go to the creating of the mighty commonwealth he contemplated. What soon followed was very different and profoundly disappointing. In the next half century much talent would be appropriated for military uses, and the new journal, just being launched, would be more preoccupied with perplexing international affairs than was expected. Its first period of this sort—from 1914 to 1919—did set it firmly in the intellectual foreground. So close was the rapport with Wilson that, while his presidency lasted, it was regarded as a kind of unofficial spokesman. Frequently suggestions appeared in its pages in advance of official action and clearly seemed to be a foreshadowing of what followed in Washington. It was widely believed that it was used for floating trial balloons. Its circulation was then the largest it ever had. When Wilson consented to the Versailles treaty, he was abruptly abandoned by the *New Republic.* Never afterward did it have the cachet of apparent White House approval; those who had looked to it for advance intelligence canceled their subscriptions. It went on, still guided by Croly, but no longer with such ebullient hope in the national future.

The magazine had published a few book reviews and articles of mine before 1928,[24] but I had not been a member of the editorial group. After fourteen years, the editors were still regarded as interpreters of progressive aspiration. Necessarily, however, they were

---

24. The only article of mine chosen for the *Anthology* was one published in 1926 ("Chameleon Words," August 25).

now sharply critical. They embraced no dogma and were properly skeptical of imported panaceas. All of them, moreover, were gifted and serious writers, and this was one of their attractions for me.

I am not certain now about the precise time of my first invitation to dine at the unpretentious house on West Twenty-second Street, opposite the General Theological Seminary, where from the first the editorial offices had been housed. It may quite well have been, as I seem to recall, that H. N. Brailsford, one of the contributing editors, whose articles on British affairs were published with some regularity, was a guest of honor and sat on Croly's right; at any rate, I sat on Croly's left and looked across the table at Robert Morss Lovett. Flanking him—although I may have this evening confused with later ones—were Oswald Garrison Villard, owner and editor of *The Nation,* and Norman Hapgood, then the editor of *Colliers.* I cannot exactly recall how many of the editorial board were present, except that George Soule, who was already a friend, sat on my left and John Dewey just beyond. But I believe that Walter Lippmann, Stark Young, and Francis Hackett were there. The talk, in such company, was becomingly responsible, yet somehow rather lively than grave, ranging widely, both in subject and in geography. It was something new for me to join in discussions likely to foreshadow the immediate appearance in print of responsible pronouncements. I was by then used to thinking of the country as a whole, with reference to tradition and incident, and trying to visualize alternatives to policies deplored by Progressives; but here the technique was projected upon the whole world by professionals in political discussion. I felt as though now I had graduated to something like a higher level in my chosen work.

I felt then, as others did, that since Americans had a continent of their own, they would soon have a much more secure repository for their common culture. Internecine wars on the scale of the one just past were not won by the victors. The Allies, in fact, were no better off then the Germans, who had lost. Reparations and debts were a plague to statesmen who, if they knew how to dispose of them, had little freedom of action. It was the Coolidge view that our allies had "hired the money" and ought to repay it, and the majority who supported him agreed. Germany could not meet the bill for reparations, and the Allies were not disposed to pay us.

These issues were endlessly discussed among us at Columbia. The Coolidge attitude was being brought nearer to reality by the Dawes and Young missions. The international bankers were selling quantities of foreign paper—notably German bonds—in American markets. This movement of capital outward enabled Europe to buy at least some American products, which they could not have done if the flow had been in the other direction. But this was temporary. These obligations—like the war debts—would never be fully repaid. Economists knew this. How could a less productive Europe, confronted with tariff barriers repeatedly made more severe by the Republicans, accumulate dollars to repay their debts? It was good business for bankers, which was why it was carried on. That it must come to a dead end in the same impasse as the war debts was certain.

This was one of our preoccupations. Such matters were being discussed weekly in the *New Republic*. With Brailsford present, I am sure we must have talked about other issues as well. For Brailsford had been for a long time—and would be for a long time in the future—obsessed by restrictions on liberty, and wherever in the world it was in jeopardy, he felt compelled to intervene.[25]

Dinner in that house, with Croly presiding, was an occasion of some small state. Those gathered around the table were gifted and voluble, conscious of their responsibility for interpreting traditions of tolerance, cooperation, sympathy, equality, and freedom. They had come together through trials of competence, secure, of course, in the Straight endowment. All were ambitious to further the causes Croly had so eloquently defined, to bring to bear, week by week, the knowledge and wisdom of the intellectual community on organized affairs.

A French couple kept the house, and the food and drink were good in the French style. The service was dignified; and the ritual moved with the conversation, the host quietly giving the lead. His thin hands moved among the dishes, his distinguished head rather shadowed from the centered light, his eyes, kind and inviting, were turned first upon one, then upon another of his guests. They were at their best in his presence, and gave what they had to give quite easily, finding it fitted to general experience in his neat summaries.

I had hoped to be asked to come again. I thought that perhaps I might because a suggestion, in an after-dinner aside, had seemed to

---

25. Twenty-two years later, in 1950, I should be invited by Kingsley Martin to lunch with the editors of the *New Statesman* as they discussed the editorial attitude the journal ought to adopt concerning Germany in the aftermath of another war. And Noel Brailsford would be there, too, still arguing that even Germans should be free.

excite Croly's interest. I was beginning to have, I said, a kind of connection with the Smith preconvention campaign. It might develop into something more. I proposed to bring the experience into the *New Republic* circle, to give and to take. Who knew but that both might benefit. There was some possibility that the journal might in this way come to have, as it had had in Wilson's time, that disproportionate influence its position as the representative of progressivism entitled it to. Smith's success was not probable, but if he should succeed, he would need the help of experienced Progressives. I did not yet understand him fully, nor did Croly, but we were not long in discovering the national reactionary behind the New York liberal.

The spring of 1928 had its excitements. When it became apparent that Smith, now serving his fourth term as governor, would very likely be the party's nominee for president, the usual scurrying around for experts began; and no one else so readily available had my familiarity with agriculture. Smith had never considered its problems himself. This was not strange. A governor of New York in the booming twenties might be aware—as Smith was—that the prevailing prosperity was not shared by a good many people, but he would not be likely to think of farmers as having special disadvantages. He had been born and raised on the lower East Side of New York. No one had to tell him that there were slums, that wages were insufficient and hours of work long, or what women and children underwent in the sweatshops of those days. His record of melioration for this kind of thing was notable, and had, finally, earned him an enviable record as a practical liberal. His accomplishments were the more remarkable because all the time he had remained a Tammany chieftain.

He liked to recall that he had joined his local Democratic organization as a ward heeler and had worked his way up. He had done all the things an ambitious politician must do, helping to carry on the machine's complicated system of small favors in return for votes. Finally he had become one of the governing crowd. He must have known all about how such a system is habitually perverted: how contractors bargained for jobs, how criminals were sheltered for a price, how the regulations protecting workers from hazard could be evaded by politicians and employers working together. No one ever said that he had had any profit from it; and when he came to be governor, he knew the kinds of law and law enforcement necessary to put an end to the abuses. Because he was himself a chieftain and was never in the slightest degree irregular, it was impossible for his colleagues to punish him. Getting to power must have cost him many a bad moment. It is not necessary to join in corruption to be touched by it; just knowing about it makes one an accessory, and Smith must often have closed his eyes to what was going on. Once arrived, though, he had set out to make changes. And his constituents, because he also had a genius for communicating with them in the New York vernacular, supported him.

He was perhaps a more popular governor for always having had a hostile legislature to deal with. It underlined and emphasized his determination to bring decency into labor relations, into factory and shop standards, and into public business. Because he was so knowledgeable and so vigilant, he would have been a good governor anyway; the Republican majority, always opposing his eminently practical proposals for reform, made him a nationally recognized one. He was quick witted, even if almost, in the academic sense, illiterate, and had a capacious memory. He also possessed a talent for absorbing what was told him, however difficult or complicated, and an ability to translate what he learned into popular jargon—a definite political asset.

His regularity in Tammany Hall was matched by his regularity as a Roman Catholic; that this was an almost insuperable barrier to the presidency went without saying. It had probably kept him from gaining the nomination in 1924, but religious prejudice was itself a kind of challenge to many Americans of a liberal sort—to Franklin D. Roosevelt, for instance, who had nominated him in 1924 in a notable speech. The miserable failure of John W. Davis, the Wall Street lawyer who had been given the nomination, had made it seem almost certain that Smith would be nominated in 1928. It was hoped that, in spite of booming security markets, the notorious Harding corruption would be remembered and that Smith might have a change of election.

Then, as Belle Moskowitz realized, there were the farmers! She had discovered, to her surprise, that rural voters outnumbered urban ones. Belle was Smith's good angel. She had worked to convince him that the New York reforms, now famous, were necessary, and she had had the executive ability to make them effective. In everything having to do with these affairs, she was his alter ego; besides, she had gradually moved into wider authority as he had learned to trust her. She —with Judge Joseph M. Proskauer working at the higher party levels —was now in charge of his preconvention campaign. When I was formally asked to meet with her, I was pleased; from what I had heard, it was better to see her than to see the governor himself, since it was she who would decide, in such an unfamiliar field, what ought to be done.

Farm policy was obviously no simple matter. It required some delicate adjustments in the whole economic system. Of this I think I convinced her in our first talk. She was a reformer herself and inclined to think that middlemen were responsible for the farmers' difficulties. If they were, there must be some way of regulating them, just as the sweatshops had been brought under regulation in New York. She grasped my explanation that there was a gross maladjustment between the whole of agriculture and the whole of industry and that it was necessary to reestablish a rough equality—farmers exchanging goods with city workers, enabling each to buy what the other produced.

After thinking about it, she objected that this meant raising the price of food, and it was so high now that many people had too little to eat. I explained that everyone who was employed had at least something to eat. The cause of unemployment was that farmers had so little purchasing power. If even in times that were called prosperous, there were four or five million who were unemployed, it was because the twenty-five million rural people had so little income that they could scarcely buy anything. Their machinery wore out without replacement; they could not keep up their buildings or even buy the new clothing the garment makers in New York might have made. She saw that. But she was still afraid of higher-priced food. And so, she said, would the governor be. I said I had no doubt that packers, millers, and the textile merchants played both ends against the middle, keeping farmers' prices down and consumers' prices up, but mere regulation would not readjust the balance. Nothing but real help for the farmers could do that.

Prices cannot be operated on directly, I said; that is, they cannot be fixed, not in our system. But the same effect might be gotten by guaranteeing farmers minimum prices for corn, wheat, cotton, and so on. How could the government do that? By judging, I said, how many acres of wheat or cotton the nation needed, by seeing that only so much was planted—at least for domestic consumption. Prices would take care of themselves if the present heavy surpluses were liquidated and an orderly planting program worked out.

She said it sounded pretty drastic. Wasn't there a simpler way? Yes, I said, the Republican way. They proposed to dump the surpluses abroad and keep on dumping them at any price they would bring, paying the farmer out of government funds the difference between what was received and what had been agreed would be a fair price. My scheme, I thought, was more realistic. There might be some small exports, but foreign markets were already resistant: there were farmers abroad, too, who would not like competition from subsidized American products, and they had influence on their governments. We had to meet our own problems honestly and at home. The fact was that our farmers grew more of certain products than was wanted. American workers were ill fed, but that, in turn, was because farmers could not, so to speak, employ them. It all went back to the need for orderly management of what was really a fair exchange of farm products for industrial goods. The balance was now upset and would stay that way unless something was done. Farmers, I insisted, were the underprivileged in our economy, and I was convinced that their difficulties were holding back the whole. They must somehow be assisted.

I had written a number of articles on this theme, but when asked outright to shape a program to be used by an aspiring candidate for the presidency, I was appalled by the limitations. Such a suggestion would have to be politically acceptable as well as practical, which was more complicated than it appeared at first. Farmers' incomes might be lifted by limiting the supply of the products they raised, but they themselves would resist that solution. They wanted relief, but they thought of themselves as having a right to do as they liked. The Department of Agriculture had been trying voluntary limitation, and it had not worked. On the other side, trying to reduce the prices paid by farmers for what they had to buy would be just as bitterly rejected by business, and workers would join in opposition. Yet there were two sides to the balance, and the public finger had to press down the one or lift up the other. Or, possibly, do both.

It was arguable, of course, that public intervention was responsible for maintaining industrial prices at too high a level. This may have started the trouble. Industries had been protected by tariffs, and industrial monopolies had been allowed to control their own prices. Lowering tariffs and breaking up monopolies would have been better Democratic doctrine than the kind of management I advocated. But such a program probably would not be effective. The farmers, for one thing, believed, against all reason, in high tariffs. Furthermore, after huffing and puffing about monopolies since 1890, Americans had very little to show; monopolies still existed. No, something more drastic was needed.

I tried faithfully to think of something. I finally took Belle a memorandum containing what I called an Advance Ratio Price Plan. In effect, it was an anticipation of what afterward was generally called "parity." It was my idea that farmers should be promised in advance certain prices a year for the product of a certain number of acres—calculated on an average that would yield the amounts consumers had shown they would buy. Farmers could grow more, but they would be allowed to market only as much as their certificates called for, that is, as much as would on the average be produced by the acres they had planted. This was crop control. But an allowance was to be made over this for what was sold abroad, and on a liquidation day, they were to get a proportionate share of these returns.

It was not a bad plan, considering that it was worked out in Hamilton Hall of Columbia University without the help of any of the many experts I should like to have consulted. There were agricultural colleges in all the states, and there was a Bureau of Agricultural Economics in the Department of Agriculture. I said that a serious program ought to be devised as a joint effort. I thought I had a good idea, but it needed people of experience to say what was wrong with it or to suggest the many administrative devices it lacked. As it stood, it was no more than an outline. Presumably Belle talked it over with the governor, but I never saw him. Although her group kept in touch with me, and, in fact, talked with me about other economic problems, nothing came of the agricultural proposal. When the Houston convention met, the professionals descended on the now-nominated candidate and sold him their bill of goods: no limitation on supply, copious dumping abroad, and all the rest. I afterward heard that George Peek, a farm machinery manufacturer from Illinois, was the chief salesman; later I would meet him.

As I look back at this effort now, it seems to have most of the elements of the farm relief scheme so painfully worked out some years later, but that is of no more than minor historical interest. Smith was not—and did not deserve to be—elected. Hoover was to face the consequences of Republican policy, outraged farmers along with all the rest. I was to write what for me was a notable series of campaign comments in the *New Republic* and to become a contributing editor. I speak of this, I realize, as though it were accession to the College of Cardinals. But that would hardly be too inflated a description. The editors, as far as I was concerned, were an anointed company. A contributing editor was not so important as might be thought by outsiders. I could write more often for the journal, but whatever I wrote still had to pass editorial scrutiny just as it always had. However, in 1928, during the months until midsummer, I made frequent comments.

After the convention, I abandoned politics and went abroad for a year. I was due for a sabbatical and was certain by then that Smith would not be elected and would not be a good president in my terms if he were. That judgment was not reached carelessly. On the contrary, it was the product of close contact with his advisers, of running comment by Croly, of serious study of the issues, and of careful watching of the man himself as he approached his apotheosis.

I had wanted very much to believe that Progressives had found a leader, but Croly knew better. He had written an article on Smith in February, a doubting analysis. Because he brought to bear his sense of our institutions, and because he suspected Smith's credentials, he had been pessimistic. I had perhaps shaken his certainty by an early enthusiasm, but Croly proved to be right in every way. It was an educative incident for me, and I have always been grateful for it, although I recall the transition with some retrospective pain.

Smith, Croly said, did have an unprecedented popularity in his own state, the result of belonging to a homogeneous community: not the city but Tammany Hall, although the two tended to be confused. Smith had risen above his environment and shown admirable capacities. New Yorkers liked to think of him as an urban Lincoln—the rags to riches saga with an East Side birthplace substituted for the traditional log cabin. This was a mistake. He had been a smart Irish lad with a talent (which had then seemed to be his only one) for amateur theatricals with a vaudeville flavor. When he turned twenty-one, the leader of his district, Tom Foley, got him appointed to a petty job with the courts. He had never since—except for two years between terms as governor—been off the public payroll. His relatives had been similarly taken care of. His whole life had been shared and contained between Tammany and the church. At thirty he had been sent to the state legislature, a complete product of his parish and district organizations.

Smith had had no idea, Croly said, of what he might do as a legislator, no consciousness of public responsibility. But since he was freer in Albany than he had been in New York—except when he was given orders—he began to be educated merely by paying attention to the business before him. He was still the comic actor, still without intellectual interests, but he had a sharp mind and soon began to understand what legislating involved. He had returned year after year to Albany—beyond the time, in fact, when Tammany ought to have given him a better job. His first nomination for governor in 1908 was hardly a suitable reward for his faithfulness; he had not been expected to win. But he had pulled through with a narrow margin. Since then, because of the record he always pointed to with such effect, he had always run hundreds of thousands of votes ahead of his Republican opponents. His Democratic constituents and also many independents supported him. He had carried out an amazing list of reforms without being regarded by anyone as a reformer. This magic, worked in the empire state with its immense political weight, was what had made him a candidate for the presidency.

Croly thought there was not much in this except political legerdemain. The nation needed something more than a politician, ready as he might be to adopt certain reforms if they seemed necessary. Actually Smith's popularity came from his possession of a talent for acting, not for good ideas. There was doubt that Al Smith of Broadway and the Bowery could become Alfred E. Smith of Washington. He would, in such a translation, no longer be to the manner born. His acting on such a stage would be likely to fall flat, and everyone would then realize that he had no other resources. His long apprenticeship in New York legislative and executive business might be more a handicap than an advantage because he had no power to generalize and project this onto larger affairs.

Said Croly: "The difficulty is, I suspect, that Al Smith, as a nursling of both Tammany and the Catholic Church, is accustomed to depend too much on authority. He can move around with perfect assurance and address within ascertained and permitted limits, but outside these limits he does not know what to do with his fine intelligence." And later he outlined Smith's dilemma: "We can understand why hitherto he has disappointed so many of us as a Presidential candidate. He is not sure what to do. If he takes an aggressive line and tries to connect the Democratic party or his own foreign following to a questionable program, he probably could not be nominated. If he sits tight and plays poker, he probably can be nominated, but he cannot be elected."

Historians will remember, but there are few others to care now, that what Smith did was to play poker, but he was bluffing with an empty hand. And his acting—brown derby, vernacular speech, and all—was received very coldly in parts west of Buffalo. He was badly beaten.

I had been in Europe, then, for some time. My attempt at a *tour de force* with the *New Republic* had been unsuccessful. My articles had, I thought, pointed to the larger issues Smith should have mastered; but his political people had paid no attention whatever. I had finally dropped away from the group of advisers in New York, and when Smith embraced the familiar Republican agricultural theory, I had lost interest.

For one like myself who had been very busy for almost a decade with educational matters widening out to a hopeful interest in national affairs, the year was a valuable interlude—something like going into retreat. It was apparent that some kind of crisis was approaching. In spite of the feverish activities in lower Manhattan, rising to a higher and higher pitch, there were signs of trouble. Unemployment of serious volume could no longer be denied; employer-employee relations were worsening, so that strikes tended to take on characteristics of civil wars, and farmers were sinking lower and lower into misery. No one could predict when the harvest of trouble would begin. Some of us had anticipated it for so long and had said so often what it would be like that our warnings were no longer listened to; the "new era" sirens seemed justified by the prolonged delay. I myself went away with a modest list of common stocks whose value appreciated almost enough to pay for the not inconsiderable expense of family travel. So I must have concluded, too, that the delay would be indefinite.

We had passage on the *American Trader* of the American Merchant Line, a trim freighter with a small passenger list, which went directly to Tilbury Docks in the Thames. It was a smooth, ten-day midsummer trip, and after the busy years, the withdrawing peace was a benison. My daughters found the ship delightful, though soon enough they would rebel against travel and imperiously demand a settling down. For the moment, however, the newness and the change were a fair exchange for the Wilson harbor home they regarded as the reward for city winters.

I had been given a research fellowship to study the agricultural policy of France, but I had a year to do it in, and there was no hurry about starting. As we steamed up the Thames in an early mist one August day, our plans were pleasantly indefinite. I wanted to visit the old English universities. Beyond that, it was pleasant to contemplate some lingering in the countryside, seeing the farmers keeping up the breeds of stock and plants they had exported to us. There were many times more acres of wheat, more herds of Hereford cattle and Hampshire swine in America now than there were in England, but this was the home source. It was a kind of return.

But it was more than that, too, for my ancestors had left this land not too long ago; my paternal grandparents had been born and raised on the Surrey-Sussex border. There were many Tugwells there yet. I had the curious feeling that I had come home, in a way, to my own land. It was the land of Chaucer, of Shakespeare, of Dickens, and of Hardy. Then too, it was the home of John Stuart Mill, of the Fabians, of Shaw and Wells and the Webbs, of Graham Wallas, Hobhouse, Barker, Marshall, Jevons, and Tawney, in whose ways I was trying to follow. I was conscious of an overall Western unity. The renaissance represented by Shakespeare, Marlow, Jonson, Spencer, and Bacon had not, I knew well enough, been born here. It had appeared in Britain long after its flowering in Italy. I could begin in Bloomsbury, go on to Cambridge and Oxford, and then upstream to France and Italy. But that threads ran out to India, Africa, Arabia, and so to many other places around the world, I could hardly be said to be aware—no more than intellectually aware, at least—for although I had learned my lessons well enough, imperialism was not much more to me than an opprobrious term. I felt, as my liberal principles required, that this kind of thing was in liquidation. In spite of having observed one war for *Lebensraum*, it did not worry me. I was thinking of America as the inheritor and interpreter of the new renaissance. Industrialism was ugly, but the British factory system had been uglier; and so, probably, had been the trade of the Medicis. It could pay its debt, as they had, in a new flowering of that culture whose home place had been here.

It was a rich prospect, and I was well set to enjoy it. I was not too ill read either, in revolutionary and military history. Since my war year in Paris, I had read more of French history. The Palais Royal would mean much more to me now than it had when I had worked within a hundred yards of its gates; and I saw Versailles as part of a pageant I had hardly understood at all when we had picnicked there on lucky Sundays in 1918. It had been a long decade. I was hopeful, in the optimistic vein of my tradition, that all I could see and absorb would somehow be put to use.

First translation was from the misty bustle of Tilbury docks to the Victorian comforts of the Hotel Russell in Bloomsbury. The weather was most un-English; it was much like what we had left in New York. Since our funds were ample, we excursioned a good deal. London, with its solidity and leisurely pace, its green squares and monuments, was what it always is to Americans, aloof but not unfriendly, with an unmistakable air of possessing everything of any account. Then we went on to Oxford—an Oxford hardly to be seen any more since the city's manufacturing activities have so greatly expanded. The colleges were bedded in the pasture green of the shires; Balliol and St. Johns were just across from our hotel, crumbling slowly to reveal a kind of inner glow. A new generation of students, just descending on the town, was filling its streets, its playing fields, and its gardens. I found, wandering through the courtyards and fields, the release I had wanted. I regretted that some of my student years had not been spent here. They might have been if I had known enough to want it then; but very probably I should not have found in it the satisfactions I could imagine now. The truth is, I knew quite well that it would have been no sort of preparation for my kind of life.

Oxford may be old and ritual ridden, but from time to time, appendages are added to it, that are gradually absorbed into its fabric. So, a little withdrawn, there were some modest buildings housing an Institute of Agricultural Economics. What, I wondered, would Duns Scotus have made of that? As is always true among scholars, I was made welcome there. Those were the days when C. S. Orwin was in charge, and he and his younger helpers gave me every facility. I read there for a while and made extensive notes. The time approached, however, when school had to be considered. We went on to Switzerland.

Lausanne, even in October, was penetrated by a thin chill wind from the encircling snowy mountains, and we were drawn southward. One night in a sleeping car, rolling out into France and down the Rhône valley, we were taken into the Midi; and in the strong sun of morning, we looked out at the countryside of Provence. Summer still lingered there. The rocky coast of the Mediterranean on one side, the Maritime Alps on the other, the *Grands Express European* bore us right down to the Italian border. At noon we were lunching on a terrace in Mentone, the sea before us and orange groves all around. The hotel, just being readied for the winter season, was empty except for us, and the attention we got was overwhelming. But after some exploring up and down the coast, we found a small house in a side street in Cannes: the rue St.-Jin Jin, an amusing saint, evidently, who brought a smile to French faces at mention. And there we stayed until well along in the spring, my elder daughter living in a boarding school in another part of town.

I was away a good deal during the winter, pursuing my study. But the places where I pursued it had more than a specific interest: Paris, Geneva, Rome, and Montpellier. In Paris I did a good deal of interviewing about the ministry, in the Ecole des Sciences Politiques, and among the various agricultural and cooperative associations. Unfortunately I found no collection of documents through which I could bring my investigation out of the large air of discussion and into its specific stages. Presently I went to Geneva and worked for a while in the library of the International Labor Office where there was an agricultural section. Then I tried for more realism by visiting the French agricultural college at Montpellier, and finally I went down to Rome for a month at the International Institute of Agriculture. By spring I was on the way to having the material for what I expected to be a book on the comparative agricultural policies of Britain, France, Germany, Switzerland, and Italy.[26]

---

26. This book was never written. My fellowship was paid for by a monograph on French agricultural policy, published as a series of articles in the *Political Science Quarterly* during the next year. Events pushing me then prevented further development of the material, and presently it was out of date.

Even the most devoted student need not spend all the hours of every day in specified occupations. I was learning a great deal about things other than my subject. Now I recall my various journeys as quite other than academic adventures. My few weeks in Paris at the beginning of the winter were pleasantly Bohemian. They came at the end of a bus trip from Nice over the passes Napoleon had used on his return from Elba (our house in the rue St.-Jin Jin had a balcony overlooking the beach where he had landed and where General Patch was to land in a later invasion with, among other troops, a combat team from Puerto Rico), through Digne, Grenoble, Bresse-in-Bourg, Autun, and Melun. The Latin Quarter was gray with winter mists, and the streets were despondently foul; but nothing so superficial as persistent wetness could hide the graces of Paris. I had seen it in another winter, a grimmer season than this. Its order was an organic one, out of the mind of planners. Along the wide boulevards, the awnings were shelter enough for its admirers, with the braziers lit and apéritifs on the tables. The talk, the eternal talk, was hardly less than in the warmer seasons.

Almost at once I ran into the inevitable Americans. Allen Tate, for instance, was having a year of resuscitation, and we were faintly acquainted as fellow contributors of the *Nation* and the *New Republic*. He, of course, had a circle, and they took me about, although I had almost nothing in common with them. On the occasion of one of our meetings, these friends introduced me to a short, oldish, fat man who looked, I thought, a good deal like pictures I had seen of H. G. Wells. I presently woke up to the realization that I had been talking casually for an hour or two with Ford Madox Ford. I was flattened. I knew him from far back as a collaborator of Joseph Conrad but also as the author of a magnificent war tetralogy; I had *The Last Post* in my baggage, as a matter of fact. I only saw him once again, and if he displayed a certain surprise that an economist should show lively interest in literature and in his work in particular, he made no comment. He was a tireless raconteur but had gone a good deal to seed, liking too much the adulation of the young and spending too many hours, I suppose, beside his favorite brazier on that betraying corner of the Boulevard St.-Germain.

I called on André Siegfried, whose *America Comes of Age* was currently being read, but he was studying Britain now and no longer had much interest in America. Edouard Dolleans was a good deal more cordial, and we reached a mutual liking, which resulted in correspondence for years to come. As for other French intellectuals, the inability of most of them to be other than condescending made any kind of interchange difficult. I was baffled, as I had been before, by this complacent provincialism flying on occasion the tattered banners of old imperial glories. It prevented Frenchmen, realistic as they held themselves to be, from understanding what was happening to the world, their parts of it particularly. A French professor presented set lectures, carefully written in his study, and amply studded with references to authority. They were beautifully delivered, strictly shaped, and there was no denying their conclusions. But the premises might be wrong and the subject, in view of everything, so trivial as to be frivolous. Education, like much else in France, was antique and brittle; learning was meticulous but not wide.

Some others of my Columbia colleagues were in Paris at this time—among them Will Ogburn—just finishing a series of studies of postwar France. Frenchmen who read it would learn more about their country than they had ever known before. There were courtesies over the interchanges involved in this, but I doubt whether policies were much influenced by any of the voluminous findings.[27]

Cannes, as much as I experienced of it, was agreeably dull. I had not quite realized—no visitor does quite realize in advance—the enormity of the hoax involved in presenting the Côte d'Azur as a winter haven. The sun shines often, but the *Mistral* often whistles down from the Maritime Alps. Ice frequently ground among the clumps of seaweed on the shore a few feet from our door, and several times our waterpipes froze. Still, aside from some discomforts, it was a good time. There was always the mountain backdrop, and the mimosas bloomed early. I bought an old Renault whose career was fast coming to an end, but it carried us back into the mountains and along the byways of Provence. It did this with reluctance; still, with a kind of triumphant effort, it always landed us back in the rue St.-Jin Jin, even if long after dark, when the furies seemed to be riding the wind out of the mountains toward the open sea, and the flimsy house was frigid.

I learned something in Provence that every New World visitor needs to learn. We forget, with our space and openness, the sheer

---

27. This series was edited by Carlton J. H. Hayes. Ogburn's volume, published in 1929, outlined the economic development of postwar France.

preciousness of land. Our grandchildren will doubtless realize it, but our generation was still not far from the pioneers who broke virgin prairies or slashed and burned whole forests. The peasants I saw here were piling stone upon stone of mountain terraces whose first courses may have been laid in Roman times. What does a man who inherits a hundred generations of patient toilful management and can hardly extract a living from his holding know of the highly capitalized farming enterprises in America? And how can Americans appreciate the jealous protectiveness of a peasant with three acres along the Mediterranean littoral? A searching eye could see, low on the mountainsides, flowers, fruits, and even wheat, cultivated in strips a few feet wide or in tiny valley fields, irrigated by small canals, in ways unchanged from times when memory runneth not to the contrary. If the eye followed toward the higher slopes, it could see narrower and narrower terraces until finally, there were only the ruins of others. Even an infinitude of labor had not been able to hold them against time and erosion. Toward the very top, where sheep and goats now ran, there were faint but regular circling traces, the marks of battles long lost with the elements.

Provence, outside its watered strips and fields, had a long, dry summer when everything green wilted or burned in the cloudless heat—a country somewhat like our Southwest for cactus and mesquite, sage and greasewood. Melting snow and stored rain, gathered and channeled downward at uncounted cost—uncounted because generations of labor had been anonymously absorbed in reservoirs, terraces, and dwellings—made it seem to the visitor a kind of paradise. But it must have been anything but that to the peasant who tried to make a living there. The illusion was heightened by the perfume industry centered in Grasse. There were whole fields of jasmine, tuberrose, carnation, and lily. To the visitor a field of roses was a bed of flowers; to the peasant, I could imagine, merely a poor-paying crop.

The English had made the Riviera a pleasure resort in Victorian times when the profits of empire were large and untaxed. A statue of an English lord still stood overlooking the harbor square in Cannes. There was no better-beaten path in the world for the well-to-do than that from Dover to Calais, on to Paris, and thence by the Blue Train to Provence. In these between-war years, the English were still everywhere, but there were Americans, too, those who preferred the Riviera to Florida or southern California. The cult of the sun could be pursued with appropriate lavishness on the artificial beach at Juan-les-Pins or on the rocks at Cap d'Antibes. There were painters everywhere, trying to catch the light and color.

I worked in the mornings. Here, in fact, at Clyde King's invitation, I wrote the most thoughtful of my general essays about agricultural policy. I called it "Farm Relief and a Permanent Agriculture." As I read it now, I realize that by then my conception of policy was already shaped. It was, of course, only suggested, because my space was limited. If anyone had had the foresight to imagine that an associate professor of economics from Columbia, on sabbatical leave in Europe, would have an influence on important decisions a few years hence, he could have known to what end that influence would be directed by reading my short essay written in that Mediterranean winter. Speculation about what I thought would, later on, be fairly feverish for a while among those whose interests would be affected; but in those days, the scanning of every sentence I had ever written would be for the purpose of culling from them such discrediting sentiments as could be patched together. It would be clear enough that I was coming to the conception of a national policy transcending all local and particular privileges and that this interest would have to be embodied in a system of regulation.

Wherever a lever could be found, the disadvantaged would have to be lifted up and the privileged made to give way. This involved abandoning the idea that individual interests came first and that what was best for all could emerge from the effort of everyone to get the best of everyone else. If these were discrediting sentiments—and my detractors would be quite certain that they were—they were mine, and I would stick with them.

That spring, after my visits to Geneva, Montpellier, and Rome, we went north again to Paris and to Oxford. After a month, I went down to Dorchester and carried out an old project, put away for just such a time. I reconstructed for myself Hardy's Wessex and worked out the locale of the novels I knew almost by heart. I fairly wallowed in antiquarianism. As far as I was concerned, it was the best time of the year. But presently I had to go back to France; the study I was making still required a few weeks in Paris. We spent most of the summer there after an interlude at Dinard-St.-Malo, and since it was very hot, it was not very comfortable for the girls. I did get my work done, and besides, there were some excursions into the countryside: a day at Chantilly, a week at Barbizon with all its recollections, explorations at Chartres, along the upper Seine valley, and around and about Versailles and St.-Germain.

In Paris I heard that my only sister had died suddenly, and I knew that this would be serious for my father, who had been extraordinarily devoted to her. How serious it would be I could not know. When I saw him again, he had aged prematurely; he never recovered his characteristic resiliency. He would fall an easy victim to the economic troubles of the next few years and slowly decline, sorrowing and lonely in spite of grandchildren and, indeed, of all that could be done to comfort him. In this way it was a sad homecoming. But it had been a year I had needed, important in shaping and firming my attitudes.

For the second time in my generation, a season of jeopardy was about to open. It compelled us to give up all our ordinary preoccupations until we had survived it. There had been hard times in the past; but, being optimists, Americans had never prepared for more of them. This one, although the admission was to come with dragged-out reluctance, was a very unusual storm. It was, in fact, to be known in our lifetime as the Great Depression. In 1893 and 1907 recovery had been mostly by the cruel passive processes of deflation. There had been lessons, but few of them had been learned. It was even believed that enough was known about business cycles to avert their worst effects. It turned out that this was not true, and that our resolution was infirm even about what had to be done. The trouble was that, as in so much else, there were differences about who should be required to do what. When the requirement pointed to the powerful, the powerful successfully resisted with long-accumulated strength any measures requiring sacrifice. The first years of our ordeal—indeed most of its history—could well be written in terms of a struggle to evade the responsibilities imposed by economic sickness.

Certainly the evidence of coming trouble had appeared before— as early as 1921—when agricultural prices had collapsed in a postwar debacle. Although it would be untrue to say that protests then had been ignored, nothing really remedial had been done, because it suited the managers of industry to maintain the advantage they held over farmers. It was useless to argue, as some of us had, that injuries to rural America would eventually affect the whole economy. The interests of each were not bound to the interests of all in any visible way. We had an additive attitude: the belief that individual prosperities added up to a whole prosperity, even when it was obviously true that profit had been gotten from exploiting others who had to be counted in the whole, and that subtraction was more in order than addition. We had not learned how to be (in Graham Wallas's phrase) a Great Society. We were to learn it slowly and painfully during the years ahead. Even after prosperity had returned, we still had not devised the instruments necessary for stability.

The first startling notice that a chain reaction had set in came in the fall of 1929. One day security prices tumbled; they recovered a little, then fell again and again. Then panic set in: not only did Wall Street brokers require more and more margin payments of those who had no funds, but also creditors everywhere, small and large, fearful of their loans or with commitments of their own to meet, began to demand that debtors pay up forthwith. The economy had been running on credit. Everyone owed everyone else. The structure was like a distended sponge, and now it was being squeezed remorselessly by an unseen hand. Enterprisers whose loans were called in resorted to emergency measures. They reduced expenses at once: they stopped buying; they discharged employees. And so the panic spread. The attempt to reduce most transactions to a cash basis left few transactions that could be carried out at all.

Hoover and his official family, together with the business community, tried to still the spreading fear with reassuring words. There was nothing unusual happening; it was all merely a "readjustment." The economy was "sound"; there was enormous productive capacity to support its securities; there was no reason to distrust the wisest leadership in the world. These words were denied by events almost before they were spoken. Enterprises everywhere were failing; before long banks were having to close because what they were asked to pay out in cash was more than they could realize by calling in their loans. Their portfolios of investments were suddenly seen to be loaded with worthless securities, many held by small banks. These, of course, were the first to fail.

Morningside Heights was a kind of grandstand for viewing the unfolding of this vast tragedy. Somewhere below us—downtown—

the financiers were trying to shake themselves loose from the general debacle. Over in Harlem, under the roofs we overlooked from our Faculty Club, the small people were finding such adjustment as they could to loss of jobs and the incomes they had provided. Below us on another side—toward the Hudson—a sprawling Hooverville soon spread along the riverbank across the railroad tracks. Before long there were thousands of shacks put together out of orange crates, beaten cans, old pieces of rubber, leather, or cloth, their denizens gone back to cave man status, scrounging in neighboring garbage heaps for food and fuel. We read, even in newspapers reluctant to report the facts, that New York was no worse off than communities everywhere else. The whole nation was gripped by the disease, and it showed every sign of becoming worse.

It went on and on. Hoover was still protesting, and volunteer agencies were handing out bowls of soup and crusts of bread as 1929 ran into 1930. The soup lines lengthened in 1931, as did the lists of ruined businesses and closed banks. The railroads were in receivership now; and the insurance companies' investments were obviously becoming worthless. Here and there formerly prosperous people were found starved and frozen to death in their homes. It was an incredible decline from the confidence and the speculative fevers of 1928 when everyone seemed to be eligible for riches with a small down payment on a few blue-chip stocks. We read, too, about farmers in the West preventing foreclosures—good, reactionary Republicans who had voted for Hoover, and back of him for Coolidge and Harding. They were the victims of their own political judgment, and they were resorting to force.

Except for the vicarious suffering anyone must feel with such events going on all about him, we at the university went along as usual, watching, analyzing, commenting, but actually not being hurt. We lost such investments as we had accumulated, but mine, for instance, had been no more than something for the future. Our homes, our family livings, were secure as long as the university was secure. The staff was reduced as student enrollments declined, but those of us who remained did not even suffer a salary reduction. The trustees' ultra-conservative investment policies saw us through.

It was different for my father. His business was paralyzed along with the rest; his chain of small banks discovered that investments of depositors' funds in railway and public utility bonds, in Peruvian or other foreign issues, could not be recovered. After twice replenishing capital out of their own pockets, the directors themselves were bankrupt. They could do no more, and the banks closed their doors. They had done the honorable thing as small businessmen, but the big businessmen they had trusted had let them down. When it was over, my father was almost as poor as when he had started, and now he was old. His world of enterprise had collapsed and he with it. He would live on, broken and helpless, for another fifteen years.

This tragedy removed a source of security I had always felt without knowing it: the knowledge that I would have his support if it should be needed. He was able for some years to hang on to the house in Wilson even though it soon began to show signs of neglect as the paint peeled and the gardens were no longer so well tended. Eventually it was sold, and my parents retreated to a house in the village. Happily it was an old and dignified one, and they were comfortable at least and in the midst of old friends. But this came a little later; while I stayed at Columbia and after I went to Washington, the house and garden by the lake were still a family refuge. I myself in those years began to lose touch, since I could no longer be there during vacation time. My travels had taken me away for two summers, 1928 and 1929. I spent some time in Wilson during 1930 and 1931, but by then I was away a good deal, and my stays were interrupted. I never afterward had one of the old seasons on the harbor.

In 1930 and 1931 I was carefully composing a book. My intention was to make a concise synthesis of economic realities and to see what public policy was required by our contemporary situation. I felt that unless the depression was allowed to drift into a complete breakdown, there was no chance of adopting public ownership on any large scale and of bringing our large industries under a common policy. Some way short of this had to be found to set up among industries and with agriculture mutual relationships allowing all of them to operate as part of a whole. The lack of this connective tissue, I thought, was responsible for the sickness we were suffering. I finished this book in 1931 and called it *The Industrial Discipline and the Governmental Arts.* Its last chapter outlined a central establishment for maintaining interconnections. Columbia University Press agreed to publish it, but I was meticulous in the revising, and by the spring of 1933, it was just in the galley-proof stage.

At almost the same time, another considerable enterprise reached the publication stage. In 1931, I was asked by E. E. Day, who was then in charge of the Social Science Division of the Laura Spellman Rockefeller Foundation, to undertake a reassessment of social science teaching in American universities and to make a report on possible revision. This could be, Day said, a guide to the foundation in its distribution of funds, at least, and might considerably influence the teachers. In view of everything—my known radicalism, if it could be called that, and my dissatisfaction with the orthodox approach to this subject—it required courage, I thought, to select me for such a task. But there were, I could see, some reasons for it. I had been one of the shapers of the Columbia program; I had written a text, *American Economic Life,* illustrating a new approach; and also, with the depression deepening, many people finally realized that our troubles went to the very foundations of our economic system. Something dramatically new might be received with more tolerance than at any time in the past. At any rate, I undertook it with enthusiasm.

In preparation, I visited a representative list of universities to find out how such subjects were currently being taught. Some six months were devoted to traveling; I went pretty well around, especially anywhere that new ideas appeared to be sprouting, making notes as I went, and considering what I had learned. In discussions with teachers of economics, political science, sociology, and social psychology, I collected such ideas as I could and discussed them with contemporaries. There was dissatisfaction everywhere with the kind of preparation students were being given. Often some kind of new approach was either being made or being planned, many of them inspired by our start at Columbia. The universities were poor, like all other institutions, for the depression had hit them hard, but I found courage and a willingness to make a new start. The enthusiasm I started with was added to by every conversation I had, and gradually, I acquired the conviction that something of a really helpful and remedial sort could be done with the immense resources of the foundation and the enthusiasm of all these widely scattered colleagues. I hoped I might suggest something of a genuine alternative to what was now so unsatisfactory.

The report for the Foundation was prepared with the assistance of several colleagues. Leon Keyserling, who had been a student in the college and had recently finished his work at the Harvard Law School, undertook to assist me in the editing and, specifically, in the study of the social objectives in the American college; my friends T. C. Blaisdell, C. W. Cole, and Joseph McGoldrick were assigned, respectively, economics, history, and political science as college subjects.[28]

Several others made comparable studies of education at the college level in other countries.[29] Altogether it was a formidable undertaking; when the study was finished with the assistance of Keyserling and the others, I had a good deal of satisfaction in it because I felt it had paid, as well as I could pay it, the substantial debt I owed for the privilege of collaborating in a decade of educational change at Columbia. It appeared, finally, in two handsome volumes published by Columbia University Press.

My own essay was almost a book in itself, although the compression was considerable. I tried to comprehend in one limited statement the essence of the American aspiration, to show how it had sometimes been perverted, and to suggest how a full-running vigor could be guided into genuine progress. I put into it all my knowledge of our history and literature, our way of life, and our talents. My specific suggestion was that there should be a definite turn toward the future for educational materials. Rather than rummaging around so industriously in the past, it might be possible, by exploring where we wanted to go, to assemble a wealth of materials concerning future alternatives and put students to work sorting them out. In the process they would necessarily make up their minds about a good many matters, but they would also learn that easy solutions are not to be found and that an experimental and tentative approach was essential. Since we were considering the social studies, and since society was always in flux, there would never be a lack of materials. It had not been easy for us at Columbia to put together the course in contemporary civilization; but with persistent effort and steady support, we had achieved a good deal. It remained to complete the task by showing how the past built up to the present and moved through it into the future. The best part of an education in the social studies would consist, I thought, in the

---

28. Leon Keyserling was, later on, after service as Senator Wagner's secretary and in several government agencies, to become chairman of the Council of Economic Advisers; T. C. Blaisdell, who would go to Washington with me and move around a good deal, was to become assistant secretary of commerce; and C. W. Cole would become president of Amherst College and later ambassador to Chile.

29. Horace Taylor, Germany; Bartlet Brebner, Canada; Jacques Barzun and Robert Valeur, France; Boris Schoenfeldt, Russia; Shepherd B. Clough, Italy; J. H. Wuorinen, Scandinavia.

effort to anticipate these thrusts into the future, to judge their promise, and to devise techniques for shaping them to our aspirations.

In the printed volumes containing my essay and those of my colleagues, I did not include my specific suggestion to the foundation.[30] This was that an institute be set up, a kind of service organization, where, along with original efforts to push out into the probable future, the materials could be gathered and prepared for making the study of the future as vivid as the study of the past, thus solving the most difficult practical problem colleges would meet in trying to go over to a new orientation. What became of my suggestion I never knew. Nothing resulted from it; indeed, I never heard of it again. It must still be somewhere in the files of the foundation along with reports of other hopeful reformers.

That this effort came to its most difficult phase when I was beginning to be engaged on another and larger enterprise prevented me from being as disappointed as I otherwise should have been by its reception.[31] As it was, my long interest in education was about to be suspended for some years, but I could not foresee that then. The report was one of the most considerable efforts I had ever made.

It was no accident that *The Industrial Discipline* and *Redirecting Education* were completed just as the Great Depression reached its climactic phase. My own processes were a reflection of the nation's disorganization, a reaction to it, a violent revolt, I might say, against allowing competitive wastes to erode our institutions. We ought to prepare a generation to resist, to take things into their own hands. That was my contribution; and it was at that juncture that I was invited to Albany where Governor Franklin D. Roosevelt was preparing to become a presidential candidate. I was asked to say what could be done, and what I said was at least listened to by a political leader who might actually do something about it.

---

30. *Redirecting Education*, 2 vols. (New York: Columbia University Press, 1934).

31. Not by E. E. Day, who had assigned my task. He seemed to think I had made a creditable investigation and had made an entirely logical suggestion. At least he said so. Day and I would meet again in a year or two under other circumstances, when he would be one of Mr. Hoover's envoys and I one of the President-elect's handymen. Perhaps I should note that Day's abilities were later utilized to the full when he became president of Cornell University.

Separation—1933

By 1933 my work at Columbia had evolved in a predictable direction. I had at first been immersed in the progressive improvement of the course in contemporary civilization to the exclusion of other interests, but within a year or two I had been called on to develop a sophomore course in economics. By then, too, I was assisting in a new venture—honors work for the seniors.

This idea also spread widely as a university activity. Its first promoter was John Erskine, professor of English Literature; but Mark Van Doren and several others, including Hawkes and Coss, the originators of Contemporary Civilization, were also involved. The idea was that seniors with high standing might be directly introduced to the great achievers of the past. There were those in the university who had made their works a lifelong study. The honors students were to have the benefit of this scholarship. My part in this as an economist was to direct the conversations about the French Physiocrats, the German nationalists, and the English expositors of political economy. These were our progenitors. For philosophy and science, others began further back with the Greeks and Romans. It was a working principle that original masterpieces should be confronted and understood.

This was a demanding assignment. As can be imagined, political economy—the dismal science—was not the best received of the subjects we explored. For me there was the added difficulty that although I had the necessary interest in how it had happened that Adam Smith, descending through the English economists—Ricardo, Malthus, the Millses, and, more lately Jevons, Marshall, and our own Francis Walker—had monopolized American economic thinking, I was more and more appalled by the repeated affirmation that the "principles" of the English economists actually governed the world of affairs. These principles were expounded exactly as were the laws of physics. A dozen texts used in college courses repeated in other words the English ideas.[32] I was becoming more and more skeptical of these

32. The more widely used texts just then were those of John Bates Clark, Richard T. Ely, Frank N. Taussig, and H. R. Seager—all called *Principles of Economics.*

"laws." They seemed to me misleading for students who hopefully were being given an understanding of behavior in the market place and productive facilities of our systems. Nevertheless, they were interesting *tours de force*, and I had no difficulty in expounding them as historical instances of attempts to reduce complex phenomena to rules.

I had a sudden respect from my elders in the graduate faculty because of my participation in the honors work. My skepticism about laissez-faire principles was, after all, not the conclusion of an amateur. It seemed that I had been well schooled in the classics, and if I regarded Adam Smith and his successor Marshall as irrelevant to the commercial world, it was not out of ignorance. Before I became a full professor, my seniors had surrendered to the extent of assigning me a graduate seminar in economic theory. This met weekly in the evening, and since I could limit it to a dozen students, and because they were mostly ones who were rising to a professional interest as future teachers or, since we were in New York, analysts or consultants in the headquarters of American industry, the discussions proceeded from genuine dedication and earnest study.

These were my academic employments, but after 1929 the country's terrible troubles made it impossible to resist opportunities to do something about them. This, I suppose, was one reason I agreed to Ray Moley's suggestion that I join him in conversation with Governor Roosevelt as he prepared for his presidential candidacy.

I have written about my experiences in this service (*The Brains Trust*, New York: Viking, 1968) but not about its continuance between Roosevelt's election and his inauguration, a stretch of more than three months of a rapidly degenerating economy and futile government efforts to stem the flood of business failures. The account of this perilous transition deserves a more serious account than it has yet had. Here I can speak of it only briefly and as part of what I should later regard as the trauma of separation from Columbia. At the time it seemed something I must do as a public service and because a president-elect chose to depend on me among only a few others to bring him information he needed and sometimes to argue for the policies it seemed to call for. Separation from Columbia was something I did not think much about at the time. I was only doing what academics had frequently been called on to do.

The real break from the university came on the morning of March 3, 1933, when I joined a mixed company of some fifty of the future administration family at the Roosevelt house on Sixty-fifth Street. We had been invited to travel on his special train from New York to Washington. On the next day the Democrats, after twelve years, were to take over the White House.

Looking back, I would wonder why I had gone along. To be an assistant secretary of agriculture was no considerable honor, and the chance of being very effective during the depression was not very good. I did have some reason, however, to believe that Roosevelt had begun to see the crisis we were in as the dividing phenomenon between an unplanned and a planned economy. It seemed clear to me that it was those free ventures for profit—the central characteristic of business—that had caused our tumble into depression. The obligations of international bankers, the heavy load of agricultural surpluses resulting from overproduction, and the decline of industrial activity —all could have been prevented by the planning we knew perfectly well how to do.

I more than half thought that our discussions in Albany had persuaded the new president that such spells of paralysis as we were now having were avoidable. This one had resulted from a flood of goods that could not be sold because prices did not fall when new efficiencies lowered costs. Because low production and high prices were preferred to high production and low prices, inventories had swollen, factories had closed, and unemployment naturally resulted.[33]

My going to Washington was partly a matter of momentum. Along with Moley, I had been kept busy since the election early in November with duties mostly, but not always, minor. Some were important. For instance, we had had a good deal to do with negotiations concerning the international debts left unsettled since the war. They were then an issue with political implications that no one knew how to handle but that would not long be put off. It was extremely unpopular to show the least leniency to our former allies. At the same time it was obvious that they had no intention of paying. The stupidities of the Versailles treaty were festering. Impossible demands for reparations had come to the inevitable conclusion. But if Germany could not pay them, Britain, France, and Italy had no compunction

---

33. I had developed this theory in articles that Roosevelt had read and commented on. It had been the main subject of our conversations in Albany. These articles were published in *Political Science Quarterly, Bulletin of the Taylor Society,* and the *New Republic.*

about not paying us. Hoover had proposed a moratorium, and Roosevelt had refused to agree. He had, in fact, temporized. Berle and I had assembled his data. We thought payment could be made if there were a will to pay, and if the public debts were given precedent over the private ones. The international bankers were busily asserting that the European governments lacked the necessary resources, but the fact was that their obligations to our bankers were being met. It was true that the transfer problem was difficult. Our high tariffs prevented payment in goods, but that was all the allies had to pay with. It was all very complicated and confused by conflicting propaganda.

The debt situation was only part of the general chaos that had deepened during the last few months. Its most publicized manifestations were financial. On the morning of March 3 as we rolled toward Washington, all the nation's banks were closed. The new president's first job would be to resuscitate such of them as could be rescued from their own follies. We were at the absolute low point of demoralization. Roosevelt had considered an entirely new start with a nationalized system. He had concluded that he could not risk the possible consequences of prolonged paralysis. Business must somehow be resumed, and there must be no delay. With assistance from a good many experts—holdovers mostly—we had worked out a program. He was fairly confident that it would work well enough to start things going again.

Roosevelt obviously meant to savor the moment he had waited for for so long. How, I wondered, could he be so confident? About a third of the nation's working force was unemployed, and many millions of families had little food and uneasy shelter as winter was passing into spring. Before cold weather came again something had to be done to improve their situation and renew their courage, and he would have to do it. It seemed impossible, but if he feared failure, he showed no sign of it.

Besides having been busy with negotiations between the old administration and the new, Moley and I had had many discussions with the president-elect about the moves he had to make as the crisis worsened. These had not been very satisfactory, nor had they seemed to me to be sufficient. I had been unhappy about the evasions of the campaign and had no reason to anticipate any more recognition of our desperate situation in the months to come. I knew by now what he felt he had to do was simply to help financial institutions out of the morass they had fallen into, perhaps with some reforms of no fundamental significance. I doubted whether unemployment relief would be adequate, since the unfortunate promise of a drastic cut in expenditures and a balanced budget had been so categorical. As for agriculture, his ambivalence was unrelieved. He held to the conviction that nothing could be done until the leaders of the farm organizations could be brought to agree on a program. It would be up to us to persuade them that our adjustment device ought to be supported. During the lame duck session just concluded, it had failed to emerge from the Senate's agricultural committee. The chairman had meant to see what favors he could extract from the new administration, but also no concentrated pressure had come from the farmers' lobbyists. Questions settled were less agreeable to these operators than ones still unsettled. The moment of agreement had not yet appeared; it was not clear when it would.

It is true that our work for Roosevelt since the election had been quite different from that during the spring and the months of the campaign. Actually we had been his only helpers. We were concerned with impending actions more than with what those actions must be. One series of conferences had had to do with the upcoming world economic conference scheduled to be held in London in June. Hoover had had two commissioners working on the agenda, and I had been delegated to deal with them.[34]

Our conferring had involved my shepherding them to Hyde Park after explorations and rather unsatisfactory discussions about the agenda. We concluded that the London meeting ought to be postponed since we were so unready, but Roosevelt disagreed, so we went on with the preparations. For this purpose, I was asked to assemble a group of experts to determine what our proposals ought to be, and I had done this. E. M. Patterson, Walter Wheeler Stewart, and a number of others had joined me in several preliminary discussions when Roosevelt suddenly informed me that he intended to make Bernard Baruch head of our delegation; Baruch would take over the preliminary work. I briefed Baruch very carefully and warned him about the differences that were likely to show themselves. For one thing, Roosevelt would not allow the debts to be discussed there. About these he had in mind to invite heads of govern-

---

34. These were E. E. Day of the Rockefeller Foundation and Professor John H. Williams of Harvard.

ment to Washington soon after the inauguration. This left for the conference matters of economic interest—trade and finance mostly. Baruch accepted the assignment, and I notified all my experts, but neither they nor I ever heard any more about it. Baruch never held a meeting, and by inauguration time we were facing an impending conference concerning international problems without any real preparation having been made. Roosevelt was evasive when I protested. What he did not tell me, but what I guessed, was that Baruch was not to be the chairman of the American delegation after all. I did not realize then but had begun to suspect that a kind of delicate evasion of Baruch's claims was going on. That financier had a prestigious place in Democratic councils. He had been chairman of Wilson's War Industries Board during World War I and was known to be a financial supporter of many legislators. He had been an ardent advocate of Smith for the presidency but had suddenly come around to Roosevelt's support only after the nomination had been won. Nevertheless he meant to have the place in the new administration he felt entitled to as a party elder. That place, he had expected, would be as secretary of state. But it was soon known that Cordell Hull was to have that premier post in the cabinet.[35]

Was Baruch sulking? Was that why he had never called a meeting of my experts? He was not among the elect on the inaugural train. I did not know, and Roosevelt was not saying, what Baruch's recognition was to be. I distrusted him. He wore the image of Wall Street and could be expected to have sympathies for the international bankers who had their own interest in the debt settlements and in the maneuvers about finance then going on. But I could not guess what conclusions Roosevelt was coming to, nor, I thought at the moment, did he.

Why, with all my dissatisfactions, was I going to Washington at all—and especially to be an assistant secretary in the Department of Agriculture? I had very nearly refused—had, indeed, told Moley it was not for me. What had changed my mind was Roosevelt's persuasion. We had done a lot of talking, he said, now was the time for action. And there would be much for me to do. It was true that

---

35. A detailed account from the point of view of a careful observer and sometime participant of the events associated with the debt question, the Economic and Monetary Conference, and subsequent policy arrangements may be found in the account of Herbert Feis, *1933: Characters in Crisis* (New York: Little Brown, 1966).

I knew more than anyone else what the preliminaries had been, even more than Moley, whose interest in economic matters was minimal. Then, too, I was mostly responsible for the agricultural policies that were taking shape. The legislation nearly passed in the session just preceding inauguration had been the result of innumerable conferences and repeated rewritings; but it had at last taken shape. Our hope that it could be gotten out of the way before other emergency measures would have to be taken had been frustrated by the one reactionary and egotistical senator, chairman of the agricultural committee, Ellison D. Smith (Cotton Ed) who was holding out for a liberal assignment of patronage.[36] Now the bill had to be revived, and this was my assignment.

Henry Wallace, who was to be secretary of agriculture, was largely unknown. How he would deal with the complicated maneuvers of bill writing and passage Roosevelt did not know. I had been, I think, the first to urge his appointment and begin the assembly of support for it. Now I was agreeing to be his assistant. As I saw it, I was to pass on to him the responsibility I had been carrying, doing my best to help in the early stages of reform. That was all. Then I would withdraw. The incongruity in politicians' eyes of an agricultural official from New York City was obvious, and I had no disposition to struggle for recognition.

As events unfolded during the interim months, the agricultural problem had retreated further into the background of public consciousness, which had never been very alert about farmers' troubles. Roosevelt, however, recognized it as the most important of the calamitous conditions to be overcome even if business failures and unemployment got most of the attention. The farmers might have to wait while others were attended to, but that they must not wait long, he knew very well.

My first responsibility, then, was to resuscitate the adjustment legislation and assist in assembling the support for its passage. That

---

36. We also suspected what turned out to be true: that he had close relationships with speculators who were strongly averse to the regularizing of agricultural markets. But we had not been able to penetrate the senatorial defenses. He simply refused to allow his committee to consider our legislation. He was later outraged by my appointment as undersecretary and was only appeased, as Roosevelt told me, by his own agreement to "the appointment of a couple of murderers" as federal marshals.

I should now have to work through others was understood, since I was to be only an assistant secretary. Meanwhile, Roosevelt said I should do some drastic reforming of the department. He had not given up his notion that it could be reduced by at least the 25 percent he had promised. He had also amazed me by insisting that most of its research should be stopped. All that, he said, could better be done at the state colleges. That prejudice I recognized as coming from Cornell, the bastion of reaction in agricultural policy. I wondered how we had persuaded him to accept the domestic allotment idea, since to the Cornellians it was anathema; in fact, he had resisted until I had assembled for his inspection ample evidence from such authorities as M. L. Wilson and later Henry Wallace, together with the studies I had been making for years. Even now I knew that he would demand an almost unanimous assent from farm leaders and legislators. Since I believed more than ever, however, that rescue of the country from its deep distress depended on the rescue of farmers from the impasse they had fallen into, I had no difficulty in accepting this commitment, and it went a long way to explain why, with all my reservations, I decided to go on working with and for him in Washington even though it meant a temporary separation from Columbia.

I had one considerable fear. It was that, in spite of his professions of fiscal conservatism during the campaign—his promise, for instance, to "balance the budget"—that Roosevelt intended something startlingly different. I suspected that he had listened with approbation to the arguments from the Cornellians—relayed to him by Henry Morgenthau—that the real lift for the farmers could only come from cheapened money. It was easy, they told him. It could be done by managing the price of gold. If the government established a monopoly of the metal, it could determine its price, and since gold was the basis of our currency, dollars could be made worth less by paying more for gold. Berle and I had argued about this at length with him, believing that gold was no longer an all-important determiner of monetary value.

There were echoes in this of old populist demands for cheap money. Since farmers were always debtors, they would benefit by being able to pay their debts with dollars worth less—and easier to get—than when the debts had been incurred. Much of American political history had revolved about this issue. The Cornellians were convinced that the value of dollars was indeed determined by the price of the gold they represented. We had argued the fallaciousness of this, but Roosevelt, we were quite aware, had not been convinced. That he did not really support a "sound money" policy had been suspected by conservatives and had contributed to the uneasiness of the financial community during the winter and spring. Unexpectedly, and for no good reason, I had been held responsible by my conservative colleagues, most of all by H. Parker Willis, the most prominent among financial theorists, for giving Roosevelt such ideas. I had, in fact, arranged for Willis to talk with Roosevelt during the interval. Unfortunately, Willis had been heavily instructive in elementary finance, and Roosevelt had taken a dislike to him. Nevertheless he had asked Senator Carter Glass, to whom Willis was advisor (he had supposedly drafted for Glass the legislation setting up the federal reserve system during the Wilson administration), to be secretary of the treasury. Fortunately Glass had refused, but the invitation had been one of those incongruous decisions he had made as he was shaping his cabinet to pacify the senatorial elders who had sponsored his candidacy. That is, it was incongruous if he did have a hidden intention to follow the advice of Morgenthau and meant to adopt the Cornellians' scheme.

What Roosevelt would do about almost every pressing issue was uncertain; even those of us who had had long discussions with him were often in the dark about what he was settling on. Since I was acutely aware of this, why I went to Washington I have never quite been able to explain. It looked like trouble and confusion. I can only conclude after the cogitations of years that I could not justify nonparticipation even with the prospect of not having much to say about the actions to be taken. I must emphasize this even though it may seem to exaggerate my estimate of the importance I attached to my view of things; but certainly my estimate of the crisis we were in and of the choices to be made turned out to be substantially correct. I felt that traditional laissez-faire had reached its final debacle in the persisting depression. What Herbert Feis (economic counselor of the state department) reported was probably a fair estimate:

Tugwell was in and out of Washington the next fortnight [in February] seeing Hull, Stimson, myself and others. For the first time, during a day-long excursion into Virginia, I was struck by his advocacy of various proposals which would necessitate dictation and control by the federal government. His cold idealistic purpose and intellectual distinction made their mark on me. But at the end of the day I could not shake off the impression that he cared too little for individual liberties and had too little tolerance for individual inclinations, faults and follies.[37]

This remark about me is also a remark about himself and many others—fine people, well fitted into existing institutions—who were frightened by their breakdown but refused to consider any suggestion of a composed order. It was my belief that it was overconcern for those "liberties" that allowed the crisis to happen. I recalled that the Supreme Court, many years before, had interpreted one of the post–Civil War amendments (the Fourteenth) in a peculiar way. That amendment had prohibited the states from making or enforcing any law abridging the privileges or immunities of citizens and from denying any person "equal protection of the law." The relevance of this pronouncement was that what had been intended as a prohibition of racial discrimination was used now to prevent laws from reaching corporations. They were, said the Court, legal persons and were fully entitled to those individual liberties Feis spoke of.[38] The effect of this was to extend the wonderful tolerance of idiosyncracy we inherited from the British to tolerance of the idiosyncracies of business organizations. They were even allowed to treat their smaller competitors and their customers pretty much as they pleased. This permissiveness, I thought, when extended to predatory businesses, was responsible for our chaotic economic situation. It was too costly a confusion to tolerate any longer.

There was another characteristic of business enterprise arising from this same protective doctrine that seemed to me a denial of prevalent professions of fair play. When miscalculations and bad management resulted in business decline or failure, the first to suffer were not those who were responsible but workers, whose only part had been to contribute their labor to the enterprise. If what was being made did not sell, offices and factories closed: but higher up the managerial ladder, the penalties were less. For a worker, his living

---

37. Feis, *1933: Characters in Crisis,* p. 79.

38. The first discussion of equal protection as applied to economic regulation was in the Slaughter House cases in 1873 (16; Wall; 36). As C. H. Pritchett has remarked, "The Court proved very reluctant to use the equal protection clause as an instrument for the protection of the civil rights of Negroes and, at the same time, eager to invent uses of it as a bar to business regulation." There is a good deal more to Pritchett's examination in *The American Constitution,* 2d ed. (New York: McGraw-Hill, 1968).

was involved and his loss was absolute. For his superior, there might be a reduction of income but no hungry family, no eviction, no idle time without even guarantee of recall when circumstances improved.

This was manifestly unfair, but it was an accepted part of the system. It was not difficult to see how change could be brought about: unemployment and disability insurance, old age protection and, if necessary, public employment. These should be paid for by taxing the incomes of those who now escaped responsibility. This had been the burden of our urgings about policy, and we at least hoped that with the lesson of the depression for support, Roosevelt would accept his commitment. To participate in these reforms would be satisfying. That something of the sort would happen whether I went to Washington or stayed at Columbia was true enough, but I felt so strongly about this unfairness that participation seemed something I ought not to avoid. Besides I had been speaking rather fiercely on this subject and had had some approving listeners. When Roosevelt said to me that we had talked a good deal and now it was time to act, and he included me in both categories, it seemed to me an admission. It made the prospect of participation irresistible.

When Ray Moley told me that in the administrative list Roosevelt was developing, I was included, I was not exactly surprised, and I must admit that the assistant secretaryship of agriculture was my own selection. There were several other alternatives, but since I was intimately concerned with a farm relief act—having worked on its formulation and passage through the House and been disappointed by its failure in the Senate—I felt a particular responsibility for seeing it carried through. About the administration of the department, too, I thought that I might well accomplish something worthwhile.

Naturally I discussed all this with my friends. Presently Frank Fackenthal, who could be said to be actively in charge of the university's administration and with whom I had had many friendly dealings, asked me if I would not talk with the president as well as with him. I had never had a personal talk with Butler. To me, as to most of the junior faculty, he was a remote presence who dealt with trustees, with distinguished figures abroad and at home, but who allowed administrative matters to remain in the competent control of Fackenthal, Coss, and other deans such as Hawkes.

My interview with him was informal and pleasant. His office looked toward 116th Street as it crossed the square still to be surrounded by the buildings known now to students. The room had recently been refurbished by associates who had deplored the drabness following many years of use. I had heard of the project, but still I was once again impressed with the many talents of Coss, who had been in charge. There was color and comfort. He was a big man, grown corpulent, but handsome in the confident way of prideful directors. He said he had been told I was about to join Roosevelt in the new administration, but since I was a useful member of the faculty, he hoped I would soon be returning. We should always try to be of service, he went on, but the university had its claims, too. He himself had had to choose several times. He had been offered appointments, even the ambassadorship to the Court of St. James, and had been urged to contend for the highest elective office as a Republican candidate. Believing he could be more useful at Columbia, he had always refused and had been satisfied with his choice. The university had become a great institution of learning, and prudent management had protected it against the worst ravages of the depression. It received no public moneys, but New Yorkers had fostered it faithfully. Its growth had been temporarily interrupted, but its members had no cause to be concerned about the future. I could, of course, have leave, but I must expect to come back presently. Columbia was my home.

I was much moved. I went back to my office and told Moley to see that I was taken off the list. He must have told Roosevelt, because I was sent for and, at the end of a long day, an hour or two was cleared for a talk. The agricultural appointment was nominal, he said; I was one of those he would need for sensitive jobs. He went on to remind me of the crisis we had to work out of somehow. He repeated: we had talked a lot, now we must act.

I felt I could not refuse, but when I joined the party entraining for Washington, it was with the clear intention of leaving Columbia only temporarily. And actually my university work came to no abrupt close. I came back once a week for the rest of the academic year to meet my seminar. By fall, however, I was deep in the entanglements of office. When, later on, I should incline toward coming back, Roosevelt would write to Butler, asking for further extension of my leave. That happened twice, in fact; but the last time I went back to no welcome from the elders. Finally the head of the economics department, Roswell McCrea, would ask me to resign, and, of course, I did. But that was when I was no longer very welcome in Washington either. I had lost both my academic and my governmental reputations.

I never had an opportunity to tell Nicholas Murray Butler how right he had been and that I should have taken his advice. I owed him such a confession.

Afterward I recalled with some contrition a casual meeting just beside Alma Mater with Robert Livingston Schuyler (imagine those names in New York City!), professor of History. He was one elder who was considerate of juniors, and I was fond of him. He said he had heard of what he called my defection and then went on to say: "You might remember that a Columbia professor can't be promoted!" I never had a chance, either, to tell Bob Schuyler that I should have known he was not speaking as lightly as his smile suggested.

Afterword

by Otis L. Graham, Jr.

Rex was always writing a book—his colleagues at the Center for the Study of Democratic Institutions, where I was a Fellow, took that for granted. I had not known that he sometimes worked on two at once, until one morning in April 1978, when the lunchtime conversation on the sun-drenched terrace of the old Center building in Montecito took a turn toward his days as a college student. Rex, then eighty-seven, retained an agile mind and a remarkable memory, and his recall of the details of both the physical and the intellectual geography of the University of Pennsylvania in 1911–15 was startling. The conversation disclosed that he had completed a manuscript on his years from Penn to his enlistment with Franklin D. Roosevelt in 1932.

It was, for me, an exciting discovery. He had been working steadily upon a revision of his anthology on the presidency and upon a long essay examining the process of revising the Constitution. I had assumed that this might complete his writing, that the gap in his own life story would never be filled. His *The Light of Other Days* (1962) had covered his boyhood and ended in 1910. His writings on the FDR era conveyed much autobiographical material, enabling us to follow his career from 1932 through the 1930s. *The Stricken Land* (1947) described his career from 1941 to 1946, when he resigned as governor of Puerto Rico, and *A Chronicle of Jeopardy* (1955) told of involvements in politics and arms issues in the Truman years. He had left occasional gaps in his autobiographical accounting and would never write of his life in the Chicago and Santa Barbara years. But the largest lacuna seemed to be the period 1910–32, years of his formal education, early professional life as a professor and author in that

245

yeasty era stretching across Progressive reform, war, and booming 1920s. Always reluctant to talk of himself, Rex in 1978 appeared content to leave us with Bernard Sternsher's brief treatment of the 1910–32 years in *Rexford Tugwell and the New Deal* (1964), which he had frequently pronounced to be entirely reliable and sufficient. Then on that morning in 1978 we learned that, in his eighties, he had found the time to fill that biographical gap himself.

It required strenuous argument to induce him to bring me the manuscript the next day. Rex insisted that I should be reading more important things. He delivered the pages at my insistence, and I found the book irresistible from the first paragraphs—a matchless firsthand account of places, personalities, ideas, public issues, and politics from reform-era Philadelphia to FDR's New York. Grace Tugwell and I insisted that the manuscript be published, and Rex entrusted his box of typescript to the two of us, turning his mind to the next project. One year later he went under the knife for minor surgery and died of pneumonia. The publication of *To the Lesser Heights of Morningside* by the University of Pennsylvania Press completes the oeuvre of this remarkable American.

That era of moral, political, and intellectual revival we call the Progressive Era was composed of many themes. Yet historians have discerned a clarifying pattern in the rich political thought of that long generation of reform. On the overarching issue of political economy, of how to cope with the power of the large corporation, the Progressives inclined toward one of two basic outlooks. In one view, all large organizations were a threat to fundamental liberties, and the continuing assignment of democratic government was to monitor the economy and dismantle concentrations of economic power while avoiding the curse of bigness itself. In the other view, industrial size was inevitable and its efficiencies desirable. The duty of popular government, therefore, was to develop the skill and power to discipline the corporation (along with labor, or any other aggregation of massive power) to social purposes. The first vision of a liberal political economy appropriate to the twentieth century was well expressed by

Woodrow Wilson in the campaign of 1912. The second was sharply counterposed by his opponent, Theodore Roosevelt.

Rex Tugwell lived his entire intellectual life within the latter, or "New Nationalism" tradition. To this tradition he made contributions on both intellectual and administrative levels which, taken together, place him in the very front rank among shapers of the contemporary political economy. The social vision out of which he grew and to which he contributed in over twenty books, through his tutoring of a president, and by a sequence of positions of administrative authority, was that of a democratic society managed by officials responsible to the public. The early shapers of his own social outlook were men like Charles Van Hise, Lester Frank Ward, Herbert Croly, whose books the young Tugwell rapidly absorbed. The teachers whose influence he gratefully acknowledged included Scott Nearing and Simon Patten at Pennsylvania; William F. Ogburn, his colleague at the University of Washington; John Dewey and Wesley Mitchell at Columbia. Tugwell saw himself in what he often called the Collectivist tradition, contrasting it with what he called the Atomistic outlook of those who would rely upon antitrust crusades to somehow restore the lost role of the market in social guidance. Both were within the "liberal" camp, but Tugwell would often capitalize the Progressivism of the New Nationalism to distinguish it from the lower-case progressivism of the Wilsonians and trustbusters with whom he so profoundly disagreed.

The struggle between these two large versions of the liberal political economy was emotional and deep, though intellectually disorderly. Tugwell had a way of summarizing this struggle in vivid outlines even when the choices were not so clearly perceived, for he wished always to clarify the consequences of this theoretical battle within the liberal mind. The presidential campaign of 1912 had given the two philosophies a relatively sharp focus, but soon the complexities of American economics and politics forced the victor, Wilson, to abandon any serious effort to design a set of policies in accord with any consistent theory. As war engulfed the nation, no clear choice had been made between the two divergent channels of liberal thought, despite Wilson's inclination toward the New Freedom ideology. More than any other individual, Tugwell resurrected and extended that debate in the 1930s.

The world war involvement, with its requirement for immediate and comprehensive social mobilization, appeared to settle this debate that had divided liberal reformers. After sampling the heady ideas of the prewar era, the first taste of social responsibility for many young men and women of this generation was not in attacking corruption in some progressive urban campaign, as their elders had done, but in mobilizing the society's total energies. The government, in wartime, *must* direct the economy, accomplishing by administrative and bureaucratic intervention what markets and moral exhortation could never achieve. Amid considerable confusion, the job was done. An army was recruited and placed in French fields, backed by awesome material resources diverted by government action from private channels. As historian William Leuchtenburg has shown, eighteen months of war mobilization had confirmed the New Nationalism in the minds of an entire cohort that would in 1932 construct the New Deal. America, the war seemed to prove, could not return to the village society and laissez-faire economy of the distant past. She must, in the twentieth century, be a planning society, with all major economic activities guided from the center.

Just as the collectivist idea had demonstrated its timeliness and viability, the emergency was over, and Wilson led a retreat from social management. Every war agency was dismantled, and the era of weak government began. Both the New Nationalism tradition as well as the moral uplift and trustbuster forms of liberalism went into eclipse. Business, operating in such markets as existed, would chart the national future without interference. Progressives of all kinds scattered, some into disillusionment and cynicism, some into such constructive minor activities as could be found, some smugly claiming that their work had been completed and that the business civilization was its expression.

Tugwell, twenty-eight when the war ended, was not engulfed by this cycle of reform weariness. He succumbed to a brief illness at the war's end, brought on more by his chronic asthma than by the spiritual disorientation that afflicted so many sensitive people at the end of the ordeal. Weeks of reading and walking on his father's New York farm revived him. His work as a social critic had just commenced as the nation slipped from reform to reaction.

A year on the economics faculty of the University of Washington was ended by his appointment at Columbia in 1922. There, with the encouragement of relatively light teaching assignments, he began to write the series of books that this volume brings to a total of twenty-three. An agricultural economist by early training, his mind turned readily to large reflections upon the changing nature of the

U.S. economy and the governmental implications of that change. He was a rising member of the Institutionalist school in economics, which recognized John R. Commons, Wesley Mitchell, and Thorstein Veblen as seminal thinkers. They stressed institutional factors in the production of economic outcomes, as against the older classical school, which stressed markets and the irresistible thrust of rational calculations by the maximizers of profit. To the Institutionalists, traditional economists and businessmen were describing a world that had ceased to exist. Progress had occurred at breakneck speed in technology and business organization but very slowly in human behavior and outlook. This "cultural lag" prevented the business, academic, and governmental establishment from perceiving how impaired markets had become. Economic activity, to the Institutionalist, did not flow cleanly and rationally in the channels cut by profit-maximizing individuals and firms in open competition. Those channels had become blocked by myriad institutional arrangements —monopolies, trade associations, unions and professional associations, codes, cartels, governmental regulation. Thus men acting in association were already managing the economic future—working through but also around market forces. In such a world, institutional intervention—by the State—was required to insure socially optimal outcomes. Believing that the whole was greater than the sum of the parts, Institutionalists rejected the idea that millions of marketplace decisions added up to social good and concluded that society must always be viewed and managed as a system. Tugwell was to write: "The cat is out of the bag. There is no invisible hand. . . ."

This was Tugwell's point of departure, as the boom era of the 1920s rushed toward its shocking collapse. His many articles and three books of pre–New Deal years (*Industry's Coming of Age* [1927], *Mr. Hoover's Economic Policies* [1932], and *The Industrial Discipline and the Governmental Arts* [1933]) marked him as a literate, committed theorist of a socially managed economy. He was a supporter of the vital and evolving body of ideas produced by the New Nationalist side of progressivism. The eclipse of those ideas in post-war reaction, as it turned out, was to last for only one brief decade.

Had the Democratic presidential nomination of 1932 gone to Newton D. Baker, as it very nearly did, Tugwell would surely have remained a Columbia economist, a prolific writer of books on agriculture as well as the larger economy. Since he wrote with grace, wit, iconoclasm, and policy engagement, he might well have become an economist writing for the general public as did a somewhat later Institutionalist, John Kenneth Galbraith.

But Roosevelt became the nominee, and displayed an unexpected thirst for innovative and comprehensive social ideas. Tugwell had been introduced to him early in 1932 by Raymond Moley. The New York governor and the professor struck it off at once on both personal and intellectual levels. Tugwell filled Roosevelt's need for the guiding ideas of social strategy as an economic system came crashing down.

There were others in Roosevelt's Brains Trust, itself a group of shifting composition in which politicians, professors, and loyalists of no particular intellectual credentials jostled one another. Moley, Tugwell, and Adolph Berle—three Columbia professors—were the original core, owing to the clarity and force of their ideas, their literary facility, and fortunate timing. Roosevelt had most need of ideas and writers in the long campaign for nomination and election, and his Columbia Brains Trust members saw somewhat less of him when the unruly tumult of governing began in March 1933. Tugwell and Moley took positions within the administration, and Tugwell's relationship to Roosevelt was the most lasting.

While he never claimed as much, it seems that of all Roosevelt's early Brains Trust advisers, Rex Tugwell made the strongest impact. The hysterical Tugwell-haters always exaggerated his influence within the New Deal out of a basic misunderstanding of the intractable pluralism of national policymaking and of Roosevelt's own invincible eclecticism. But despite a polity in which large ideas about the organization and purposes of political economy have never had the influence accorded social theory in European politics, the early 1930s were a time when theorists had unusual access to power. In this setting Rex Tugwell and his ideas made a rare imprint upon American political history.

The story of Roosevelt, Tugwell, and their collaboration in the shaping of the New Deal has been told in rich detail by several authors—Bernard Sternsher in *Rexford G. Tugwell and the New Deal,*

in the three volumes of Arthur M. Schlesinger, Jr.'s history, by Tugwell himself, and in a number of historical monographs by various authors. Tugwell shaped the new president's thinking and public statements as speechwriter and idea broker, and in the winter of 1933 Roosevelt asked him to make the transition from adviser to administrator. With some misgivings, Tugwell became an assistant secretary of agriculture. (There was no White House staff of any consequence in 1933 to which advisers like Tugwell or Moley could be appointed.) From that post Tugwell influenced both departmental and larger policies, maintaining a close interest not only in the design of the farm program but also in the National Recovery Administration, conservation, food and drug regulation, social security, national planning. In many talks with Roosevelt, he gave a boost to some programs, advisers, and plans, and discouraged others, playing a central role in the push and pull of ideas around the president. In his years within the New Deal (Tugwell left the government at the end of 1936), he never lost Roosevelt's confidence and involved himself energetically in a broad and unpredictable range of issues.

He was, by every account, an unusually confident person, sure of the basic soundness of his analysis of the larger crisis and of his own administrative abilities. To men of insecure ego or sharply divergent outlook, his confidence was often called arrogance. Brilliantly articulate in person and on paper, Tugwell had the rare gift of incisive comment on complex problems. He was never windy or boring—as professors were universally expected to be. Roosevelt, a man of complete and imperturbable self-confidence, liked the Columbia professor's powerful and integrated social outlook, his flexibility and innovative turn of mind within his larger view, his aggressive appetite for bold departures.

Inside the New Deal there was more to do than to continually reinforce the president's leaning—always partial, vacillating, and doubtful—toward the planning end of the liberal philosophy and away from the atomistic, antitrust inclination. From 1934 to 1936 Tugwell headed the Resettlement Administration, a remarkable and unique effort to encourage new settlement patterns in both rural and suburban places. The story of this enterprise is brilliantly told in Paul Conkin's *Tomorrow a New World* (1957). Yet Tugwell's energy and disciplined work habits matched his appetite for engaging the entrenched interests preventing social advance, and he found time to lead the long fight to strengthen the Pure Food and Drug Act of 1906.

This campaign brought him the animosity of the food and drug industries and their newspaper allies, and this would end his political usefulness. Just before the campaign of 1936, he convinced a reluctant Roosevelt that it was time for the New Deal's most controversial administrator to resign. Tugwell finished out the 1930s in some interim business activities in New York, then as head of the New York City Planning Commission. Columbia had not wanted him back. The assignment as governor of Puerto Rico came in 1941. To the end he and Roosevelt remained warm friends, though Tugwell was never again on assignment near the center.

His career was far from over when the Roosevelt years ended. Ahead of him, after Puerto Rico (he resigned as governor in 1946) lay efforts as a historian of the New Deal, biographer of Franklin Roosevelt, critic of the nuclear arms race, innovative director of the planning program at the University of Chicago, writer on planning, on the presidency, and on the necessity and possibility of comprehensive Constitutional revision.

But the public image of Tugwell remained that of the Brain Truster to FDR, and it was clear to his friends that, at least emotionally, he shared that assessment of his own life's center of gravity. Actually, his career could not have been assessed as he left government service in 1936. This is not only because too much of his own work lay ahead, but also because we still struggle for a clear perspective on the place of the planning idea to which he gave such powerful expression.

A negative assessment of the 1932–36 career of Rex Tugwell might easily be offered. It would allege that the "collectivist" ideas of Tugwell and the other planners in the New Deal merely confused the situation, were poorly implemented, and by 1935 were rejected by "the Second New Deal," which turned toward decentralization, antitrust, and economic management by Keynesian fiscal policy rather than through centralized direction. In this perspective, Tugwell had urged policies that Roosevelt did not and probably could not have imposed upon the sprawling and poorly understood economy.

A negative assessment might go farther. It could be argued that the puny programs in population resettlement left little mark. Market forces emptied out rural America, and suburbia was built without reference to Tugwell's flimsy experiments.

Tugwell himself, in his historical and autobiographical writing, would occasionally cheerfully concede that the "collectivists" and planners had "lost." Yet he seemed imperturbably confident that the liberal tradition would eventually be forced to give up its dalliance with the Wilsonian yearnings and choose a planned economy, a holistic approach to policy and society. He, along with others less gifted and less fortunately situated, had urged a planning philosophy upon the New Deal. The timing had been premature.[1] Tugwell was content for his ideas to await the verdict of the future.

Thus critical judgments contrast with his own conviction that time would vindicate his analysis of the correct political economy for modern America and would make his (and other planners') efforts in the 1930s a fertile set of experiments rather than a regrettable diversion. There is much to be said for his sense of history's verdict, expressed privately to friends though never committed to paper. What was this planning idea that he lifted out of the progressive tradition and urged upon the 1930s? And how are we to evaluate it? In *Toward a Planned Society: From Roosevelt to Nixon* (1976), I have addressed that question in some detail. It is a story of multiple initiatives and much confusion, since no single mind or agency controlled the movement for planning on a national level in the depression years. Yet Tugwell's view of where the planning imperative pointed was remarkably consistent.

The 1930s were a time of emergencies. Even those who concluded, as did Tugwell, that the crisis had made social planning inevitable did not pretend to know exactly how this might be implemented. Tugwell was armed with a set of principles but hardly with a blueprint for social management. He assumed that our modern economy was chronically unbalanced by the institutionalized power

---

1. In his many books on Roosevelt, Tugwell vacillated between the view that "Franklin" had been right to reject a clear choice for planning given the circumstances, and the view that the economic catastrophe opened opportunities for system change that Roosevelt had allowed to slip by. The bulk of his writing stresses the difficulties of political leadership in the 1930s, not Roosevelt's lack of mental clarity and determination. But Tugwell always wrestled with the judgment.

of special interests. Accordingly, the national government must intervene in at least the large-scale agricultural and industrial sectors in order to influence prices, wages, profits, and to channel investment more wisely than had the scramble of shortsighted entrepreneurs who operated within a narrow and self-serving balance sheet. His support for New Deal programs in agriculture (the AAA) and in industry (the NRA) did not mean endorsement of the actual forms these programs took. Here he was often critical. He urged Roosevelt to see the economy whole, to mesh his interventions so that they were systematic and matched the system's maladies.

In broad outline, he had decided what needed to be done to make planning possible. One finds his thinking most succinctly expressed in the chapter, "Government and Industry," in *The Industrial Discipline and the Governmental Arts.* With federal chartering of corporations as a lever to influence investment decisions, with social control of prices, with a tax on undistributed profits in order to force corporations to go to the capital markets, the government would have sufficient tools to iron out the business cycle and ensure continuous expansion. Note that deficit spending was not a part of his reform package. He sought structural repairs, while Keynesian policy left the structures of power essentially unchanged.

The idea of planning was certainly not original with Tugwell. Yet his formulation of these ideas for his colleagues was especially forceful and adroit. Perhaps his most creative contribution to the evaluation of the national planning idea was his exploration of the potential of public policy in altering settlement patterns. He had anticipated the dislocation of farm populations that would follow from advancing technology and had instinctively assumed that individuals and families would benefit from and need social help to guide the building of new living and working places as they were cut loose from traditional farm employment. He once told me, with vivid recall, of that fog-shrouded morning when "the Brothers Rust" rolled out their new mechanical cotton picker in a field just west of Memphis, Tennessee. Upon its demonstration, Tugwell mused that he must hurry back to Washington to figure out what to do with the poor blacks and whites whose displacement was now imminent. His subsequent efforts as head of the Resettlement Administration (RA) encompassed new, planned suburban communities, the resettlement of rural people in subsistence homesteads or cooperative farming communities, and "mixed economy" planned communities where individuals might combine farming and wage earning in light industry. The program was instantly controversial and much ridiculed. It was rarely noted that Tugwell disagreed with FDR's hope of launching a major "back to the farm" movement, assuming, as an economist might be expected to do, that industries were in urban areas for reasons of efficiency and that people must move to them rather than hoping for a major flow of jobs the other way. But he was enthusiastic about the planned suburban community idea, and both the rural and the suburban experiments of RA pursued ideas for community design and diversified small-scale agriculture that are only now coming into their own as alternatives to the sprawling suburbs and large-scale commercial agriculture that have dominated since World War II.

Roosevelt borrowed from Tugwell's planning ideas, and the New Deal to some extent reflected them in strategy and structure. In agriculture they led to better results than in industry, where NRA-style "planning" was an economic mess and a political disaster. The central planning institution that Tugwell urged upon the president was never allowed to emerge, despite some stubborn presidential support for a small coordinating institution that went by several names and was eventually remembered as the National Resources Planning Board. Congress was not ready for such an institution in the constellation of governmental units, and, of course, the idea of planning had a very weak hold upon the American mind. For some, these ideas were an unfortunate detour in the 1930s. Tugwell and many others saw their expression and incomplete implementation as a valuable part of the learning curve for twentieth-century liberalism. That the planning idea received at least this disjointed and partial trial owed much to Tugwell's influence.

Even before Roosevelt moved to the White House in 1933, the Columbia professor had developed a reputation for "radicalism" in hostile sections of the press, among trade associations and businessmen, and on the Hill. "Rex the Red," "the Sweetheart of the Regimenters," he would be called, labels that I once laughingly mentioned to him only to detect a rare wince of discomfort. On the whole he had expected to be both disliked and caricatured, and he took these emotions as reliable signs that he and the others were indeed close to dead center in their aim upon institutional reordering. He never shared his critics' tendency to lash out at individuals, even the most irresponsible business and financial leaders. He conceived of human misbehavior as social rather than individual, deriving from man-made systems that had fallen far out of touch with reality.

Was he a "radical"? From one perspective, his detractors could not have been more confused in making such a charge. On the conventional political scale, Tugwell was a liberal—just as his friend Roosevelt, who was also called a Communist in some quarters. He had no interest in socialist doctrine, and rejected public ownership of the means of production except for isolated experiments such as in the Tennessee Valley. He believed that American industrial capitalism was a splendid engine of prosperity, if properly tuned and adjusted, and both growth and prosperity were always his goals. Like the very capitalists who disliked him, Rex Tugwell had no use for Marx and would later in life take no strong interest in the truly radical "no growth" ideas that flowed from the minds of E. F. Schumacher, Herman Daly, and others. His ideas on fiscal policy were staunchly conservative. He had always believed in a balanced budget and saw Keynesian fiscal manipulation as a deplorable way to float a flawed economy over the hard places without making the required, difficult institutional rearrangements.

Like his conservative critics, he had always endorsed hard work and discipline, for individuals and institutions. It is often forgotten that many of the New Dealers disliked "welfare" intensely, Roosevelt and Tugwell in the lead. Tugwell wrote in *The Battle for Democracy* (1935):

> The most you can do for people is to discipline the institutions and forces which are inimical to the individual and so to provide freedom for action. You cannot forever go on providing subsistence for the idle at government expense. This will never be more than subsistence and it will eventually kill the thing we are trying to foster.

Like other American conservatives, he loved the American land and believed fervently in the primacy of the national interest. He was divorced in the thirties, which in those days added to his image as iconoclast and unreliable professor. Married to Grace Falke from 1938, he was ever the devoted husband and father. I suspect, without hard evidence, that he had trouble voting for George McGovern in 1968.

Yet there were grounds for the conviction that Rexford Tugwell was a subversive, a disturber of things as they were. He had indeed written as a young man that little poem promising social reconstruction, which ended:

> I am sick of a nation's stenches,
> I am sick of propertied czars . . .
>
> . . .
>
> I shall roll up my sleeves—make America over!

And in December 1931, he had said: "Business will logically be required to disappear. This . . . is literally meant. The essence of business is its free venture for profits in an unregulated economy."

This intellectual leaning was less threatening than perceived. He had not meant that private property or even enterprise in pursuit of profit would or should disappear. He felt that unlimited opportunity for abuse of the free market should be ended and tight social controls put on the level of profits and permissible uses of land or other instruments of economic power.

Quite radical for their time, such sentiments paralleled the subsequent track of American history, as social regulation intensified. Tugwell was located on the managerial edge of modern liberalism, quite ready to assume greater social influence, as a public official, among those who would run the country. He distrusted markets, which he saw as irretrievably rigged to produce antisocial and astigmatic decisions. He also distrusted congressmen and "politicians" from subnational jurisdictions, whom he saw as hopelessly parochial and lacking in national vision. And, of course, he had no confidence in a nation run by businessmen, for they answered to narrower and more self-seeking motives than others in the polity. Reflecting the planning tradition out of which he arose and to which he contributed, he believed always in intellect, in forethought, in the rational mind viewing affairs from the top.

He held a perspective on recent history that may not only illuminate what was done in the 1930s, but also clarify future choices. The depression had destroyed laissez-faire, but the New Deal, in reconstructing the political economy, had not chosen clearly between planning and Wilsonian trust-busting progressivism. As a result, a system he called "partial planning" evolved, in which powerful occupational groups eliminated real competition in their sectors, often with the aid of some government program or tax/regulatory subsidy. Half the economy was planned, to achieve private purposes. The other half of the citizens, unorganized, remained in a disorderly competitive sector. Subsequent writers, such as John Kenneth Galbraith and Theodore Lowi, have expanded upon this insight. To Tugwell, the choice that had been avoided in the 1930s would eventually have to be made by liberals. The post–New Deal system of partial planning was seriously flawed and would last only so long as the era of abundant resources and Cold War spending acted together to maintain growth. As the 1980s begin, it appears that the political economy that he knew to be flawed has indeed developed fatal systemic disorders, and the election of 1980 brought to power a regime willing to choose between market capitalism and planning. Should that strategic course not lead to a healthy political economy—and Tugwell never for a moment believed that Herbert Hoover's world could be restored by a California actor or anyone else—then the progressive coalition would again face the choice for planning.

This final volume of Rex Tugwell's autobiography is published at a time when confidence in social intervention has plummeted from the peak of the 1960s to a low mark bringing to mind the 1920s. One might suspect that the decade of the 1980s, like the 1920s, will be a time when Tugwell's social outlook will be ignored, when not actively attacked.[2] But if we think again upon that earlier season of weak government and faith in unregulated capitalism, we are reminded that there are cycles in the realm of political ideas. Should we

---

2. Of *To the Lesser Heights of Morningside* it may most urgently be said that this is a book President Reagan should read. He has repeatedly asserted that "fascism is really the basis for the New Deal," and in the late 1981 specified in a televised interview that he meant that Roosevelt's advisers (though not FDR, Reagan conceded) had admired Mussolini, and that their planning ideas were fascist. This ignorant and absurd idea could have been laid to rest by a cursory study of the 1930s or by reading John Diggins's *Mussolini and Fascism: The View from America.* But I urge Mr. Reagan to read this book for a lesson in history and political ideas.

come again upon a time when the "natural" workings of the market-place, the social outcomes produced by a turbulent and flawed modern capitalism, are unacceptable to large numbers of people, Tugwell's life and thought will come into a new importance.

There is much in the liberal tradition from FDR to Jimmy Carter that, in retrospect, chastens the interventionist impulse, indicts the performance of public bureaucrats, casts doubt upon the wisdom available in Washington and on the campuses. But Tugwell as both writer and administrator cut a track down the other, better edge of the liberal experiment. He always believed that there was much social good to be done by the public sector, by those who used a balance sheet that went beyond mere money after expenses to include more fundamental things: the viability of the ecosystem; the education, health, and character of the citizenry; social cohesion; the arts and sciences; justice.

Across his career he demonstrated an uncanny ability to discern the indices of social damage not reflected in the business balance sheet, indeed rarely on any governmental budget or agenda. He had always believed that action should follow thought and was adept at devising ways for the public, through government, to address the social flaws that the marketplace would not treat. Lodged in the Department of Agriculture when he was not advising Roosevelt on speeches and strategy, he spread out an agenda that went beyond the rescue of commercial agriculture to include an attack upon tenancy, a new economic base for those locked into submarginal lands, the purchase and rehabilitation of abused and wasting acreage, the protection of the fragile high plains where traditional wheat farming had made the dust bowl, the stricter regulation of food and drugs, which no consumer could adequately screen for fraud or potential harm. Here was social intervention where the payoff was high. To these areas where the market had failed, Tugwell brought a style of public administration and patterns of thought that were inventive, open to new ideas, flexible in the face of unflattering facts. In time, his long and broad career should again serve as a major source of insight where men and women take democracy seriously.

Index

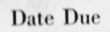

Date Due

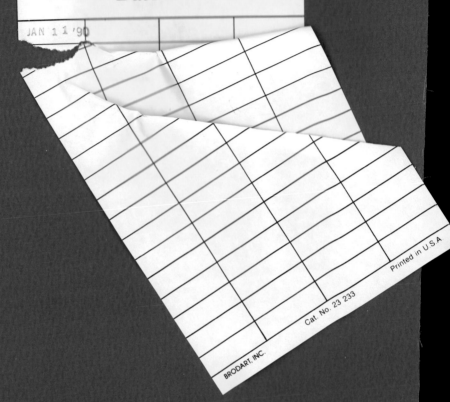

BRODART, INC.

Cat. No. 23 233

Printed in U.S.A.